P9-ELG-478

SEVENTEENTH CENTURY STUDIES
SECOND SERIES

SEVENTEENTH CENTURY STUDIES

SECOND SERIES

BY

MEMBERS OF THE GRADUATE SCHOOL
UNIVERSITY OF CINCINNATI

EDITED BY

ROBERT SHAFER

PROFESSOR OF LITERATURE AND FELLOW OF THE GRADUATE SCHOOL
UNIVERSITY OF CINCINNATI

Essay Index Reprint Series

BOOKS FOR LIBRARIES PRESS, INC.
FREEPORT, NEW YORK

First published 1937
Reprinted 1968

LIBRARY

APR 10 1968

UNIVERSITY OF THE PACIFIC

181083

LIBRARY OF CONGRESS CATALOG NUMBER:
68-16976

PRINTED IN THE UNITED STATES OF AMERICA

PREFACE

IN the first series of these Studies, published early in 1933, I explained the nature of my connexion with them and the extent to which I am responsible for them. I need not repeat that explanation, though I should say that the studies now published are based upon doctoral dissertations.

It first occurred to me that Francis Osborn should be worth looking into some ten years ago, as I stood in a bookshop idly turning the pages of Judge Parry's edition of the First Part of Advice to a Son—a book, as I have since learned, much harder to find than several of the seventeenth-century editions of Osborn's principal writings. My eye had lighted upon a paragraph beginning: "A few Books well studied, and thoroughly digested, nourish the Understanding more, than hundreds but gargled in the Mouth, as ordinary Students use." And then, turning back, I had read: "Huge Volumes, like the Ox roasted whole at Bartholomew Fair, may proclaim plenty of Labour and Invention, but afford less of what is delicate, savory and well concocted, than smaller Pieces." These and some other sentences suggested that Osborn might have been sadly misrepresented in such brief accounts of the man and his work, or allusions to him, as could then easily be found; and in 1931 I suggested to Mr. Betz that a critical survey appeared to be in order, and perhaps a reprint of Advice to a Son, or of a collection of passages from this and Osborn's other books. It soon became evident that we were not alone in our interest, and Mr. Betz, in rewriting a part of his dissertation for the present volume, has been able to profit by the valuable articles of Mr. W. Lee Ustick printed in 1932 and by the somewhat amateurish yet devoted and useful work of Mr. John E. Mason. Mr. Ustick, Mr. Mason, and other scholars, indeed, are concerned only incidentally with Osborn while engaged in exploring the whole field of books of parental advice in England; but they have done much to confirm our impression that Osborn is practically the only English writer in *this kind besides Halifax and Chesterfield who still possesses more than historical interest and deserves to be better known on his own account.*

Mr. Betz has something to say of the instant popularity of Advice to a Son, *but we would like to know more than we do about the early editions. There is a copy in the Thomason Collection in the British Museum which may safely be assumed to be an example of the first edition, both because of Thomason's known habit of purchasing books and pamphlets promptly upon their appearance, and because on the title-page of this copy he has crossed out the "6" in "1656" and has written in "October. 18. 1655." Another copy dated 1656, and now in the Library of the University of Cincinnati thanks to the Taft Memorial Fund, was purchased in the belief that it too was an example of the first edition; but upon comparison with the copy in the Thomason Collection it was found to be printed with different type, and to show a few textual changes. The Library of the University of Cincinnati also possesses a copy of the fifth edition dated 1656, with a Preface in which it seems to be referred to as the fourth edition. We therefore conclude that our other copy just mentioned must be an example of the second or perhaps of the third edition; but more than this about editions earlier than the sixth, of 1658 (with which is usually found the first edition of Part Two, 1658), we have not been able to learn. I should be glad to hear of other copies which might help to clear up this small bibliographical problem. The British Museum has nothing between the first and the fifth editions.*

Miss Hartsock's study of the philosophical and ethical background of Dryden's plays is another instance of a task undertaken without knowledge of closely related work elsewhere under way. Most of Miss Hartsock's conclusions had been reached and a first draft of her study had been written before we learned that Professor Bredvold was engaged in preparing a comprehensive survey of Dryden's intellectual milieu. We soon heard from Professor Bredvold, however, that, for reasons with which we find ourselves in disagreement, he had concerned himself very little with the plays. Consequently, as Miss Hartsock has said in rewriting her study for this volume, her work is in part complementary to that of

*Professor Bredvold and in part a criticism of his position. I venture
to think that students of Dryden and all students of the currents
of seventeenth-century thought will find her work interesting.*

 *The third study here printed goes back for its origin to a
conversation in London, a good many years ago, with Dr. A. W.
Evans, the accomplished author of* Warburton and the Warbur-
tonians. *Dr. Evans thought it a pity that Jeremy Collier should
still be known to students of literature only for his* Short View
of the Immorality and Profaneness of the English Stage, *and
expressed a wish that his several volumes of essays, "very lively,
human, and wise," might be reprinted. I knew nothing of them,
but luckily spied a complete set a few days later in a shop on
Charing Cross Road, and carried the books home with me that
autumn. Though I found I could not agree that a new edition
would be likely to be wanted, I did come to feel that Collier's essays
and sermons deserve careful study, for the light they shed on
currents of thought at the close of the century, and also as an
indispensable preparation for any real understanding of the man.
The* Short View *itself, as Miss Ressler says, has usually been
misjudged; and I hope it will be recognized that she has taken a
long first step towards showing the extreme silliness of the
conventional attitude exemplified by Mr. Bonamy Dobrée in his*
Restoration Comedy *when he superciliously refers to Collier as a
"frenzied divine."*

R. S.

19 March, 1937

CONTENTS

PAGE

PREFACE   v

FRANCIS OSBORN'S "ADVICE TO A SON," *by Siegmund A. E. Betz*   3
    I. Ideas   10
   II. Osborn and Chesterfield   42
  III. The Advice-*Genre*   50

DRYDEN'S PLAYS: A STUDY IN IDEAS, *by Mildred E. Hartsock*   71
    I. Dryden and His Century   71
   II. Dryden and Hobbes   88
  III. Dryden and Montaigne   144
  IV. Conclusion   170

JEREMY COLLIER'S ESSAYS, *by Kathleen Ressler*   179
    I. Infallibilities and Metaphysics   179
   II. Psychology: From Spirits to Certainties   208
  III. Morality and the Social Scene   235
  IV. *Modus Vivendi*   261

FRANCIS OSBORN'S *ADVICE TO A SON*

By SIEGMUND A. E. BETZ, PH.D.

FORMERLY UNIVERSITY SCHOLAR IN ENGLISH
UNIVERSITY OF CINCINNATI
ASSOCIATE PROFESSOR OF ENGLISH
LINDENWOOD COLLEGE

FRANCIS OSBORN'S *ADVICE TO A SON*

F RANCIS OSBORN is not, doubtless, an "important" seventeenth-century figure, although in his own day and for some years thereafter his name, if not one to conjure with, was at least provocative of opinion and comment. He was, in a sense, the Abraham Cowley of prose—receiving acclamation from his contemporaries but neglected or, occasionally, abused by subsequent generations. His *Advice to a Son* was important enough when it appeared to cause the Chancellor of Oxford University to prohibit its sale, and to occasion a writers' squabble of considerable magnitude and interest. Samuel Pepys reports Sir William Petty to have said that the "three books . . . the most esteemed and generally cried up for wit in the world" were Osborn's *Advice,* Browne's *Religio Medici,* and Butler's *Hudibras.*[1] Anthony à Wood deemed it worthwhile to collect all of Osborn's published works, and to trouble himself about the authorship of disputed pieces.[2] No such enthusiasm is recorded of the eighteenth century, although an edition of Osborn's *Works* appeared as late as 1722. Among other more important factors that I shall discuss later, the man's style was then no longer able to arouse friendly interest. Yet Boswell confesses an admiration for Osborn's work, though only in connexion with Johnson's caustic denunciation: "Were a man to write so now the boys would throw stones at him."[3] Swift mentions Osborn as an example of a writer affecting fashionable court phrases which later become unintelligible, and disparagingly contrasts him with other seventeenth-century authors.[4]

And indeed, by eighteenth-century standards Osborn's work cannot rank stylistically high, though by no means so low as Swift

---

[1] *The Diary of Samuel Pepys,* ed. by Henry B. Wheatley, London, 1918, IV, 22.

[2] *The Life and Times of Anthony Wood, antiquary, of Oxford, . . .* described by Himself, ed. by Andrew Clark, Oxford, 1891-1900, II, 5.

[3] James Boswell, *The Life of Samuel Johnson,* ed. by Roger Ingpen, Boston, 1925, p. 416.

[4] *Tatler,* No. 230.

or Mr. A. A. Tilley, writing in the Cambridge *History,* would have us believe.[5] Its greatest merits in this respect are a vigour and a pungency too unpolished and irregular to be called epigrammatic. These virtues—strengths is perhaps a better word—are not those of the humorist, however. Of all seventeenth-century writers Samuel Butler is probably the closest to Osborn in thought. Yet as one reads the work of the two men one is instantly impressed with a vast difference in tone and temperament. Samuel Butler's humorous comparisons are given for their own sake. In Osborn there is something quite different. There is an edge of bitterness, of cool, objective sarcasm in contemplation, but no more than an edge; and as one reads one senses that not even for a moment did Osborn experience the sheer imaginative joy in wit that lightens the seriousness of Butler's social purpose.

The very nature of Osborn's style in fact suggests the method of study that must here be used. Since he allows one to see only the mountain-peaks of his thought, one must perforce reconstruct the surrounding terrain. Both source-hunting and the conventional tracing of intellectual development would be ineffective in Osborn's case, the first because Osborn is not important enough to make the labour profitable, the second because his work is too much of a piece, the consistent body of ideas of a mature thinker. The most profitable approach to an author of Osborn's calibre and type is that of a humanistic study which attempts, first, to disengage the essential quality of his ideas from their obscureness and to reconstruct the whole body of thought of which Osborn has set down for posterity interesting and characteristic fragments; second, to clarify these ideas in terms of the intellectual *milieu* of the seventeenth century and to state their permanent significance.

For after all, Osborn, like any reflective writer of more than ephemeral interest, was not the product only of an age, but also gave expression to certain unchanging ways of thought which have still their pertinence. The age into which he was born, however, had not a little to do with shaping him, and his life ran its course amid stirring times and scenes. His grandfather, father, and brother successively held the office of Treasurer's Remembrancer

[5] *The Cambridge History of English Literature,* Cambridge, 1912, VIII, 431.

in the Exchequer, and the family had distinction enough to receive handsome emoluments for its service to the state. Francis Osborn's father, Sir John Osborne, was the first of the name to reside at Chicksands Priory, Shefford, in Bedfordshire. Francis, born 26 September, 1593, was the youngest of five sons. "At ripe years," says Anthony à Wood, "he frequented the court, became a servant in the Pembrochian family, and at length master of the horse to that most noble count William earl of Pembroke."[6] How long he continued in this position cannot be ascertained; at any rate, he entered into the life of London in the spirit of other young country gentlemen who came to the city to seek their fortune. He frequented St. Paul's, the daily meeting place of "the principall *Gentry, Lords, Courtiers,* and *men of all professions not meerely Mechanick,*"[7] as he says. For a time, at least, he was employed in the office of the Lord Treasurer's Remembrancer. In 1641, says Wood, Osborn, "having been puritanically educated, had public employments . . . conferr'd upon him. . . ."[8] The same authority also states that Osborn "did run with and truckle to the times in Oliver's raigne, and accepted of petty offices under him. [He was] one of the seven for the countie and city of Oxon that was a judge as to all prisons and persons committed to any prisons in comitatu vel civitate Oxon 1653."[9]

The date of Osborn's removal to Oxford is difficult to establish. Desire to publish his writings and to supervise the education of his son at the University, and perhaps circumstances arising from a lengthy litigation over an inheritance, determined the step. Despite his antipathy to universities, Osborn speaks of Oxford with great affection in one of his letters to Sir William Draper, his brother-in-law, through whom he had obtained preferment under the Commonwealth, and for whom he evidently felt warm friendship. During the latter part of his life Osborn seems to have

[6] Anthony à Wood, *Athenae Oxonienses,* ed. by Philip Bliss, London, 1813, I, 706.

[7] *Historical Memoires on the Reigns of Queen Elizabeth and King James,* London, 1658; *Traditionall Memoyres on the Raigne of King James* (hereafter designated *Memoirs-James,* as the *Traditional Memoires on the Raigne of Queen Elizabeth* will be designated *Memoirs-Elizabeth*), p. 65.

[8] Wood, *Athenae, loc. cit.*

[9] Wood, *Life and Times,* I, 185.

gone to London frequently, and was a "great acquaintance" of the philosopher Hobbes.[10] He died at Draper's house in Nether Worton, near Deddington, Oxfordshire, on 11 (or perhaps 4) February, 1658-59, and was buried in the church there. He was survived by three daughters and the son to whom his *Advice* was addressed. This son, John Osborne, remained at Oxford as a fellow of All Souls College until 1654, when he received the degree of B.C.L. His career as a barrister was distinguished; after holding various important Irish positions and refusing in 1691 the office of Chief Justice of the Common Pleas in Ireland, he died, it seems, as King's Serjeant-at-Law in the same country.[11]

As far as can be ascertained, Osborn published only during the last eight years of his life. The earliest pieces were two anonymous pamphlets which appeared in 1652.[12] *A Perswasive to a Mutuall Compliance under the Present Government. Together with a Plea for a Free State Compared with Monarchy* (Oxford), was dedicated to Cromwell. The "perswasive" endeavours to prove the authority of the Parliament to be valid as that of a *de facto* government; the "plea" as that of a *de jure* sovereignty. The other pamphlet, *A Seasonable Expostulation with the Netherlands, Declaring their Ingratitude* TO, *and the Necessity of their Agreement* WITH *the Common-wealth of England* (Oxford), like the *Perswasive* of the first pamphlet, is generally mild in tone and urges the mutual

[10] *Brief Lives, chiefly of Contemporaries,* set down by John Aubrey . . . ed. by Andrew Clark, Oxford, 1898, I, 370.

[11] Materials for the biographical sketch have been gathered from Osborn's works (including the very interesting letters to Draper, printed apparently only in the 1722 edition, which contains also a memoir by an unknown hand) ; from Wood, *op. cit.,* and Aubrey, *op. cit.;* and from the following modern sources, to which I here acknowledge my indebtedness: Sir Sidney Lee's article in the *D.N.B.;* Judge Edward Abbott Parry's introduction to his edition of *Advice to a Son,* London, 1896; and G. C. Moore Smith's edition of *The Letters of Dorothy Osborne to William Temple,* Oxford, 1928, Appendix IX. (Dorothy Osborne was Francis's niece.)

[12] Wood, *Athenae Oxonienses, loc. cit.,* assigns both to Osborn without question. For the *Perswasive to a Mutuall Compliance* there is further authority. In an edition of *Advice to a Son* published in 1656 (either the second, third, or fourth edition) at the end of the preface "TO THE READER" appears an announcement: "Publish't of late by the Author of this ADVICE, *A Perswasive to a Mutuall Compliance under the Present Government.*"

advantages that England and the Netherlands could enjoy through a peaceable alliance.

In 1656 Osborn published the first part of *Advice to a Son*.[13] The work became popular at once and within two years ran into five editions before Osborn finally forsook the anonymity under which he had at first issued it. In July, 1658, "the vice-canceller (Dr. Connant) [of Oxford] caused all the booksellers to appeare before him, and commanded them not to sell any of Mr. Osborne's booke. He was complained of then by severall ministers in the country that [he] bred severall principall[s] of Atheisme in country gentlemen. The book afterwards sold the more."[14] In 1656 also appeared *Politicall Reflections upon the Government of the Turks. Nicolas Machiavel. The King of Sweden's Descent into Germany. The Conspiracy of Piso and Vindex against Nero. The Greatness and Corruption of the Court of Rome. The Election of Pope Leo the XI. The Defection from the Church of Rome. Martin Luther Vindicated,* "By the Author of the late *Advice to a Son*" (London),[15] a book of politico-religious essays, of which the first is the most considerable. In reply to the misogyny of *Advice to a Son* there appeared in 1658 a scurrilous, nonsensical parody of, and attack on, Osborn, *Advice to a Daughter. In opposition to the Advice to a Sonne. Or Directions for your better Conduct through the various and most important Encounters of this life. Under these general Heads, I. Studies, &c. II. Love and Marriage. [I]II. Travell. [I]III. Government. V. Religion. Conclusion,* "By Eugenius Theodidactus" (London). The author was one John Heydon, astrologer and Rosicrucian. Its method is the familiar seventeenth-century point-by-point refutation, interlarded here, however, with a plethora of abusive epithets. It was com-

---

[13] All references to either part, and quotations, refer to the editions of 1658, the last printed before Osborn's death. The full titles are as follows: *Advice to a Son. Or Directions for your better Conduct, Through the various and most important Encounters of this Life. Under these Generall Heads. I. Studies, &c. II. Love and Marriage. III. Travell. IV. Government. V. Religion. Conclusion.* The Sixt Edition. (Oxford.) (This will be hereafter simply designated *Advice* in all notes.) *Advice to a Son. The Second Part.* (London.) (This will be hereafter designated *Advice—Second Part* in all notes.)

[14] Wood, *Life and Times*, I, 257.

[15] All references throughout the essay are to this edition (designated hereafter in notes simply as *Politicall Reflections*).

piled in a white-hot fury, requiring only sixteen days to complete, as its author boasts, and its frequently unintelligible jargon contains little that could have seriously injured Osborn's reputation. But that Heydon should not be given much credit for even the lucid passages is evident from Thomas Pecke's defence of Osborn, *Advice to Balam's Ass; or, Momus Catechised, In Answer to a certaine Scurrilous and Abusive Scribbler, one John Heydon, author of Advice to a Daughter,* By T. P. Gent (London, 1658), which proclaims that large passages of *Advice to a Daughter* were filched from John Cleveland, Sir Thomas Overbury, and Sir Walter Raleigh. In one place,[16] indeed, which Pecke, however, fails to notice in his point-by-point answer, Heydon, who since he is writing anonymously can praise his other works to his heart's content, even quotes a passage of Raleigh's *Instructions to His Son* as part of one of his own earlier publications. The climax of Heydon's impudence, a second edition of *Advice to a Daughter,* "With a Word of Advice to *T.P.*", which appeared in 1659 (London), contains no definite attempt to meet the accusation of plagiarism.

Undaunted, and perhaps rather encouraged, by this attack, Osborn in 1658 issued a sixth edition of *Advice to a Son,* and published *Advice to a Son, The Second Part,* in each case forsaking the anonymity he had maintained, but which it was now futile to continue. In the same year he also published *Historical Memoires on the Reigns of Queen Elizabeth, and King James* (London). The memoirs are an analysis of the temper of England under different monarchs. At times Osborn's method is to tell some incident from which he can draw a shrewd conclusion about government in general. Elsewhere outstanding characters are sketched in brief, and the way in which their careers illustrate the spirit of the times is indicated.

In 1659 Osborn issued *A Miscellany of Sundry Essays, Paradoxes, and Problematicall Discourses, Letters and Characters; Together with Politicall Deductions from the History of the Earl of Essex, Executed under Queen Elizabeth*[17] (London), dedicated

[16] P. III.

[17] All references throughout the essay are to this edition (designated hereafter in notes simply as *Miscellany*).

to his niece, Elizabeth Draper. In this collection of literary fragments are represented many types of seventeenth-century prose.
In connexion with the letters there is some incidental verse, rather
perfunctory in quality. The *History of the Earl of Essex* is much
in the vein of the *Memoirs*.

Osborn has been credited with three other works: *The Private
Christians Non Ultra, or, A Plea for the Lay-Man's Interpreting
the Scriptures,* "Written by Philolaoclerus" (Oxford, 1656); *A
Dialogue of Polygamy,* "Written Originally in *Italian:* Rendred
into *English* by a Person of Quality; and Dedicated to the Author
of that well-known Treatise call'd, *Advice to a Son*" (London,
1657); *A Modest Plea for an Equal Commonwealth against Monarchy. In which the Genuine Nature and true Interest of a Free-
State is briefly stated: Its Consistency with a National Clergy,
Mercenary Lawyers, and Hereditary Nobility examined; together
with the Expediency of an Agrarian and Rotation of Offices
asserted. Also, An Apology for Younger Brothers, the Restitution
of Gavil-kind, and relief of the Poor. With a lift at Tythes, and
Reformation of the Lawes and Universities. All accomodated
to publick Honour and Justice, without injury to any Mans
Propriety, and humbly tendered to the Parliament,* "By a Lover of
his COUNTRY in order to the Healing the Divisions of the Times"
(London, 1659). About these apocrypha Wood[18] presents considerable gossip and guesswork. There is no very good external
evidence for assigning any of the pieces to Osborn, and in every
case internal evidence of form and content makes such authorship
unlikely. The most interesting is the *Modest Plea,* whose probable
author, William Sprigg, treats many subjects that were close to
Osborn's heart.

[18] *Athenae* I, 706-7.

I. IDEAS

EDUCATION

THE range of Osborn's predilections and animosities—for such his vigorous opinions at first glance seem—is not extremely large, and falls conveniently into three divisions representing his views on education, on politics, and, most significantly, on philosophy and religion. In all of these his naturally strong independence takes the form of a dislike of institutions. He distrusts state, church, and school, and his bitterness extends even to the simplest of all institutions, the family. For Osborn, organized society is a necessary evil, and is itself dependent on the evil propensities in human nature for its existence—the social doctrine of Hobbes, it will be remembered.

In some respects Osborn anticipates Rousseau quite as much as he reflects Hobbes. Generally, however, he abstains from offering solutions of his own for the problems he states; although his *Politicall Reflections on the Government of the Turks* is little else than a greatly prolonged and elaborate hint for a Machiavellian Utopia. Among his chief characteristics are practicality and a restraint that inhibits any tendency to let a particular point of view dominate his mind too far. This latter tendency, which in some cases prevented his carrying his arguments to their logical and necessary conclusion, and therefore prevented his realizing his true position as fully as he might, was in other cases instrumental in giving him some of the calm sagacity of Halifax's "trimmer": *"This innocent word* Trimmer *signifieth no more than this, That if Men are together in a Boat, and one part of the Company would weigh it down on one side, another would make it lean as much to the contrary; it happeneth there is a third Opinion of those, who conceive it would do as well, if the Boat went even, without endangering the Passengers; now 'tis hard to imagin by what Figure in Language, or by what Rule in Sense this cometh to be a fault, and it is much more a wonder it should be thought a Heresy.*"[1] Osborn's intellectual equanimity, however, comes not so much from a genuine desire for the safety of the "Passengers" as from his desire for an objective point of view.

Theories of education, like those of religion and government, reflect the cultural and philosophical ideas of their proponents. And in education innocently ignorant but dangerous proponents of unsound doctrines are perhaps as frequent as in government and religion. Few men take the trouble to track down the ultimate origin of the ideas they adopt, and still fewer attempt to understand or to regulate their practical conduct in the light of its historical and philosophical relations. One need only call to mind some of the educational practitioners of the twentieth century, who make elaborate promises about the future generations that are to preserve and perfect an enlightened democracy; glibly prophesying the size of tomorrow's figs from today's thistles, as though children reared according to doctrines that in the last analysis are behaviouristic and Marxian will somehow grow up venerators of Shakespeare and Plato. Osborn and his contemporaries seem to have had much more native wit, for in general they saw whence their ideas came and whither they were going. In religion, Osborn's perception of his own true position, of the true terminus of his logic, was defective; as for government, his attitude was limited by a sceptical disgust; but in the practical and concrete matter of education—the very *raison d'être,* after all, of such books as *Advice to a Son*—Osborn knew his ground thoroughly and stated his position with clarity and good sense.

It is not a position agreeable to the most enlightened thought of our day, nor was it to that of Osborn's; but it does represent an attitude which was common in the seventeenth century, and which, although it may not receive one's sympathy, is nevertheless capable of exposition and to some extent of justification. Educational practice then as now was the result of experiment imposed on tradition, but the circumstances of the time tended to halt the development in institutional procedure that had been the result of the labours of the early English humanists, so that private individuals often made considerable efforts to direct the studies

[1] *The Complete Works of George Savile, First Marquess of Halifax*, ed. by Walter Raleigh, Oxford, 1912. p. 48.

of their children in fields neglected by the regular curricula of school and university; in some cases, also, especially talented students, like Milton, outstripping the intellectual pace of the institutions they attended, were their own educational experimenters. The first kind of experimentation apparently had entered into Francis Osborn's education, and in his *Advice* he recommends the second to his son.

With regard to education in institutions, he is, despite his "practical" prejudices, sometimes rather sensible. He regrets that he was not given the benefit of a public-school education, the social aspects of which seem in his mind to outweigh whatever intellectual advantages private instruction may possess.

> Though I can never pay enough to *your Grandfather's* Memory, for his tender Care in my *Education,* yet I must observe in it this Mistake; That by keeping me at *home,* where I was one of *my young Masters,* I lost the advantage of my most docile Time. For not undergoing the same Discipline, I must needs come short of their Experience, that are bred up in *Free Schooles;* who, by plotting to rob an Orchard &c. run through all the Subtilties required in taking of a Towne: being made, by use, familiar to *Secrecy,* and *Compliance with opportunity*; Qualities never after to be attained at cheaper rates, then the hazard of all: whereas these see the danger of Trusting others, and the rocks they fall upon, by a too obstinate adhering to their own imprudent Resolutions: and all this, under no higher penalty than a Whipping: And 'tis possible, this Indulgence of my Father might be the cause, I afforded him so poor a Returne, for all his Cost.[2]

This approval of institutional education does not extend, however, to the universities, which, in their present state at least, he condemns.

> *Cambridge* or *Oxford* . . . like *Stonage* [*i.e.,* Stonehenge], the *Pyramids,* and other *Rarities,* may well be worth a *visit,* but not to be made *Habitations* or places of abode. It not *residing* in the power of any *Tutorage* to inculcate a *wisdome*

[2] *Advice,* pp. 1-2.

beyond the extent of its knowledge, and the ability it hath to back its *Rudements,* by visible *experience*.[3]

The *Faculties* of *Soul* and *Body* . . . [are] observed at long running to receive seldom amendment, often *Detriment* from the Restrictions of *Art:* unlesse in things like *Painting* meerly *Delusive,* or *Grafting,* and *Planting* wholly Laborious. These being Imbellishers, if not Restorers of *Nature,* whereas the *Liberall Sciences* (as the *Schools* call them) Labour to Confine *Experience* within *Generall Rules,* though found to be as Diffusive and Numberless as the Accidents and *Events* depending on Motion.[4]

Despite his violent attack on university education as it was practised in the seventeenth century, Osborn is fair enough to admit that, with all their deficiencies, the universities are the natural centres of learning. He admits, too, that, after all, even the kind of erudition he approves is naturally to be sought in them : mathematics and medicine, which he counsels his son to study, are both university subjects. Those who would despoil the colleges he does not encourage, "For though thousands are found to bury their Talents in the ocean of *Controversies,* and an implicit adhering to the writings of the *Ancients* . . . yet all ages do afford some that scorn to be tied up to Patternes, but inrich the world with such new *Inventions,* as may not onely expiate the Charge, but the Ignorance of all *Foundations*."[5] He finds justification for the universities in the *possibility* of their merit, much as he questions its *probability*.

The reason for Osborn's attitude in this matter can perhaps best be stated in terms of his theory of the nature of education. In all his work one can perceive traces of Hobbes's philosophy and psychology, and these are especially marked in the case of his ideas concerning education. He thinks of every man as clearly in conflict and in competition with his fellows, and of the purpose of education as being instruction in means to gain an advantage over them. Just as the desire for advantage is instinctive, so is the growth of the mind largely a matter of instinctive response

[3] *Advice—Second Part,* p. 64.
[4] *Miscellany,* p. 83.
[5] *Politicall Reflections,* pp. 115-16.

to external stimuli. For example, he advises his son to "Beware what Company you keep, since *Example prevailes more than Precept,* though by Erudition dropping from these Tutors, we imbibe all the tinctures of Vertue and Vice: This renders it little less than impossible for Nature to hold out any long Siege against the batteries of Custome and Opportunity."[6] It is clear from this and other passages in Osborn's work that he considers education an external social influence exerted on the natural impulses of the individual. But in this same passage one can perceive that Osborn's ideal method of education would be to lead the natural impulses in their proper, easy channels. This philosophy accounts, too, for his emphasis on practical experience. Education by practical experience as Osborn understands the term excludes the notion of a moral conformity to an ideal spiritual law—the educative principle of the older dualistic tradition—and substitutes a system of trial and error, which through rewards and punishments develops habits of prudent action.

The errors in educational principle of which Osborn accuses the universities are not without effect on the commonwealth. For Osborn, education must be useful to the state as well as to the individual—useful in the very practical and essentially materialistic way that he never ceases to advocate. In the first place, the supply of graduates, which far exceeds the demand, annoys Osborn almost as much as their poor quality. Like John Earle in his *Microcosmography* and Chesterfield in his letters, Osborn feels contempt, too, for the scholar's lack of social grace, and finds him unable to cope with the practical situations of life. England is overrun by clumsy pedants, who are the curse that indiscriminately bestowed education always entails. Osborn points to the Turks as an example of a nation, who, despite the tyrannic character of their government, have at least the advantage of control in education. By combining legal and ecclesiastical functions in a single learned class, and by limiting learning through the prohibition of printing presses and other devices which lead to such abuses as are current in European universities, the Turks

[6] *Advice,* p. 39.

have been able to make learning of real civic value.[7] As far as England goes, great men come from its universities, but their greatness owes nothing to the formal processes of education.

That this concern for the state does not make Osborn of the party of the idealistic Italian Humanists, and English successors such as Elyot, is evident when one remembers his distrust of courtiership and his tendency to make Machiavellianism a *private* rather than public policy. Even more significant is his lack of sympathy with their conception of learning and its value to the individual. Assuming as he does that learning is not in itself a worthy end, and that it is at its best merely an embellishment of life or a thin summary of experience, he feels strongly the justice of the attack he makes upon "pedantry." He says, "Such as make *Learning* a full Imployment have their *Judgement* so over-awed by *Antiquity,* that like *Players* they dare present nothing in publick but what their *Poets* have left them written."[8] At its face-value, this is sober, if somewhat unoriginal, comment. In the light of other remarks of Osborn's, however, it indicates clearly his position with regard to humanistic education. He shows no signs of understanding literature as the substance of an educational discipline. Aside from occasional condemnations of contemporary writings and some praise of Bacon, Raleigh, and writers of similar ideas, literary comment is rare in his works. His notion of classical literature seems limited to historical and philosophical writers. The manner in which he brushes aside foreign-language study, together with his sceptical attitude towards the cultural value of travel, confirms this judgement.

According to Osborn, therefore, learning is bad for all classes. An aristocrat becomes useless to himself and to the state; a plebeian, on the other hand, unless he is eminently qualified for intellectual pursuits, is made dissatisfied with his normal rank, and becomes dangerous as well as useless. Osborn recommends, indeed, a *"mixt Education,"* including a variety of subject-matter

---

[7] *Politicall Reflections,* p. 111 ff. Osborn's admiration for the efficient, if nevertheless tyrannic, Turkish government is interesting when one compares it with the avowed republicanism of his 1652 pamphlets. There seems to be a genuine development here in the direction of Hobbist absolutism.

[8] *Miscellany,* p. 80.

and well strengthened with much practical experience, since such an education alone will enable a man to rise to any position without betraying the fact that his new station in life is foreign to his original environment.[9]

Coördinate with Osborn's dislike of institutions is, of course, his hatred for tradition, which every permanent institution tends inevitably to embody. Osborn hates traditions largely with the spirit of Ananias in Jonson's *Alchemist*. And indeed, in his casual dismissal of art, in his disapproval of hawking and duelling, and in his bourgeois care for profit, Osborn is quite the stage Puritan. The connexion between education and tradition is a complex matter, of whose difficulties seventeenth-century intellectuals, including Osborn, were well aware, since tradition largely influences both the purpose and the method of education. He realizes that contact with a curriculum determined by classical standards must of necessity create a characteristic mental and moral outlook for the student. And he is aware of the great depth to which this process extends. He seems to contemn the pedant not as a man afflicted with an unfortunate but curable humour, but as a man whose whole life has been spoiled by improper influences. It is because he realizes how great the influence of the universities is, that he would prevent its exercise in directions he deems wrong. Hence he finds the universities guilty of pernicious traditionalism. For the vicarious racial experience of scholarship and its ideal of appreciative culture Osborn has little respect. History, a study in which tradition and reason labour together to determine both scientific and humane truth, Osborn considers unworthy of serious attention. Literature he apparently thinks a mere toy. And that he should thus despise the educational subject-matter of the universities is only natural, for the end he proposes for education is not the enrichment of personal experience or the definition of humane truth, but the acquisition of useful information and skill in manipulating one's fellow men to one's own advantage.

Osborn's ideal method of education, accordingly, is based on experience—experience unqualified by any except the simplest kind of traditional sanction. *Advice to a Son* does not indicate in

[9] *Advice*, pp. 4-5.

detail Osborn's formulation of his method. The book is based on the father's experience, and is avowedly autobiographical; but even towards his own work Osborn takes an attitude which reveals the manner in which he would make experience replace academic education. His lack of faith in written manuals of conduct extends to his own writings, confident though he is of their merit: "But if this savours too much of the *Stoick,* You may qualify it as you please: For I doubt not, but the zeal your *Youth* doth yet retain towards the Creed and Practice of others (possibly not so well taught) may at present make much of *This* look like *Blasphemy*: But when so many Winters have snowed on your Head, as on your fathers, you will think it *Canonicall, and fit to be read to Posterity.*"[10] That is to say, the father's experience will have to be confirmed by the son's before it will be *"Canonicall,"* or valid as a guide for life.

Here, however, Osborn runs into a genuine difficulty. For if the moral dictates of religion and philosophy can be distrusted as not personally verified, then the counsels of a father can be despised on the same grounds. Furthermore, he understands that experience is a hard teacher, and that not all of those educated in her school survive the rigour of her discipline. Some concession to stable authority must therefore be made,[11] especially since his cautiousness easily makes him fear the consequences of too much and too general experience.

Experience, then, is not to be made an excuse to cover any number of youthful lapses; it is not synonymous with "wild oats." The whole tenor of the *Advice to a Son* is in direct opposition to such a confusion of ideas. Osborn's reason for writing the book is to enable his son to avoid the father's mistakes. Very interestingly he says that his son should look upon "these Admonitions, *as* markes to saile by, not *for* presages of Shipwrack."[12] Many things, accordingly, which ordinarily one would include in practical ex-

---

[10] *Ibid.,* p. 72.

[11] His longing for authority in education as in other matters is interestingly expressed in his approval of the Jesuits: "the principal business of Youth . . . is, *to be perfect in Patience and Obedience*: Habits no where so exactly learned, as in the *foundations* of the *Jesuites,* could they be fetcht thence without prejudice to Religion or Freedom." (*Ibid.,* p. 6.)

[12] *Ibid.,* preface "To His Son."

perience are carefully excluded. Travel, for instance, is condemned as leading to debauchery that is scarcely compensated by the meagre intellectual development it gives. It is of value to a man only in proportion to the previous experience he has had. Before one enters a foreign country, says Osborn, one should be familiar with the manners of one's own, and should have already acquired a sound judgement. That is, experience is not to be sought indiscriminately and without the balance of a well-ordered reason capable of profiting wisely from the lessons it can give. Finally, therefore, Osborn's principles seem to turn against themselves. Basing his theory of education on a definite rejection of tradition, on individual enterprise rather than accumulated thought, he proceeds to set up a system of learning which in practice shows signs of submitting, after all, to external restraints, of setting up tradition anew.

This apparent inconsistency, however, is due not to a want of thought on his part, but to the wrongness of his premises in aspects of life wider than mere educational procedure. That such is the case is evident when one considers some of the conclusions to which his educational theory leads him. As long as Osborn is dealing with matters that are relatively unphilosophical, as long as the point in question is ethically indifferent, his advice is that of a sensible, clear-headed thinker. For instance, his advice on how to learn to write is as follows: "The way to *Elegancy of stile*, is to employ your pen upon every Errand; and the more triviall and dry it is, the more Brains must be allowed for Sauce: Thus by checking all ordinary Invention, your Reason will attain to such an habit, as not to dare to present you but with what is excellent: and if void of Affectation, it matters not how meane the subject is, There being the same Exactness observed, by good Architects, in the structure of the Kitchin, as the Parlour."[13]

Nothing could be sounder. Notice, however, the rather less worthy character of this advice:

> make some inspection into *Physick;* which will *adde to your welcome, where ever you come*: it being usuall, especially for Ladies, to yield no less reverence to their Physitians, then

[13] *Advice*, pp. 16-17.

their Confessours . . . The Intricacy of the Study is not great,
after an exact knowledge in *Anatomy* and *Drugs* is attained. . . .[14]

One begins to suspect, in reading passages like this, that Osborn
had little faith in man's ability to achieve success by genuine
worth and dignity, nor much desire that his son acquire these
traits.

Caution and the knowledge that material profit has its dangers,
rather than any strong ethical sense, keep his counsel from becoming utterly ruthless; but that Osborn is motivated chiefly by the
gospel of getting-on is further shown by his attitude towards
manners. For Castiglione, it will be remembered, manners are the
outward manifestation of an inwardly good and noble soul. Already
in Della Casa's *Galateo* the idea of courtesy had slightly degen-
erated, and in England the opinion was fairly widely held that
polished etiquette was simply a species of hypocrisy. The curious
fusion of Puritan and Machiavellian in Osborn is nowhere made
clearer than in this: he has the Puritan's and the simple Englishman's distrust of etiquette, and he knows well enough the multitude
of courtiers' sins that it can hide. He has also the Puritan's and
the bourgeois Englishman's contempt of the Italianate refinements
of art and letters. Yet despite these opinions, he recommends that
his son learn thoroughly the tricks of courtiership and the elegancies
of manner which shall enable him to be successful in the world.
Manners have for him become, like learning and even religion
itself, a mere device for personal advancement. External polish
is, indeed, he says, a necessary accompaniment of inner worth—
not, of course, in the sense that it arises from inner worth, but
in the sense that it is essential to the practical use of inner worth.
Manners must be perfected for the very Chesterfieldian reason
that it is "in the power of a foolish Custome or Gesture to render
the most able ridiculous."[15]

To understand Osborn's conceptions of the relation of education
to the welfare of the individual and the state it is necessary to keep
in mind the background of educational theories of the English

14 *Ibid.*, pp. 6-7.
15 *Ibid.*, pp. 140-1.

Renaissance. Osborn's opinions, of course, are in part derived, by adoption or reaction, from the general stream of Italian educational theory. In other respects they are expressions of English obstinacy towards the revival of learning. To give Osborn credit for too much originality in his theories of education would be a serious mistake. The author of *Advice to a Son,* it must be remembered, was not so much an original thinker or a leader in thought, as a sensitive perceiver and shrewd recorder of social trends.

He lived in a period of great and serious interest in education when a vast readjustment was in process. In the seventeenth century at least three chief kinds of opposition to the universities can be distinguished as coming from distinct groups of men differing in interests and in educational purposes. The first of these included men like Milton, who were dissatisfied with the failure of universities to take up the new learning that had been received more enthusiastically elsewhere than in England:

> I shall produce abundant active effect at present if I can induce you, my auditors, to turn over seldomer those huge and almost monstrous volumes of the subtle doctors as they are called, and to indulge a little less in the warty controversies of the sophists. . . .
> I think there never can have been any place for these studies on Parnassus. . . .

Thus Milton in *Prolusiones Oratoriae.*[16] Other critics of the universities, however, opposed them not out of love for the things that belong to Parnassus. Powerful prejudices against university training were always noticeable in certain sections of Puritan thought. On this account, indeed, Osborn himself expresses apprehension for the safety of the universities.[17] A third group of critics of the universities, numerically perhaps the least significant, were men who like Osborn felt little or no sympathy with a mode of education that was, in the last analysis, based on a philosophy to which they did not subscribe. For Hobbes, as an example, the

[16] Masson's Translation, quoted by James Holly Hanford, *A Milton Handbook,* New York, 1933, p. 15.
[17] *Advice,* pp. 3-4. His alarm was not groundless: *cf.* S. R. Gardner, *History of the Commonwealth and Protectorate,* London, 1916, II, 322, note 2.

universities were to be made the servants of the monarch in teaching the people, through the clergy and scholars generally, and he finds that

> though the Universities were not authors of those false doctrines, yet they knew not how to plant the true. For in such a contradiction of Opinions, it is most certain, that they have not been sufficiently instructed; and 'tis no wonder, if they yet retain a relish of the subtile liquor, wherewith they were first seasoned, against the Civill Authority.[18]

This view, which Osborn might, except for his indifference to the form of the government, have shared, is similar to the Turkish notion of education mentioned above.

The first of these three attitudes towards university education is clearly on the side of humanistic training. But it should be remembered that Milton himself in his later life renounced classical culture, aligning himself with the second of the three attitudes. This and the third, indeed, were fundamentally illustrative of a widespread reaction against humanism that was proceeding on the Continent as well as in England. The third attitude is indicative of an important change. For only a little way separates Hobbes's distortion of the purpose of learning from the even more utilitarian abandonment of it. Despite superficial similarity, how far is this doctrine removed from the ideal of civic and personal virtue which had been the educational principle of the Italian Renaissance of the Quattrocento! The ideal of the wise courtier who acts so as to benefit his prince and thereby the whole of society, which had been set forth in Italy by Castiglione, had in England been expressed in such works as Elyot's *The Boke Named the Governour.* But by Osborn's time the individualism and rationalism of the Renaissance had gone far beyond their original sphere of influence. Rationalism turned its batteries against Protestantism, and individualism its batteries against the new education.

In Osborn, however, not only rationalism, but certain ingrained English prejudices found expression. Elyot had realized that the humanistic education of Italy would in England have to adjust

[18] *Leviathan, or the Matter, Form, and Power of a Commonwealth, Ecclesiastical and Civil,* ed. by A. R. Waller, Cambridge, 1904, pp. 249-50.

itself to different circumstances, since in England the town was only gradually becoming the centre of learning. The English aristocracy was rural, not urban; and Osborn, it seems, reflects something of the rural independence, the flouting of fashionable elegance, of the old country gentry. Closely related to this quality, also, is his practicality, ever an English trait and especially prominent at a time of commercial expansion such as the sixteenth and seventeenth centuries witnessed. Humphry Gilbert in his *Queen Elizabeth's Academy* had vigorously stated the need for a kind of education that dealt chiefly with the things of this world in a this-worldly way. And even Cleland in his *Institution of a Young Nobleman* had wished to temper the classical humanistic discipline with an untraditional infusion of experience.

But in Osborn's scheme of purposes the disappearance of the ideal of the courtier as adviser to his prince, as public benefactor and genuine aristocrat, is due not only to British practicality and the nationalism which had attacked humanistic education. It is further due to a state of affairs which Osborn reflects in an especially noteworthy manner. For England during the seventeenth century was divided, not geographically and politically as was Renaissance Italy, but socially and spiritually. In Italy humanism had the unfulfilled hope of a national state to lend dignity and worth to its purposes. But in England, which had already been a nation for some time, the disturbed condition of the period prevented that leisurely interest in letters which was the foundation of humanism, and the unity of political purpose among learned men, which was its social manifestation.

There was, to be sure, an abundance of scholarship and no deficiency of great minds that had mastered the technique of historical and literary study. But in general the interest of these minds was diverted, or in some cases almost impressed, into the service of political and religious factions, whose struggle, though inevitable and perhaps ultimately salutary, was destructive of the ideal contemplative scholarship which can discover and express great truths and embody them in living men who will serve the state with wisdom. How many scholars of that period, having a distaste for the literary warfare of the time, must have become, like

Robert Burton, melancholy scavengers of the débris of medieval learning! Occasionally some one like Milton appeared, who, although he was in the thick of battle, could see beyond immediate ends to ultimate purposes. But usually in this century it was the fate of great minds to be unsuccessful and unhappy. Milton's own life was a long, finally a wearying, philosophical Odyssey. Men like Osborn inevitably had their share of disappointment and grievance, and, finding little consolation in philosophy, turned from it in annoyance. Possessing intelligence enough to understand the problems of their time, they lacked the earnest nobility of purpose to strive for any solution but the most direct and personal. Osborn, as a shrewd observer and a keen thinker, saw and obeyed the necessity of the century, which led to expediency and regard for personal safety as the best plan of action and as the best aim for organized education.

POLITICS

The most outstanding instance of this regard for expediency is Osborn's advice concerning government, which he begins with a general disavowal of responsibility: "such . . . as cannot make all well, discharge their conscience in wishing it so; Government being the care of providence, not mine."[1] With this principle as a basis, he develops the system of conduct that his son is to follow in his contacts with rulers and governmental affairs. There is no general social ideal of action in what he has to say. Even personal honour, the traditional mark of the aristocratic spirit, he dismisses with his usual practicality: "nurse not *Ambition* with *your own blood,* nor think the wind of Honour strong enough to blow away the reproachfull sense of a shamefull, if possibly that of a violent Death. . . ."[2] He quotes with satisfaction: *"A living Dog is better then a Dead Lyon."*[3] Fundamentally, it would seem, Osborn prefers to have his son take no part in politics: the moral responsibility of the citizen for the safety and guidance of the commonwealth he does not recognize. The dangers inherent in political life make it folly to seek office.

[1] *Advice,* pp. 104-5.
[2] *Ibid.,* p. 106.
[3] *Ibid.,* pp. 106-7.

First and foremost, of course, this attitude towards political behaviour expresses once again Osborn's pusillanimous caution— a caution which leads him to tell his son that on the whole travel is not worth the risk it entails, and that the chance for happiness in marriage is so small that the wisest procedure is not to marry. But Osborn's political indifferentism exemplifies also another very important trait—his disillusion about mankind. In his dealings with human institutions he refuses to consider honour and virtue as dependable motives of action. No class is exempt from his general accusation:

> The truth is, if wise men will make it their businesse, they may be easily able, where the people are unsettled, to obstruct good, & promote much evil, under the specious pretences of *Religion* and *Safety*: therefore far cheaper pleased, then discontented; being otherwise in true policy, capable of no slighter security, then shall be able to cut off all hope or desire of future revenge: The consideration of which, though it cannot make me altogether approve, yet it abates my severity in the condemnation of that Legislator, said to have writ his Laws in bloud, which might be more sutable to the complexion of some times, then may possibly hitherto have been thought.[4]

Not much confidence can ever be placed in individuals or in groups: as social beings most men are, Osborn believes, like himself interested in safety and profit, and if they possess intelligence, are shrewd rather than moral. He looks upon mankind with distrust and, even in the case of his readers, scorn.[5] The body politic embodies the sum of all the irrational tendencies of its component individuals.

Caution and despair over mankind, therefore, both counsel quiet submission to authority. The moral problem of submission Osborn handles in an interesting fashion: conscience, he says, has no concern with politics, and should lay down no prescriptions for the individual's action towards the government.[6] "He that suffers

---

[4] *Advice,* pp. 144-5.

[5] See *Advice—Second Part,* preface "To the Readers."

[6] Interesting research, it seems, could still be done on the seventeenth-century attitude towards conscience; Osborn's notions might be connected with the whole

his *Conscience* to mislead him in civill obedience, makes his guide a stumbling-block; not considering that *All Governments now extant had their foundations laid in the dirt,* though time may have dried it up by oblivion, or flattering Historians lick't it off."[7] Since government is a kind of necessary evil, with which the wise man will concern himself as little as possible, Osborn says that one should not trouble himself whether his fetters are made of many links, or of only one. For the well-behaved, according to Osborn's standard, the duties normally imposed by the state will be a light burden.

Nor does loyalty to the state fare much better than personal honour and conscience. To serve the government from loyalty rather than from a desire for profit is folly; just as it is unreasonable to do more for a friend than he can be expected to do for one in the future, unless one has a debt of gratitude to pay for past favours. Furthermore, one is not by right obliged to remain loyal to a party that is falling, since ". . . All we owe to Governours is Obedience, which depends wholly on Power, and therefore subject to follow the same Fate and perish with it. . . ."[8] It is always dangerous, says Osborn, to be "overobliging" to civil authority, and especially to a king. To do good out of hope of requital is perhaps the greatest folly, since princes, like subjects, are creatures of ingratitude.

From these general principles relating to the character and the persons of government Osborn deduces an elaborate set of instructions about manners in relation to the ruler. One should be especially careful about giving advice, which should not be offered, and which even when it is requested should not be given too readily. Great caution must be exercised not to offend monarchs by putting

question of toleration, which was treated in a philosophical and psychological manner as well as in a political one, in many works of the time. Note such works as *A Discourse of Ecclesiastical Politie: Wherein The Authority of the Civil Magistrate over the Consciences of Subjects in Matters of External Religion is Asserted: The Mischiefs and Inconveniences of Toleration are Represented, and All Pretenses Pleaded in Behalf of Liberty of Conscience are Fully Answered,* anonymous, London, 1670; and *A Short Answer to His Grace the Duke of Buckingham's Paper, concerning Religion, Toleration, and Liberty of Conscience,* anonymous, London, 1685.

[7] *Advice,* p. 113.
[8] *Ibid.,* p. 118.

them at a disadvantage in repartee. Since it is always "slippery about the Throne," one should be especially careful not to reveal the faults of great men in writing or conversation. Similarly, a person acting as a great man's secretary should limit himself to the task of an amanuensis, not presuming to offer correction to his master. Two things are to be avoided—giving offence and the necessity of assuming responsibility.

Osborn closes this discussion of government with comment on the reward that those who enter public life may expect. They will see fools promoted above wise men, and their hopes for success will be clouded by the dangers to which they expose themselves. Seekers after public office become the victims of false ambition and are deluded by fame, in the pursuit of which one should not let the glamour of any particular person lead to adopting him as a model. One should rather take one's example from several persons, for only by so doing will one be apt to win universal approval. Osborn has a traditional and salutary distrust of fame, both as a desirable end to be achieved and as a reliable criterion of true worth. He advises his son not to judge things by the standards of those who are mere followers of fame and fortune. But if he should seek fame—and Osborn here, as in the case of travel, suspects that his son will probably not obey his first counsel and advises accordingly—it can be successfully obtained through a cautious use of the knowledge gained by experience.

Just as in the case of education, Osborn's sceptical attitude towards an institution is tempered by a recognition of its inherent possibilities for good, so in the case of government his cynical distrust of organized society is qualified by a definite acceptance of its necessity and usefulness. The governments of his own time Osborn considered all about equally corrupt. It is significant that in his political writings he displays little preference for one form of government over another. In advising his son, he gives counsel applicable to "free states" as well as warnings about princes. In his discussion of the reign of James I, although he announces his purpose as being to show how the present difficulties of England are due to that prince's evil and folly, he says nothing obviously prejudicial even to the most absolute monarchy. In an age when faith in traditional institutions was shaken and when new structures seemed as weak as ancient ruins, it appeared to Osborn wisest and most practical to cling fast to whatever workable systems society had devised or would devise, even though those systems were subject to inefficiency and corruption. For, pessimistic as he was about virtue and honour as effective motives in human life, Osborn found the inefficiency of men's organizations to some extent a natural consequence of man's spiritual status. "He that seeks *perfection on earth,* leaves nothing new for the Saints to find in heaven: For whilst Men teach, there will be mistakes in Divinity; And as long as no other governe, Errors in the State: Therefore be not licorish after *Change,* lest you muddy your present felicity with a future greater, and more sharp inconvenience."[9]

Osborn's conception of the origin of the evil nature in society is not, however, theological in character, but definitely naturalistic:

> The *golden Age,* so much celebrated in *Poetry,* is as remote from *Fiction* as *Miracle.* The *Earth* affording more *felicity* to a *Few* than a *Many,* which those people bordering upon the *Sun,* from whence *Mankind* is at first said to proceed, might, by reason of a *slower increase,* longer enjoy: Till by falling into conjunction with *colder Climes,* & (so) apter for *Generation,* she came to *over-stock* herself: Loosing the *universall felicity* in a *crowd of Inhabitants.* From whence sprung not onely the *Use,* but an unavoidable *Necessity* of introducing *Government,* which falling under distinct *Headships* or *Royallets,* needed no greater provocation to *Rapine* and *war,* than the *strongest* found in their *Naturall temper. . . .*[10]

At first glance this suggests Rousseauism; but Osborn looks upon the golden age as something never to be recaptured, no matter what means men may try. Nor are institutions to blame: they are the result, not the cause, of human discontent. Osborn is in general not a Utopian; he is thoroughly reconciled to government and attendant evils as they are.

> . . . *Oppression & Tyranny* is not only *Naturall* but *Necessary* to preservation. For if the *stronger Creatures* did not

9 *Advice,* p. 142.
10 *Advice—Second Part,* pp. 123-4.

spoile and devour the *weaker*, the whole masse of *Animalls* would perish by *famine*; or *stifle* for want of *roome*.[11]

Submission to the powers that be, therefore, is not only profitable and safe, but also philosophical.

It should be noted, however, that submission to the state does not arise for Osborn from any conception of social coöperation. He ever writes from the point of view of the contemner of mankind, and the course of action he wishes to teach his son is the most desirable behaviour not of one man among others, but of an intelligent man among the masses of stupid, inferior beings. He is interested not in an ethical peace with the universe but in a practical peace with the powers that be on earth. Nor does he ever establish fully and clearly a system of ethics or ideals that will integrate the purpose of the state with the needs and rights of the individual citizen. Osborn's utilitarianism—his professed concern for *"the good of the Generality, Voted, by all Right and Reason, the Supreame Law,* And for whose Salvation *Innocency* himselfe was willing to die"*[12]—is really a socialized form of his concern for personal safety. Just as the individual is forced to the use of reasoned circumspection and care to protect himself against the dangers of the world and his own folly, so is the community compelled to avail itself of a system that will protect it from external attack and internal rebellion.

The trend of Osborn's political thinking is towards Hobbesian absolutism, and one is not surprised to find him saying that ·"the *Keyes of the Church can hang no where so quietly, as at the Gi[r]dle of the Prince,"*[13] and that Henry VIII did not need the sanction of the clergy for his divorce. His praise of religion as a servant of the state has something of a sinister note: ". . . *Law* can promote no *Good*, nor prevent *Evill*, but what is open to *publick cognisance*; whereas *Religion* penetrates so low, as to erect a Tribunall in every minde. . . ."[14] Furthermore, not only religion, but other social traditions as well, are legitimately subservient to the purpose of increasing the prestige of the state.

[11] *Advice—Second Part,* pp. 154-5.
[12] *Politicall Reflections,* p. 34.
[13] *Ibid.,* p. 29.
[14] *Ibid.,* p. 22.

"If *the good of All* . . . be the *Supreme* Law, & grounded upon that of *Nature*, whose chief businesse is to intend the *preservation* of the *whole* . . . why should such be blamed, as take the most probable ways to promote peace,"[15] even if these ways are not perfectly in accord with an ideal truth. Custom, education, and ignorance are the three social villainies that Osborn decries as the foes of clear thinking. But he admits they play a useful part in the efforts of the "Magistracie" to establish its power more firmly, and with characteristic ethical callousness concludes that to use them for what they are worth is the natural privilege of rulers, being in their case especially justifiable because it may promote the common welfare.

Further evidence of Osborn's close relation to Hobbes is to be found in his ideas concerning the relation of ethics to law. Since right and wrong are, according to him, mere matters of custom, and since the state is the supreme authority to which all men owe obedience, it follows that the ruler has the privilege of declaring himself the arbiter of right and wrong. The state, as the legitimate judge of custom, and as the guardian of education and religion, has all the most powerful means of social influence in its hands and has the right to use them as it pleases. The question of the ruler's conscience and moral responsibility Osborn ignores, but does make clear that he believes virtuous character not very frequent among princes.

It is not surprising then to find Osborn expressing views that are beyond question Machiavellian. The Turkish customs of disposing of offending magistrates by "clandestine deaths," which have the supreme advantage of removing the abuser of an office without, by the publicity of formal impeachment, casting disgrace on the office itself, and of strangling superfluous princes to prevent political factions, he commends, and in the essay entitled *"Some* Advantages *may be deduceable from* Court-Factions,"[16] he observes that a single unopposed party prevents all mitigation of oppression, going on to say that he has heard that "Divers persons of *equall authority,* though *both wicked,* do in experience *produced* [sic] *more* justice then a *greater probity* in a single *Indi-*

15 *Ibid.,* p. 38.
16 *Miscellany,* p. 240 ff.

viduall . . . ,"[17] at any rate in such a time as his own. Government should not be entrusted to human passions: bribery is better than love, fear, and hope, as a civil tool. Osborn's "Discourse Upon Nicholas Machiavel. Or, An Impartiall Examination of the Justness of the Censure commonly laid upon him"[18] gives sufficient evidence of his having really read and understood Machiavelli. Whatever wickedness there is in Machiavelli, Osborn says with malicious wit, must be somewhat excused by the consideration that Machiavelli was employed as an ambassador. The content of *The Prince,* however, is in itself justifiable, because more wickedness can be found in the lives of real monarchs than in that of Machiavelli's ideal prince: "he that knowes not how rare a Commodity *Probity* is, in the Market of Princes, is no fit Reader, much lesse a competent Judge of *Machiavell.*"[19]

Osborn's notion of the supremacy of the government is in many respects consonant with Bacon's conception. Both writers advocate a tolerant Erastianism with regard to ecclesiastical policy; both assign to the government definite responsibilities and almost unlimited authority. But enthusiasm for a particular form of government, and faith in its powers for good, are absent from Osborn's thought. He is thoroughly disillusioned about princes. Not only James, Bacon's idol, but most monarchs, are corrupt. Nationalism, too, which in Bacon is unlimited, makes no appeal to Osborn, who gladly praises the methods of the Turks and considers European civilization as everywhere nearly equally afflicted with bad government. In Bacon the Renaissance enthusiasm for the state preserved some of its Italian eagerness to make an art of government. But for Osborn, as has already been said, government was a necessary evil, whose avowed purpose was seldom properly fulfilled.

And this brings us back to Hobbes, in whom, of course, Osborn has his closest parallel. Although he may have gathered from Bacon something of his tolerant spirit towards varieties of religion and some appreciation of the practical problems of government, it is essentially with Hobbes that he agrees. Both men see the state as

[17] *Miscellany,* p. 241.
[18] *Politicall Reflections,* p. 125 ff.
[19] *Ibid.,* pp. 136-7.

connected with the natural dissension of mankind. Government is related to an effort to escape from the misery of unorganized social life. Osborn and Hobbes agree further in giving the state supreme authority, to which obedience is due in everything. They are alike prone to give the Church into the hands of the state, religion having—at least on earth—the very practical use of making subjects submissive to their rulers.[20]

Osborn and Hobbes illustrate a prominent characteristic of seventeenth-century rationalism—its distrust of human instincts, and its policy of submission to prevailing institutions simply because no remedy is at hand. A curious situation arose from this submission, however. To all superficial intents and purposes both men defended Church and state vigorously; but the slightest reading between the lines will show that their defence of the Church was largely a mere gesture; and a careful examination of their defence of the state shows how far thought of such quality as theirs threatened the stability of existing institutions. It is to the credit of seventeenth-century intelligence that Osborn's work, which ostensibly defends the Church, should have been condemned for atheism, just as Hobbes's *Leviathan* was rejected by the royalists whose cause it defended. And as they saw through the arguments of these two, so may the more intelligent conservatives of the seventeenth century have perceived that to the same category belonged Samuel Butler, who like them was a rationalist with a message.

PHILOSOPHY AND RELIGION

If one defines a man's philosophy as his conception of the ultimate sanctions lying behind his beliefs and actions, one must admit that in Osborn's case this conception has not been explicitly and fully stated, but must rather be reconstructed from hints and

---

[20] Nevertheless, although it is obviously with Hobbes that Osborn agrees in the substance of his political thought—his conceptions of the state as the result of mankind's viciousness, of the supremacy of the civil government, of the subordinate position of the Church—the *basis* of Osborn's ideas is perhaps more nearly Baconian. Hobbes prided himself on the deductive character of his philosophy (*cf.* A. E. Taylor, *Thomas Hobbes*, New York, n.d., pp. 35-6), and refused to let the observation of life supplement logic. Such an attitude must certainly have been for Osborn a crowning instance of the pedantry he abhorred.

fragments of ideas. The same unwillingness to classify and to integrate information which keeps Osborn from really entering into the scientific spirit, prevents him from ever setting down in a systematic fashion his philosophical ideas. Yet though his ideas change, they change not through mere whim or fashion. Beneath them there is a strong, intelligent consistency that gives to his pronouncements an air of sober evaluation—a consistency arising not from thoroughness of philosophical method, but from a uniformity of philosophical temperament.

The independence of Osborn's thought is even more clearly brought out by the significant way in which he departs from the philosophers whom he comes closest to resembling. He does not have Hobbes's bland confidence in the infallibility of logic. And in many matters he has too much distrust of all evidence to attempt the application of Bacon's scientific method to any practical problem: he falls back on personal experience and the rough approximations of cool common sense. He lacks the atheist's unwholesome stubbornness and the scientist's wholesome curiosity. This lack of curiosity, however, is evident only in the case of "natural knowledge"; in social, political, and religious matters he shows interest enough. The central subject of thought, for him as for the humanists, was man, as an individual and as a component of institutions.

His shrewd circumspection is matched by an equally great objectiveness. Though Osborn is interested in government, he prefers to have nothing to do with it. Although he conforms to the Church, he is free in his sympathy with other religions and understands the position of the man with no religion whatsoever. He is eager in his pursuit of historical information, but distrusts historians because they are generally not disinterested. Some of his impatience with traditional education is due to its failure to inculcate in students this same objectiveness. It also, in his discussion of historical events, tempers his opinions with a very considerable restraint. Osborn distrusts even the passion for righteousness, which can, apparently, like its evil counterpart, disturb the cautious and impartial judgement of reason.

Yet for all his confidence in reason, Osborn appreciates fully the weakness of human intellectual powers. He dislikes tradition largely because to him it seems a presumptuous exaltation of human opinions, which are seldom supported by reason and observation. In an age when speculation was rife, Osborn urges his readers to cling fast to the closest approximation of truth afforded on earth, the reasoned evaluation of objective data. His plan of life is not, therefore, the stark opportunism that it at first glance seems. It is rather the mature conclusion of a man who, in an age when there were no great certainties, advised his fellow creatures to turn to petty probabilities, to the matter-of-fact concerns of life, and to wrest from them stability for the spirit and safety for the flesh. In all things, therefore, he champions the mean—not the golden mean of the humanistic Renaissance, but the safe mean of the English Restoration.

The most fruitful field of investigation regarding the deeper implications of his philosophy is, of course, his attitude towards Christianity. With regard to the authority of Scripture he is distinctly Anglican. He cautions his son not to be led astray by random interpretations of Scripture or by the improper use of it in skilful hands. In cases of doubt "take fixation from the *authority* of the *Church,* which cannot be arraigned of a damnable error, without questioning that truth, which has proclaimed her proofe against *the gates of Hell.*"[1] Osborn has scant praise for "the vagabond *Schismatick,*" and although, except for some denunciations of the Roman hierarchy, he has little to say about specific forms of church government, he does insist on ecclesiastical authority and dutiful submission that does not allow itself to be unduly scrupulous: "he that herds with the Congregation, though in an Error, hath *Obedience* to stand by him, whereas a Truth in the other may be rendred more peccant, through a solitary obstinacy. . . ."[2] There are even traces in Osborn's thought of a hankering for the firm government and so-called shrewd playing-up to human nature of the Roman Church, about whose adherents he has some good things to say, as he has, in fact, about Puritans, Millevaries, and Arians. Very characteristic and finely temperate is his approval of the Reformation as an acceptable middle path, "most conformable to the duty we owe to God, and

[1] *Advice,* p. 148.
[2] *Ibid.,* p. 152.

the Magistrate; if not too flegmatick, in passing by decent Cere-
monies, or too cholerick and rigid, in obtruding upon weak and
tender Consciences."[3]

He gives a good reason for opposing the persecution of the
Puritans:[4] they should have been left alone to recover sanity of
their own accord, since violent opposition tends to arouse rather
than to suppress a movement. But a deeper reason, perhaps, is one
that lays his whole religious position open to serious doubt: "*the
exposing of any religion to contest* . . . [is] *dangerous*, seeing
all at this day in veneration are under *persecution* in some place
or another, wherefore unable to silence the Reason of those formerly suborned through *contrary Education*."[5] Loyalty to the
religion of one's native country, then, is justified not only on the
basis of the supremacy of the government, but on the grounds
that fundamentally men's religions, like other cultural factors,
are determined by education. That the religious development of
the individual, apart from direct supernatural intervention, and
from the spontaneous promptings of reason and conscience, is
based on social environment has of course been acknowledged
by religious groups generally. The attitude in itself is not at all
indicative of a lack of faith. But when it is coupled with the
timorousness that Osborn shows it is a mark of faint assurance.
The elaborate cautions about behaviour towards foreign religions
with which he plies his son show how he was infected with the
fear of so many of his contemporaries—the fear of losing his
faith. He is continually advising his son not to expose his religion
to influences that will disturb faith by disproving the unique
character of Christian doctrine.

These two bases of ecclesiastical loyalty: Erastian submission
to the power of the state, and expedient submission to the most
familiar form of Christianity, are fundamentally related: each is
after all some kind of check upon the unlimited divergencies
of religious practice and opinion that resulted from the Reformation. But Osborn's submission to the Church of England is seen

[3] *Advice*, p. 157.
[4] Osborn's disapproval of Dissenters, it should be noted, is on grounds not
of doctrine, but of civil expediency.
[5] *Memoirs—James*, p. 70.

even more clearly in its true character when one recalls some of the fundamental changes that the Renaissance introduced into the belief of certain parts of Christendom. Most significant of these changes in connexion with Osborn is the readjustment of the relation between philosophy and religion, which the Renaissance almost everywhere produced.

The Catholic system of belief, which saw Earth subtly pervaded by the presence of Heaven, the Renaissance met with a determined emphasis on life apart from its heavenly relations. The conflict was not immediately apparent. The new forces of the Renaissance were so different from what men were accustomed to, that common ground for a quarrel could scarcely be found between the old and the new. Accordingly, the two systems of thought existed side by side, often even in the mind of the same man. As a result, in practice men were drawn more and more from the other world, which in theory they continued to acknowledge as more important. This mental state easily brought about a complete modification of the religious spirit.

> The passive and contemplative form of Christianity, with its constant reference to a higher world beyond the grave, could no longer control these men. . . . The form assumed by the strong religious instinct which, notwithstanding all, survived in many natures, was Theism or Deism, as we may please to call it.[6]

That is to say, for such men Heaven receded from the Earth. They often still believed in God, but they did not perceive His transcendent presence in a world that for all practical purposes seemed to go its way without Him.

So, for instance, both Osborn and Bacon see life from a fundamentally naturalistic, unreligious view-point: and both are willing to put the Church at the mercy of the state. Neither, however, wishes to give up the hopes and fears of traditional religion. Not insincerity or hazy thinking but the severance of philosophy and religion account for such a position.[7]

[6] Jacob Burckhardt, *The Civilisation of the Renaissance in Italy*, transl. by S. G. C. Middlemore, London, 1909, pp. 547-8.

[7] Then, too, the enthusiastic, extravagant courage of the Renaissance was on the wane in England, and many of the wisest saw that a hasty dismissal of faith

Osborn's idea of faith is significantly revealing. Officially he says that faith is above reason. He has *"ever thought it a* lesse impiety to limit reason, then Faith."[8] Yet he acknowledges revelation only in connexion with reason; if faith is above reason, reason nevertheless is next in rank: "he offers an high indignity to the *Divine Nature* that robs God of his honour by owning thoughts of him unsutable to the Dictates of Reason (the exactest Engine we have to measure him by, out of the Volume of his Word). . . ."[9] And it is by means of reason, whose universality proclaims it "likeliest to be the Oracle of the everliving God," that the substance of faith is to be defined. "Now if Faith be not allowed to be taken implicitly from the Authority of any Church, a freedome of choice, by consequence, will result to all, by which Salvation must be wrought out: And in this wilderness of contention we have no better guide to follow then *Reason,* found the same for many thousands of years, though *Beliefe* hath been observed to vary every Age."[10] Seen in the best light this means simply that reason and religious intuition are to work together in formulating a creed. As an example of this coöperation one may quote a passage of singular interest as well as of considerable beauty (the conclusion of *Advice to a Son. The Second Part,* "exploding atheism," as the gloss says), in which Osborn maintains that the prosperity of the unrighteous or the sufferings of the just are no good excuse for atheism. "Wherefore *knowledge* being at a *non plus (a thing she doth naturally aborre)* many, because they cannot decipher a Reason, *why Providence in this world appeares so oft in the favour* (to our seeming) *of wicked and unjust designes, and so far discourages the good, as to leave them in the hands of oppressors,* they, like inconsiderate *sea-men,* do cut the *Cable of* hope, and forsaking the *Anchor* of *Providence,* resign the conduct of all things to *Fortune,* who is yet so *constant* in her *vicissitudes* (familiar to *Gamesters*) that in *a small time* she

---

was not only indiscreet, but perhaps opposed to the higher spirit of rationalism itself. The emphasis on reason was prominent, it must be remembered, in Milton's philosophy too, and he was not a man to make two systems of philosophy and religion.

[8] *Advice—Second Part,* preface "To the Readers."

[9] *Advice,* p. 177.

[10] *Ibid.,* p. 169.

doth not onely take away, but returnes to every man his *Money* again."[11] There is, however, or rather, there may be, a hidden compensation for the just and the unjust.

> Nor can any man ghesse how an other Fares by an outward aspect taken from his Moveables, but must sleep with him & enter his bosome, which *God* doth; and can no doubt by *slacking* of *Grief* in one, and *winding up Feares* and *Jealousies* in another, make the world even. It being the *Spring* and intrinsick *part* of the *watch* that the *work-man* lookes after, and not the *case,* though it may possibly be *gold,* or some richer Materials, which the *Rabble* do usually cast their eyes upon. . . .[12]

But even in this there is a trace of the idea that if religion is nothing else it is an agreeable delusion—the feeblest of all apologetic arguments—and that it is best to believe simply in order not to take a dangerous chance for the next life. Similarly Osborn's authoritarianism is not the genuine authoritarianism of Christianity. Expediency in this life, adequate precaution for the next, rather than faith in the revelation of the Spirit, are his reasons for submitting to authority. And his Christianity is made even more suspect by an examination of his idea of the conscience. His most interesting discussion of the subject occurs in *Advice to a Son. The Second Part,* where he gives an interesting account of what is to him a plausible doctrine: "those *learned* among the *Catholikes* do not with us look upon *Conscience* as *a distinct quality or Naturall Indowment of Man,* but meerly *acquired by Custome at* the mediation of *shame* or *Losse*. . . ."[13] To them conscience is "but a meer *bubble* in the *Imagination,* which *Feare* and *Hope* by the assistance of *Use,* can *blow* like a *glasse* in what *fashion* or *bignesse* they please, shewing there, to the *Life* represented, good or bad according to the *tincture* a former suborned passion may have *dipped* them in. . . ."[14] In this same section of *Advice to a Son. Second Part,* he says that reason and affection can always find plausible excuses with which to suborn conscience. Conscience

[11] *Advice—Second Part,* pp. 185-6.
[12] *Ibid.,* pp. 186-7.
[13] *Ibid.,* p. 175.
[14] *Ibid.,* pp. 176-7.

is merely a "passion," therefore, and accurate, intelligent moral analysis of self is possible for no man. It is not surprising, then, to find in *Advice to a Son* a passage which is in reality a complete denial of permanent moral law: "All things, we stile Sin . . . [lie] in the bowels of men, as Metals do in the Earth, under an equall parity, till *Policy,* for the benefit of Commerce, stamps them with the image of the *Devill,* and on their Ranverse *Punishment* and *Shame*: No more proper to them by nature, than for Gold or Silver to beare the Impresse and superscription of a Prince. . . ."[15] His wide religious tolerance, too, it should be noted, is the result not of Christian charity, or of a confidence in the truth of his own creed so great that it fears no rivals, but of this same spirit of moral relativism.[16]

In several instances Osborn shows a disparity between his real philosophy and the Christianity he professes. And he is too wise a man not to realize that something is wrong. Speaking once more of conscience, he relates it to religion and confesses that to many of his contemporaries neither is any longer vitally significant in ethical questions. "The *sense of honour* [is] supplying in divers persons the place of *Conscience: Religion,* in our daies, being so blended in *Hypocrisy,* that tis come to signify in *Statesmen* greater *danger,* than *advantage.* . . ."[17] In another place he laments with apparently great sincerity of feeling the loss that the shaking of medieval faith has brought to the world. Perfect freedom from worry, he says, is perhaps possible only in the Roman priesthood. With this joy of an absolute faith, pervading life with the comfort it brings, for ever gone, Osborn turns elsewhere than to religion for his real guidance in life. *"But now* since the blood of the *Saints* together with their *names* are expunged the *Gates* and *Doores* of

[15] *Advice,* pp. 87-8.

[16] He does not say that no objective supernatural truth exists, but rather that human stupidity and error make its apprehension and application only remotely possible. Note the following passage: "Thus doth *Religion* run from one *Meridian* to another, thriving best at first; for after a long abode she so far sharpens and refines the spirits of men, as they are able to discover such Abuses and Errors, as may afford them a pretence to cut her own throat for what she possesses; when, God knows, it is not the *Doctrine* that is changed, but their *Apprehensions* . . ." (*Politicall Reflections,* pp. 50-1).

[17] *Advice—Second Part,* pp. 102-3.

the *Sanctuary, Good works* have lost their *value,* & nothing more in esteem than *new Opinions.* Wherefore *since in the absence* of a protection from the *Altar,* nothing remaines without able to secure us quite from the sense of *Oppression,* let us turne our indeavours towards such *remedies* as *Prudence* and *Philosophy* are found to prescribe us. . . ."[18]

This appeal to reason, it should be noted, was in essence a proclamation that his rationalism was thoroughgoing. For purity of logic (though not for the study of formal logic) he had great admiration, and he proclaimed mathematics the highest science because of its rational basis. Yet his praise of reason did not stop with an acknowledgement that it was a sure tool for the mind. He applied it to many aspects of human life; and he acquired thoroughly the cynical spirit that such rationalism usually tends to bring about. Reason, as Osborn understood it, was a reason which limits itself to certain characteristics of experience and which tries to make these "do" for the whole of life. Osborn tried to understand everlasting questions in terms of his own epoch alone; and this effort is largely responsible for the tone of unhappy disillusion that his works exhibit. More than many of his contemporaries does he show the utter ebbing of the Elizabethan love of life. In him the characteristic gloom of the seventeenth century, rarely lightened by cavalier wit, takes to itself a cynicism and a distrust of human nature that beyond mere wariness shows an irritated inability to understand the universe. Osborn's distaste for tradition is in itself an evidence of his failure to obtain satisfaction from his philosophy. Among practical men anti-traditionalism is always a latent tendency; but when a man of such evident intellectual power as Osborn turns against not only the formal tradition of learning but even against the graces of literature and art, there seems to be at work a powerful, directed reaction against some important stream of thought. Osborn's reaction was against the humanistic as well as against the romantic strains of the Renaissance, and involved an increased emphasis on the rationalistic phases of the same movement.

[18] *Ibid.,* pp. 36-7.

In addition to his animosity against learning, Osborn shows an equally strong opposition to those aspects of life that are the more usual concerns of literature. Classifying all human feeling as "passion," he adopts a tone of bitter cynicism towards sentiment and sentimentality alike. His scant and perfunctory poems do little to dispel the impression gained from his advice about love and marriage. This section of the *Advice to a Son* has deservedly been one of the main points of interest in Osborn's works, and loses little of its effect through the renunciations of an appended apology "To the Women Readers." Marriage is for Osborn, like other institutions, the result of an unavoidable necessity occasioned by civilized life. The love-instinct, he says, is implanted by Nature for the propagation of the species. In animals it assumes a role of normal and appropriate importance; in human beings, on the other hand, it leads to many varieties of folly: "our fellow Creatures, (the exacter Observers of the Dictates of Nature) promiscuously . . . [bestow love] on every distinct Female of their respective *Species*; whereas Man, being restrained to a particular Choice, by the severity of Law, Custom and his own more stupendious Folly," is carried away by "the first apparition of an imaginary Beauty," love causing "Madness in some Folly in all. . . ."[19] Both the Church and the law connive at deceiving men into an acceptance of marriage. But such persuasion is superfluous, Osborn adds, for there are always fools enough to stock the world. The section on love and marriage reveals all of the moral obtuseness that was to characterize the Restoration, without the gaiety of that later time. It is typical of a period when that part of the Renaissance which produced sonnets was no more.

The basis of Osborn's thought, it is clear, is rationalism; and for Osborn rationalism not only gave sanction to an expedient course of action, but also pointed out to him the position in which he stood. Among like-minded contemporaries regret for the faith of the Middle Ages and the beauty of the earlier Renaissance had turned to a cynical bitterness long before Osborn began to write. But in Osborn's bitterness and dissatisfaction there was an element of thought that many others had not—the clear perception of the

[19] *Advice,* pp. 48-9.

historical significance of what was going on: he speaks of the Reformation and the invention of printing as heralds of the downfall of the old order, and despite his contempt for antiquity there is regret for the times that are gone. In fine, rationalism was for Osborn a useful, though limited, weapon of thought. Although it was by no means a telescope whereby he might discern clearly the prospects of the past and future, it served well as a compass to tell him in what direction he was going for the present. If he failed to develop his system of philosophy completely, it is still to his credit that he at least saw the world of his contemporaries as in some respects it needed to be seen. Rationalism such as Osborn adopted is, as the best seventeenth-century and the best modern thought perceives, a dangerous guide to life. But when all is said and done, it remains a better thing than the undisciplined emotionalism of thought and action which has since the eighteenth century been sounding its own noisy praises throughout the civilized world.

II. OSBORN AND CHESTERFIELD

MR. W. LEE USTICK has called Osborn's work the prototype of Chesterfield's letters to his son,[1] and·this relationship, obvious to anyone who has read both authors, reveals one of Osborn's most significant aspects. It is surprising, however, to find that nowhere in his letters, so far as I have been able to ascertain, does Chesterfield refer to Osborn, fond though he is of quoting favourite books of counsel, as may be seen from his emphatic reference to the political maxims found in the *Mémoires* of Cardinal de Retz.[2] The similarities of general style and tone, and even of phraseology, lead one to hazard a guess that there is, however, a closer connexion than is obvious on the surface. For example, with regard to behaviour in Roman Catholic countries Chesterfield and Osborn respectively say:

> When I was in Roman Catholic countries, I never declined kneeling in their churches at the elevation, nor elsewhere, when the Host went by. It is a compliance due to the custom of the place, and by no means, as some silly people have imagined, an implied approbation of their doctrine. Bodily attitudes and situations are things so very indifferent in themselves, that I would quarrel with nobody about them.[3]

> To the *Eucharist,* met in the Streets (through which it is often born to the houses of the Sick), Costome, no less than the Injunction of the Magistrate, obligeth all to kneel, or bow: The which if a Stranger neglects, he is liable to the Inquisitors: Now if it be an Idol, St. *Paul* saith *an Idol is nothing*: And if it renders the Meat offered unto it no waies

[1] In "Advice to a Son: A Type of Seventeenth Century Conduct Book," *Studies in Philology,* XXIX, July, 1932, p. 409.

[2] See Letters 1551, 1557, 1582, 1746 (an undated enclosure in a letter to his son, which lists sixty-seven of the Cardinal's maxims), *et al.* References are to the six-volume *Letters of Philip Dormer Stanhope, 4th Earl of Chesterfield,* edited, with an introduction, by Bonamy Dobrée, London, 1932.

[3] Letter 1660.

distastfull to a sound Conscience, how should it deprave me to be uncovered, as the rest are? It being palliated, if not absolutely decided this way, in the case of *Naman,* and the Duke of *Saxony*; whom *Luther* permitted to assist the Emperor *Charls* the fifth at Mass, onely to preserve a temporall Dignity, covering it with the title of Civil respect.[4]

If one were to take from Osborn's writing its pre-Dryden involvedness, or from Chesterfield's its fine Addisonian elegance, one would have in an overwhelming number of instances the same thoughts in much the same words.

Two explanations occur to one why Chesterfield should display seeming or even real ignorance of Osborn's work despite such similarity. Mr. Bonamy Dobrée, in his introduction to the letters, has pointed out that Chesterfield, though he must have been thoroughly familiar with his grandfather Halifax's *Advice to a Daughter*, and though there is so much alike in the characters of the earl and his grandsire, "mentions him only once"; and goes on to say that "the reason is pretty clear; a man who quotes his grandfather will certainly be looked upon as a bore."[5] The Marquis of Halifax's parental advice is markedly similar in tone to Osborn's, and one explanation of Chesterfield's apparent independence of Osborn is that perhaps it was from Halifax rather than from Osborn himself that he gleaned the seeds of Osbornian doctrine, which, in the intellectual environment that Chesterfield enjoyed, soon enough developed into something resembling the original plant. But the very fact that Chesterfield avoided referring to his grandfather suggests possibly a general tendency to avoid reference to sources uppermost in his mind. So, for example, as Mr. Dobrée has shown, Chesterfield in his philosophy is remarkably dependent upon Cicero's *Offices*. Yet I have been unable to discover that in the letters to his son he quotes the *Offices* at all,[6] although he does quote from the *De Oratore*. There is no very convincing reason for supposing, therefore, that he did not know Osborn; and there is the evidence of abundant parallels tending to show that he did know him. It must be remembered, too, that Osborn and Chester-

[4] *Advice*, p. 92.
[5] Dobrée, *op. cit.*, I, 14.
[6] Nevertheless, in Letter 1653 he warmly recommends the chapter on decorum.

field, though they agree completely in their estimates of women, universities, and human nature, are at odds over the intrinsic worth of courtliness and of classical learning. Accordingly, since Chesterfield's letters were written to serve as outlines for Stanhope's education, the boy being expected to look up the books his father mentioned, Chesterfield would naturally have avoided naming the *Advice to a Son,* which, despite its philosophical similarity to Chesterfield's own views, certainly would have exerted a strong influence against many of the traits the earl was anxious to inculcate.

To understand rightly the relationship to Osborn (and conclusions here are quite independent of, and much more important than, questions of source-relationships), it is necessary to take up once again the task of evaluating Lord Chesterfield. The task is, perhaps, more vexing and ungrateful than difficult or tedious. The popular estimate of the man has so often been shown to be wrong that no recapitulation of the argument against it is necessary. What critics have tended to forget, however, in their eagerness to fix responsibility for the monster-myth about Chesterfield, is consideration of the whole question of why, despite its erroneousness, the traditional calumny clings with such extraordinary tenacity. As yet no one has done for Chesterfield what Carlyle and Macaulay did for Cromwell. Despite explanations of the affair with Johnson, despite charitable interpretations of his counsels regarding fornication, and despite revelations of the man's political honesty in a corrupt age, the old dislike abides.

In the first place, much of it is due to the spirit of democracy which since the French revolution has made elegance and aristocratic standards suspect in Europe and America. Democratic standards have encouraged a cult of crudity and have led to such developments as that which in the United States has been aptly designated the mucker-pose. Then, too, there is the British abhorrence of things French, of things that are or seem to be hyperelegant: this is a different thing from the first attitude, but in the present case works for the same end. Deeper than these causes, however, lies a relationship between Chesterfield and an element of European consciousness older than Rousseau or Anglo-Saxon nationalism. That element is Christianity. Chesterfield was the kind of man who in a pagan society, like that of the ancient Rome he so wholeheartedly admired, could never be considered other than eminently sane, just, and admirable, but who in a Christian society, despite a host of virtues that demand praise, must appear at the least faintly despicable. The reasons for this are easy to discover. That Chesterfield's fine control of his emotions, his good taste, his political uprightness, his willingness to sacrifice personal vanity to kindliness, the genuineness and honesty of his feelings, which never were allowed to become undisciplined enthusiasms (note, in this connexion, his dislike of Methodism)—that these qualities certainly constitute him something very much like a Christian gentleman cannot be denied. Yet it is no less undeniable that he was without Christian faith, hope, charity; and that he was completely without any sense of dependence on divine grace. The deficiency is glaring, and inevitably has rendered the whole man suspect, despite his justice, prudence, fortitude, and temperance.

His certain and indisputable possession of these moral virtues, moreover, was not the result merely of accidental circumstances of birth and environment; Chesterfield never relied on his natural impulses and inclinations as being sufficient to produce the ideal of perfection that he had before him. Rare enough to deserve considerable attention are men who so thoroughly as Chesterfield have exercised man's power to know and to shape himself. As Mr. Bonamy Dobrée has said,

> Who is there . . . that feels strongly one way or another about Hervey or Harrington, Pulteney or Bubb Dodington, or who cares immoderately about that much more important figure, the Duke of Newcastle? They did not create themselves, therefore they do not stand for anything. Chesterfield, on the other hand, stands for something very definite; he is the pattern of a certain type of man, embodying an idea which must always be an integral part of any society, though its value must fluctuate with the need for it. It is the idea of the consciously civilized, controlled man, as opposed to that of the savage, or impulsive man. . . . One cannot help siding either with or against it as one cannot help either admiring or despising the unbridled enthusiast; one cannot remain indifferent. It is because this constructed character takes visible

form in the letters that they are still important. . . . Wesley
was important for what he represented, Chatham for what
he did; but Chesterfield yet persists through having been
what he made himself.[7]

His desire to construct a character was to be fulfilled, furthermore, in terms of materials of an uncommon sort. It was to a
large extent Chesterfield's extreme sensitiveness that led to his
near-failure as a politician and his condemnation as a parental
adviser. The quality of his mind was in no sense of the word
coarse. He perceived with wonderful clarity that education was
dependent on a host of subtle influences which even the detailed
guidance of a father could never impart, but which must come
from an intuitive understanding of the nature of men and things;
that good manners required study and yet must, in the final
reckoning, be unstudied: he had, therefore, Osborn's fear of the
pedantry that loses a genuine feeling for life.

Like Newman a hundred years later, he was born with a mind
that inevitably was impressed with the world and expressed its
views of the world in terms of subtle perceptions that the greater
part of mankind cannot appreciate; and like Newman, who in
most respects certainly is Chesterfield's antithesis, he was misun-
derstood and maligned because of that very quality. Both men
had a certain subtle honesty which even to other intellectual, honest
men must have seemed like casuistry and "slipperiness." Chesterfield's ability to be on good social terms with men who were his
political enemies is a case in point. He was not, in the ordinary
sense, ambitious. " 'I want those two great prevailing springs of
action, avarice and ambition,' he told Lord Marchmont. . . ."[8] The
development of his personality was not shaped by unphilosophical,
crudely selfish ends. His method and manner were not Machiavellian, designed to gratify most efficiently and speedily the lust for
power and pleasure. Like his great prototype, the stoic Cicero,
he was neither an ambitious egoist nor a sentimental reformer:
his public policy flowed from a keen mind striving to discern mankind clearly, from a realization of the soundness of traditional

[7] Dobrée, *op. cit.*, I, 21-2.
[8] *Ibid.*, p. 77.

ethics, and from a desire to live life in this world as satisfactorily as he could.

His lack of avarice and ambition, indeed, made it possible for him to see the world, and particularly the world of courts, with much of Osborn's detached view. Chesterfield, however, unlike Osborn, had Roman courage rather than Post-Renaissance despair, and therefore, although he knew that courts *were,* as the old advice books and courtiers' manuals had made clear, dangerous, ungrateful places, he decided that the righteous, sober, clear-headed man could live in them and succeed.

Chesterfield's conscious and deliberate fashioning of himself, however, made him part of a tradition to which Osborn did not belong and which indeed he definitely rejected. The real background of Chesterfield's advice to his son has been admirably characterized by Mr. Paul Elmer More in a passage that deserves quotation.

> He was the late product of an art which has practically passed from the world. We are concerned to-day about our duties and our pleasures, and about the means of making life efficient; but who is concerned to mould his life into an artistic design? We write enormously of all the mechanical arts, but where is to be found a modern treatise on the one supreme art of living? It did not use to be so, as any one knows who has read the literature of the Renaissance. . . .

> There are hints of [this conception of life as one of the fine arts] . . . in Xenophon and Horace and other writers of antiquity, but its real origin would be found in the engrafting of the classical sense of decorum on the mediaeval idea of chivalry.[9]

Surely nothing could be further from this tradition of literature and life than Osborn's harsh and obstinate cynicism: Osborn, indeed, being unable to see how the human spirit, sailing a heavy, practical ship, could do more than manage to avoid shipwreck, whereas Chesterfield thought himself and his son capable of going safely into the roughest sea in a delicate bark. Osborn, of course, though he counsels expedient elegance, was the antithesis of urbanity; like certain courtesy-book writers of the sixteenth

[9] *Shelburne Essays,* Fifth Series, New York and London, 1908, pp. 216-17.

century he stands for the country gentleman who resents urban polish and what he deems superficiality. Chesterfield, on the other hand, deserves perhaps above all else the adjective *urbane*. His dislike of the country is only too clear. His description of his visit to Devonshire during his father's last illness is picturesque, though less charitable than was the wont of Chesterfield when he was somewhat older. He contemptuously says that

> the inhabitants here are as utter strangers to the sun as they are to shoes and stockings . . . [h]ad I been a Papist (as, thank God, I am not), I should have thought myself in purgatory; but, being a good Protestant, I was obliged most orthodoxly to conclude myself to be in Hell. But, reflecting, since, how little good company I meet with here, and how much I might expect to find there [*i.e.,* in London], together with the consideration of my excessive poverty, I begin to believe I am in Scotland, where, like the rest of that nation, I only stay till I am master of half-a-crown to get out of it.[10]

Of Osborn's private life we know comparatively little, whereas we know a good deal about Chesterfield's. Although this circumstance is due in part, of course, to the fact that Chesterfield was a public character and in general a man of greater importance than Osborn, there is something in the nature of the advice each man has to give which further explains it. Osborn's advice, as will be shown later, was not only a piece of specific personal guidance for his son, but also gave him an opportunity to express his views about a variety of things. It seems to have been written with an eye to publication. Chesterfield's advice, on the other hand, is direct and immediately personal: he does not content himself with describing the dangers to which the young man entering society is exposed: he gives an extended account of his own difficulties and failings. The letters, too, were never intended for printing and were in fact published against the will of those most immediately concerned. There is, because of this difference, about Osborn's work a certain oracular quality that is missing in Chesterfield. One is tempted to think of Osborn as a kind of impersonal sum-

[10] Letter 13 (To the Hon. Mrs. Howard).

mation of certain aspects of the seventeenth century. This is related to the fact that he is not at all conscious of being a made man. He is witty, and in a sense artificial, but his tone is that of a man speaking out his blunt uncultivated feelings. Significantly he is more of a determinist than Chesterfield.

III. THE ADVICE-*GENRE*

THE differences between Osborn and Chesterfield, however, give no hint of how many types of thought books of
advice in all ages have put before the world: this protean
form of literature includes kinds of counsel that stand in much
greater contrast. As is evident in Osborn's case, such writings are
not always purely personal documents. A thoughtful consideration
of Cicero's *Offices,* for instance, will suggest that it and many
similar works have a dual purpose; they are definitely personal
documents, but at the same time they are compositions designed to
express to the world at large their authors' views of life. Putting
those views into the form of advice to a son, or of a letter to a
friend, gives them something of that quality of almost nonchalant
indirectness, exemplified also in the narrative poets' plunging *in
medias res* or using a "framework" story, which is one of the
permanent bases of good art. An artist rightly enough does not
want to assume the demeanours of the preacher or philosopher. The
advice book, accordingly, is often, no less than the literary epistle, a
disguised philosophical essay.

This consciousness of an audience other than his offspring is
clearly evident in Osborn's work. The fragmentary character of his
counsel might lead one, it is true, to think his intention was merely
to provide John Osborn with "markes to saile by"—admonitions
a little out of the ordinary. But to realize how much Osborn knew
himself to be an outrager of convention one has only to glance
at the prefaces addressed to his readers which appear before the
two parts of the work. Furthermore, it is not in his essays, or
other miscellaneous writings, which are considerably more systematic, but in *Advice to a Son* that he sets down his most important thoughts. And it is perfectly natural for a man of Osborn's
temperament to choose for the utterance of his deepest convictions an apophthegmatic and fragmentary form. The academic
instinct in him was at best feeble—no *Leviathans* would sport at

his bidding. "Huge *Volumes*," he says, perhaps with something of a thrust at Hobbes, "like the Oxe roasted whole at *Bartholmew Faire*, may proclaime plenty of Labour and Invention, but afford lesse of what is delicate, savory and well concocted, than *smaller Pieces: . . . Humane sufficiency being too narrow, to informe with the pure Soul of Reason, such vast Bodies.*"[1] The popular form of the advice book, which had already been used by Lord Burleigh, Raleigh, and the great James himself, was ideally suited for Osborn's purpose.

Indeed, as will presently be made clear, the rather disorganized quality of Osborn's *Advice* is a valuable clue to its literary ancestry and that of many similar works. In the first place, advice literature really belongs to a larger *genre* which includes not only the manual of precepts but also the courtesy book and the treatise on education.[2] In the case of Osborn's work this relationship is immediately apparent when one observes that certain subjects, such as fencing and poetry, with regard to which Osborn felt little interest except in so far as he challenged tradition by his matter-of-fact Puritan opinion, are nevertheless included in *Advice to a Son*—apparently because comment on such subjects was a conventional part of courtesy books and treatises on education.

Advice to a Son shows very clearly the disintegration that had taken place in the literary type of the courtesy book. The philosophical temper of the sixteenth century in Italy, where the *genre* had originated, and that of the seventeenth century in England, where it was assimilated into other literary traditions, were aspects of the Renaissance vastly different in the influence they tended to exert on ideas of proper and advantageous conduct. As Mr. Elbert N. S. Thompson has pointed out,

> The fact is, there was less apparent need in England for the perfect courtier. In small southern states there was a general call for service, at court, in diplomatic business, or in war. But in the larger life of England men left school to teach or

[1] *Advice*, p. 9.
[2] John E. Mason's *Gentlefolk in the Making*, Philadelphia, 1935, shows very fully just what is the content of this *genre*, as it appears in England from 1531 to 1774. More limited in scope but on the other hand somewhat more penetrating in its conclusions is Ruth Kelso's *The Doctrine of the English Gentleman in the Sixteenth Century*, Urbana, 1929, to which is appended an extensive bibliography.

preach, to manage their estates or follow one of the professions. Furthermore, as men of letters outgrew the financial dependence on the nobility that hampered early humanists like Budé, their attitude toward the nobility was altered. Consequently, the court training lost its hold. Naturally, therefore, the old book of courtesy disintegrated, and its parts were assimilated by writings of other kinds.[3]

It is a far cry from Castiglione's *Book of the Courtier* to Osborn's *Advice to a Son,* not only in the conception of conduct that the two works reveal, but also in the attitude towards literature of each writer. Yet a comparison of the two works is valuable for the light it throws on the changing temper of the Renaissance as it followed its destiny on the Continent and in England.

In the first place, *The Book of the Courtier* itself is in a sense the product of a local condition as much as of the larger impulses of the Renaissance, being the result of the intimate and cultivated humanistic society that flourished in the small states of Italy. The ideal of conduct defined in such an environment would naturally be imbued with the peculiar philosophical spirit which was nourished by the rediscovered ancient literatures and which at this time was not yet troubled by the vexing individualism which soon permeated Renaissance thought and action. *The Book of the Courtier* retains much of the sublime impracticalness of the Middle Ages. If it were not so obviously indebted to the dialogues of Plato for both form and thought, one might easily be tempted to entitle it *The Mirror of Courtiership.* It is concerned with the presentation of an ideal that was sponsored by cultivated Italian society, and this alone it accomplishes; the practical achievement of the ideal, the method of educating the courtier, is neglected. Despite the abundance of concrete illustrations that Castiglione uses, his work remains an ideal discussion, whose practical value consists not in the specific instructions that it offers but in the richness of the inspiration it possesses, in its intellectual subordination of individual whim to the larger purposes of religion and philosophy. Like any medieval writer, Castiglione assumed a

---

[3] *Literary Bypaths of the Renaissance,* New Haven, 1924, pp. 152-3. I am indebted to Mr. Thompson's chapter on "Books of Courtesy" for many suggestions in the following pages.

universal moral law, a great ethical generalization, which the concrete details of life are used to illustrate.

By other writers, however, it was ancient scepticism alone that was adopted, and Platonic spiritual affirmation was suppressed. The effect of this trend in Renaissance thought upon the courtesy books is closely connected with matters that are historical rather than philosophical. The courtesy books of men like Castiglione were written with the idea of increasing the spiritual attainments of a society which was already cultivated; they were not mere books of etiquette. A certain practicality, however, they could not help having, as is evident from Castiglione's intention that the courtier give counsel and inspiration to his prince. This serving of statecraft, however, was not necessarily a monopoly of virtuous princes and courtiers, but might exist at the most Machiavellian of courts. And where Platonic spiritualism declined, the courtesy book became more and more practical and not seldom unscrupulous.

The utilitarian conception of courtiership, in turn, easily led to the development of courtesy books into simple manuals of advice. As long as the *genre* retained the philosophical characteristics of *The Book of the Courtier* it retained the form of an extended general discussion of important aspects of life; but once its purpose became utilitarian, the *genre,* it would seem, tended to assume the form of isolated bits of counsel—the most practical kind of literature imaginable. This degeneration of the type is only the logical result of the abstraction from it of part of its original purpose.

The new *genre,* moreover, filled a need which was itself the result of developments in Renaissance culture parallel to those that have been outlined above. In some periods, indeed, such literary expressions may be rather superfluous, since the principles of morality have been generally agreed upon by mankind in general. Such, for instance, was the case in the Middle Ages, when moral teaching was well-nigh uniform throughout the Western Christian world. When, however, men's repose in the moral precepts of an active teaching institution like the medieval Church is broken, argument over moral matters breaks out afresh, and not only the inculcation but the simple definition of virtue becomes the function of didactic literature. Further, when men lose trust in the tradition handed from century to century, they revert to an adherence to that simple prototype of all tradition, the precept handed from generation to generation, from father to son. Logically then, it would seem that the greater moral and religious confusion one finds in a given period, the more frequent will books of advice tend to become.

The advice books of seventeenth-century England by their very number offer strong evidence for the truth of this principle. In England, more perhaps than in any other country, was felt the need for direct, immediate practical advice. For in England the Renaissance did not reach its greatest strength until its sceptical and rationalistic elements had already acquired considerable vigour. Puritanism, which had abundant moral convictions but was deficient in authoritative unity, prepared the ground for the atheism of the latter part of the seventeenth century, since by rejecting the intellectual and cultural tradition of the older Christianity, it tended unwittingly to play into the hands of continental rationalism, which began by attacking the Roman Church, but which eventually became the foe of all religion. From the religious turmoil of seventeenth-century England emerged, accordingly, at least two types of Renaissance individualism. The first, unorthodox but deeply religious, was the individualism of Luther's private judgement. The second, rationalistic and worldly, was the individualism of the Italian sceptics, transmitted to England through French writers. A kind of advice book corresponds to each of these. Of simple manuals of devotion and sober precept there are such works as Nicholas Breton's *The Mothers Blessing,* his *An Olde Mans Lesson and a Young Mans Love,* William Martyn's *Youths Instruction,* and John Norden's (?) *The Fathers Legacie, With precepts Morall, and Prayers Diuine. Fitted for all sorts, both yong and old.*[4]

Intermediate between them and the type of advice book to which *Advice to a Son* belongs—the shrewd, worldly counsel of men like Sir Walter Raleigh—stand a few works which have some of the characteristics of the latter type, but which in general trend belong rather with the pious works of the religious advisers. The out-

---

[4] For these titles, and for some information used in the following pages, I am indebted to Mr. W. Lee Ustick's article cited above.

standing example of these is King James's *Basilikon Doron,* which, as is natural from the scholarly quality of its author's interests, reflects considerably Castiglione's idea of nonchalance, making evident the literary ancestry of the book. James puts great emphasis on religion, and despite his hostility to Puritans wrote a book that in many respects a Puritan would not have been ashamed to call his own, as Mr. Ustick points out. Pagan ethics and Christian doctrine form the basis of its moral philosophy. Like its ultimate Italian prototypes, it attempts to cover the fields of clothing, sports, and general social demeanour, and these matters it refers to a religious basis as well as a utilitarian one. The loftiness of Castiglione's ideal courtier is absent, but the work has the simple, straightforward piety and good sense which in English thought often took the place of the more high-flying virtues.

The second great class of advice books, to which Osborn's work belongs, has little or no pious counsel, and confines itself to the most practical kind of advice based on a philosophy of expediency. This naturally represents the most pronounced departure from the nobler Italian courtesy books, since it presupposes a pessimistic evaluation of mankind, and is thoroughly materialistic in its conception of the value of manners and good conduct.

The immediate continental literary counterpart of the worldly kind of advice book seems to have come from France, where there appeared such works as Du Refuge's *Traité de la Cour* (1616?). As the century grew older, increased connexions with French court life led to a general introduction into England of the Parisian idea of the courtier, which had succeeded the older Italian idea. In 1722 there appeared in London a volume entitled *Instructions for Youth, Gentlemen and Noblemen,* consisting of reprints of four treatises that had been popular during the seventeenth century. In addition to *Raleigh's Instructions to His Son, and to Posterity* and Burleigh's *Precepts* (designated in this volume as *The Lord-Treasurer Burleigh's Advice to a Son*), it contains *The Instructions of Cardinal Sermonetta, To His Cousin Petro Caetano* and *Walsingham's Manual of Prudential Maxims, For Statesmen and Courtiers.* These last pieces are both of them translations of continental works, and were known in England long before this publication. The first of the two, although it gives distinctly worldly advice, bordering at times on a rather doubtfully ethical shrewdness, makes some attempt to justify the social procedures it suggests, and is careful to define some kind of moral distinction. The other work, however, which seems to be of Spanish origin, while it admits that a moral man would never engage in such activity, describes all of the trickery and deceit that could be employed in the court. Works like this must have had a great influence in shaping Osborn's opinions of court life, and in contributing to his pessimistic evaluation of human nature generally.

The general characteristics of the second group of advice books are practicality, unscrupulousness, time-serving, and the kind of caution that comes from distrusting mankind everywhere. Religion receives mention, of course, but the disillusion that the religious troubles of the sixteenth and seventeenth centuries brought to England has penetrated deeply into the minds of many thoughtful Englishmen, and had a counterpart in a further disillusion with regard to government, friendship, love, and human nature generally. The advice that these books give, therefore, is not an advice designed to bring its recipient close to an absolute and ideal perfection; for what this is writers of such works would not and could not say; it is an advice intended to keep away from men the most obvious causes for pain and discomfort. To get along as best one could was the hope of these writers, just as to live gloriously and magnanimously had been the hope of Castiglione.

A good example of the extremely practical, ethically callous advice book is the ninth Earl of Northumberland's *Advice to His Son,* which was written at the end of the sixteenth and the beginning of the seventeenth century.[5] It appears to be the work of an experienced, thoroughly educated, and well cultivated man, but is entirely lacking in all religious sentiment, even of the purely conventional kind. Its not being intended for publication may account for its frankness in treating the evil aspects of human nature, and for its omission of the usual pious conventionalities.[6]

[5] It has been recently edited and for the first time published in full, by G. B. Harrison, London, 1930.

[6] Osborn's little couplet,

> "Now *You* are *Taught* to *Live,* there's nothing I
> Esteem worth *Learning,* but the way to *Die,*"

with which he closes the earlier portion of *Advice to a Son* is really an excellent

In content Northumberland's *Advice* is closely related to later examples of the *genre*. In form, however, it is a continuous discourse, broken into two parts. Most of the advices, on the other hand, tend to be fragmentary in character, being composed of a series of short essays, as is Raleigh's *Instructions to his Son, and to Posterity,* or of a series of loosely connected statements arranged in groups according to subject-matter, as is the first part of Osborn's *Advice.* It has been suggested above that this form is to some extent due to the degeneration of the courtesy book; but this fragmentary form suggests another source for the advice *genre* that cannot be ignored.

And this source, the wisdom literature of the Hebrews, is, in fact, very valuable for the further light it sheds on the fundamental nature of the *genre.* This is especially true of *Ecclesiasticus,* which, as a matter of fact, is largely written in the form of advice to a son; as, "My son, defraud not the poor of his living, and make not the needy eyes to wait long."[7] Mingled with such precepts there is, just as in Osborn's *Advice,* philosophical comment and explanation. Osborn's *Advice,* in turn, depends for its effectiveness on a style often resembling the Hebraic proverb couplet; so for example, "Propose not them for patterns, who make all places *rattle,* where they come, with *Latine and Greek*; For *the more you seem to have borrowed from Books, the poorer you proclaime your naturall Parts,* which only can properly be called yours."[8] With euphuism only lately dead, and with the character sketch flourishing in his day, there was abundant reason why Osborn should adopt a style that was full of contrasts and depended for its vigour on the skilful balancing of two related parts of a thought, or on the amplification or restatement of a proverb.

Now as Moulton has pointed out in *The Literary Study of the Bible,* the very term "wisdom" has an especial significance which

commentary on the relative importance of religion in comparison with that of worldly wisdom, since it admits that "learning to die" has not been included in the advice, and therefore is, after all, perhaps not so very important. Northumberland does not even include a pious epilogue of the kind that Osborn puts before this couplet.

[7] *Ecclesiasticus* iv:1.

[8] *Advice,* p. 14.

distinguishes the books with which it is ordinarily connected from other portions of Scripture. The name "wisdom" suggests

> that its literature will have a practical bearing on human conduct. A great part of such writings is made up of specific observations or precepts in matters of social and family life, or business management, public policy, and general self-government. And where such works as *Ecclesiastes* or the *Wisdom of Solomon* are occupied in interpreting history, or reading the riddle of life, they make it clear that the argument is followed with a constant reference to the bearing of the whole on conduct. It is only when a comparison is made with the kindred department of Prophecy that we see the right of Wisdom literature to be classified under the head of Philosophy, the organ of reflection. Prophecy also is concerned with conduct, but it starts always with a Divine message, on which all that it contains is based. Of course Wisdom is in harmony with the revelation contained in Law and Prophecy, but it never appeals to it. The sayings of the Wise come to us only as the result of their own reflections, in combination with the general tradition of Wisdom.[9]

The wisdom books are, in many respects, exceedingly realistic: they disentangle truth from the tangled skeins of experience, and then state it in terms of that experience. One might call them the sceptical parts of Holy Writ, for many passages of them reveal the temporary bitterness and disillusion that, whether or not it be ultimately compensated by a fresh access of joy, is, at some time and in some way, a characteristic symptom of most realistic, clear thinking about human life. As Henry Thatcher Fowler has pointed out, the wisdom literature continues the train of thought that was started in the book of Job: "the rewards sought by men are not always given in direct proportion to the wisdom and virtue of the seeker."[10] The wisdom books are efforts towards the reconciliation of revealed truth with this experience. Like Socrates, the teachers of wisdom believe that truth is approached by active doubt as well as by active faith. Proverbs generally emphasize the practical and sceptical aspects of thought and one is tempted

[9] Richard G. Moulton, *The Literary Study of the Bible,* Boston, 1896, pp. 255-6.
[10] *A History of the Literature of Ancient Israel,* New York, 1922, p. 337.

to speculate whether they may not be the kind of simple moral teaching to which mankind rather generally turns when religion and philosophy fail to provide an adequate code of moral or judicious conduct—just the situation that also calls forth the advice book. The impulse to supplement or to reinterpret traditional teachings is, of course, present at all times, but crises in the moral and religious life of the people augment the tendency and stress the individual character of the advice that is given.[11]

The wisdom literature shows this same individualistic tendency. *Ecclesiastes, Proverbs,* and *Ecclesiasticus* were written between 332 and 168 b.c.—a period not distinguished for political quiet. As is clear enough from the wisdom books, the dangerous qualities of rulers were not left to seventeenth-century England to discover. Counsel to stay away from persons of great power, to walk warily if one cannot avoid their presence, is abundant in the wisdom literature, as in the advice books, and for the same reason, the corruption of government and the political disturbances of the times. The cultural situation was, indeed, in many points similar to that of Europe at the time of the Renaissance. After Alexander's conquest the process of Hellenization began, and came to its climax in the Maccabean struggles. That is, Hebrew culture was put on the defensive against a foreign culture, just as European culture was put on the defensive against the same invasion centuries

---

[11] A striking confirmation that the advice book develops easily out of simple proverbs is to be found in Irish literature. The development here is in many respects similar to the Hebrew, and may in fact be an instance of Hebrew influence. The similarity of the "Triads of Ireland" to characteristic manners of expression of the wisdom literature is strikingly obvious, and Kuno Meyer believes that "the model upon which the Irish triads, tetrads, pentads, &c., were formed is to be sought in those enumerative sayings—*Zahlenspruche,* as the German technical term is—of Hebrew poetry to be found in several books of the Old Testament." And he quotes passages from *Ecclesiasticus* and *Proverbs* to prove his point. (Royal Irish Academy, Todd Lecture Series, vol. xiii, *The Triads of Ireland,* ed. by Kuno Meyer, Dublin, 1906, pp. xii-xiv.) Among the Irish, gnomic literature apparently took most readily the form of such enumerative proverbs. It is interesting, therefore, that there existed in ancient Ireland a class of literature corresponding to the advice *genre,* which shows here again its development from the proverb. "Among the gnomic literature of ancient Ireland," says Meyer, "the instructions given by princes to their heirs, by tutors to their disciples, or by foster-fathers to their sons form a group by themselves." (*Ibid.,* vol. xv, *The Instructions of King Cormac Mac Airt,* ed. by Kuno Meyer, p. v.)

later.[12] During the centuries immediately preceding the birth of Christ faith and morals among the Jews were disturbed. Confidence in the sacrificial system of the Temple was already shaken,[13] and a mere appeal to traditional faith and practice was accordingly insufficient: therefore the wisdom literature, with its approach to religion through practical life, arose. For its materials this literature naturally drew upon the traditional body of proverbs—the reasonable propositions of common sense and popular shrewdness —and also upon the wise sayings of the learned philosophers. The situation is again parallel to that of seventeenth-century England, where, as has been said above, there was a tendency to develop a type of literature that gave brief, apophthegmatic advice, isolated and terse, proverbial and epigrammatic. It is interesting that the seventeenth century, too, should be the century in which the essay assumed form in the English language, just as the period of the wisdom literature was the time of its development in Hebrew.[14]

That the advice books are, therefore, in general spirit similar to the ancient wisdom literature, is clear enough. A careful examination of the advice books, furthermore, shows that they owe a large and direct debt to the wisdom books, especially to *Ecclesiasticus*. This debt is discoverable in the very subjects chosen for advice, in manner of phrasing, and in shrewd knowledge of human nature.[15]

[12] *Ecclesiasticus* was, in fact, written with a definite anti-Hellenic spirit: "The mass of information which the book contains regarding Jewish religion, thought, and ethics, during a period for which we do not otherwise possess such information, marks it out as a work of high importance. The writer evidently intended to offer to his people a kind of text-book to which men and women might have recourse for guidance in almost every conceivable circumstance of life. He does this, however, with the primary object of setting in clear light the superior excellence of Judaism over Hellenism. In a sense, therefore, *Ecclesiasticus* may be regarded as an apologetic work, inasmuch as it aims at combating the rising influence of Greek thought and culture among the Jews." W. O. E. Oesterley in the introduction to *Ecclesiasticus,* The Cambridge Bible for Schools and Colleges, Cambridge, 1912, p. xxiv.

[13] *Ibid.,* p. xxxii.

[14] *Cf.* Moulton, *op. cit.,* pp. 260, 267. Moulton points out the great stylistic influence wisdom literature had on Bacon, Feltham, and Earle.

[15] Notice that Heydon says Osborn's advice "smells like a diseased peece of an *Apocripha.*" (*Advice to a Daughter,* 1658, p. 3.) On 22 June, 1614, there was entered into the Stationers' Register a book called "BATHSHEBA*es Instructions to her sonne* LEMUEL *or an exposition vpon the last chapter of*

The most remarkable parallel between *Ecclesiasticus* and an advice book is that offered by Sir Walter Raleigh's *Instructions to his Son, and to Posterity*. Any such comparison must be entered into warily, because the advice *genre* obviously will have certain favourite hackneyed themes that all the givers of counsel will use. Yet, the fact that the fundamental spirit of Raleigh is so vastly different from that of the author of *Ecclesiasticus* makes it somewhat easier to establish a relationship, since it is men who are writing in a similar spirit who may *unconsciously* say the same thing; when two men writing from a different point of view say similar things the probability of direct borrowing is much greater.

Raleigh's advice is a strange mixture of ruthless worldliness and of simple, practical piety. One recalls immediately Osborn's defence of him against the charge of atheism.[16] Raleigh is obviously disillusioned, and his pious remarks may be little more than a conventional close. But the movement from worldliness to piety suggests Jesus Sirach's movement from shrewd, sceptical (but moral) observation to the praise of the law of God. Raleigh, like Osborn, quotes Solomon with evident approval, and seems to have drunk deep at the well of the wisdom literature. He quotes also from *Proverbs,* and, at the end of Chapter VIII, from *Ecclesiasticus* without even acknowledging the source: "Make not the hungry soul sorrowful, defer not thy Gift to the Needy, for if he curse thee in the Bitterness of his Soul, his prayers shall be heard of him that made him."[17] If one abstracts from *Ecclesiasticus* all of the material chiefly theological or locally Hebraic in character, what is left is still a good-sized manual of practical advice, just such as a father might give to his son. And for nearly all of the principal kinds of subject-matter that Raleigh has in his advice, something corresponding can be found in *Ecclesiasticus*. For instance, Raleigh devotes a whole chapter to friendship, a subject that Jesus Sirach mentions again and again, in warnings as to the

the proverbs" by John Dod and William Hynde. In 1597 Thomas Middleton had published *The Wisdom of Solomon Paraphrased* (see Middleton's *Works,* ed. by A. H. Bullen, London, 1886, vol. viii, pp. 137-297). These are instances of interest in the wisdom literature and its connexion with advice books in the years preceding Osborn's greatest writing activity.

16 *Miscellany,* preface "The Authour to the Reader."
17 *Ecclesiasticus,* iv : 6.

choice of friends, in admonitions concerning duties towards friends. The whole question of restraint in speech, one of the most noteworthy themes of *Ecclesiasticus,* receives extensive discussion in Raleigh. The advice not to go surety for anyone is emphasized significantly in both works. And Raleigh's comment on mercy and justice towards the poor, is, of course, directly taken from the same source.

The Italian courtesy books and their various descendants, the wisdom literature of the ancient Israelites, and, finally, advice books written in England in the half-century preceding his own work—these formed the background of Francis Osborn's *Advice to a Son.* And that this book represents the full development of advice books as a separate *genre,* can be postulated with a considerable degree of certainty. The great fame of the book, its undoubtedly original quality, its obvious consciousness of the subject-matter of other examples of the type, all point to it as the English culmination of a literary form that had grown up out of a variety of materials in order to meet what was a pressing need of the day.

Especially convincing is the claim of Osborn's work to being the most significant of the advice books, when one remembers that Osborn is notably connected with the very conditions that have been pointed out as being the social causes for the appearance of the *genre.* He was well aware of the disturbance in politics (the 1722 edition of his works even calls him an "eminent statesman"!); he had heard the arguments of all the religious sects of the time; he had come into contact with his fellow men in important places of life in an intimate way; he knew his times as few men did. Most significant of all—to state an unhappy fact charitably—he was by natural temperament and through the influences of the day a vigorous anti-traditionalist, who felt strongly that individual effort and thought, apart from received patterns of conduct, were necessary.

What elevates him far above all the other advice-writers is the fact that he not only states his point of view, but is also aware of its ramifications. Raleigh, Burleigh, and Northumberland illustrate well enough the amoralism of certain kinds of thought during the period, and they are interesting examples of the way in which this trait was connected with the advice *genre*. But it is only in Osborn that one finds the complete and open statement of the philosophical dilemma that lies behind it. His thought is in many ways imperfect and faulty; but of all the important advice-writers he most clearly shows to the reader the relationship existing between the philosophical temper of the period and the advice books that it produced. Though he does not solve the problems of faith and rationalism, he states them well.

To the superficial observer, Osborn seems to be verily the self-sufficient wit of Newman's description:

> Every now and then you will find a person of vigorous or fertile mind, who relies upon his resources, despises all former authors, and gives the world, with the utmost fearlessness, his views upon religion, or history or any other popular subject. And his works may sell for a while; he may get a name in his day; but this will be all. His readers are sure to find out in the long run that his doctrines are mere theories, and not the expression of facts, that they are chaff instead of bread, and then his popularity drops as suddenly as it rose.[18]

Francis Osborn is, beyond question, one "who relies on his own resources," and although he does not despise quite *all* former authors, he definitely rejects the scholarly tradition of literature, and the rejection has earned for him, it seems, the doom of the shallow thinkers whose works are finally discovered to be "chaff instead of bread." This he does not quite deserve, for, much as one may be convinced that in these particulars Osborn resembles the pseudo-philosopher Newman has pictured, there is borne in upon one with equal force the realization that Osborn's writings are not quite "chaff"—that there is behind them a significant body of thought. Carefully examined, it is of extreme interest, not as something great and noble, but as something vigorous and really important. Osborn's ideas are not "mere theories"; they are based on hard, clear facts—of the kind that Osborn was fitted to perceive. He had a thorough distrust of metaphysics and even of abstraction,

---

[18] *The Idea of a University Defined and Illustrated,* eighth edition, London, 1888, p. 129.

and made no attempt to carry his generalizations into remote universal conclusions.

It is to be hoped that in the course of time mankind will conclude that the sort of philosophy upon which some of Osborn's views are based is indeed chaff. But until such a conclusion is held more generally than it is today, the principles that often guided Osborn's observation and thinking will have far-reaching intellectual and social consequences; and he will be a figure deserving study.

After all, the best introduction to Osborn must ever remain the preface to the *Miscellany,* in which he states that his purpose in writing is not to court the reader, but to give expression to a spirit that would otherwise break the containing vessel. His subjects, he says, he has chosen with freedom and with no attempt at exhaustive or scholarly treatment. He insists, as he does elsewhere too, that a man can write if he has an experience and understanding of society, even though he lack formal university training.

The bitter frankness of this document serves as nothing else could to make clear to the reader the kind of man Osborn was. He says that he cares nothing either for praise or blame, and that he cannot be held accountable for the errors in his writing,

> *being from my* Birth, *uncapable to receive the Rich* Talent *of* Learning, *look'd upon, as* The onely Key *of* Knowledge: *which if obtayned, had been Little Advantage, since I want* a Memory *wherein to* Hoord *up what I had* stollen. *And so the* Acquired Groat, *might not unpossibly* have spoiled, *and* adulterated *the more* Natural Shilling. *Wherefore, if a* Chymistry *might be found, able to* Extract *any thing useful toward the* Conduct *of* Man, *out of such* Ordinary Simples, *as* These, *They were* highly to be esteemed; *And in likelyhood,* more suteable *to every* Tast, *as* Fresh-gathered *from the* Tree *of* Experience, *then those* Sophisticated *by the* Schools, *or of a* narrower interest, *then* That, *of* the whole Society of Man.

Later, in the same place, he says,

> . . . *I remember, to have heard from Sir* William Cornewallis, (*esteemed* none of the *meanest* Witts, *in his* Time) *That* Montaign's Essay's, *was the likelyest Book, to advance*

Wisdom: *because, The* Authqurs own *Experiences, is the* Chiefest argument *in it. For as* St. August[i]ne *saith, of* Short *and* Holy Ejaculations; That they pierce Heaven *as* soon, *if not* quicker, *then more* Tedious Prayers: *So I have reaped greater* Benefit, *from concise and* Casuall Meditations, *on severall* Topicks, *then* long *and* voluminous Treatises, *relating meerly to one and the* same thing. . . .

It is his purpose

to redeem *the* World *out of a* Common Error, *by shewing,* Men *are not so* unhappy *in the* Absence of Learning, *as* Scholars *pretend.—Whose* First *Question is,* What University you are of? *And their* last, *if answered,* None: *For then, they consider the* Party *as* irrationall, *and* below Conversation. *Forgetting, That though* Books *may produce a few* rough Materialls; *it is only in the power of* Experience, *and* Naturall Parts *to Build up and* Burnish *a* Perfect Man.

This preface shows too how well Osborn understood the manner in which his work was being received, and the significance of the reception. To condemn a man for not agreeing with one, he says, is like condemning him for having a nose of a different length, since minds, like bodies, vary. He has no illusion that his fame will endure. Here as elsewhere the fugitive quality of literary fame is fully apparent to him. He is honest in admitting the possible deficiencies of his work, in confessing that argument and persuasion are of little use in the world as it is. He admits, further, the limitation of his own point of view, and satisfies the discerning reader that his work is a reasonably careful and a reasonably sincere exposition of his views. He offers his subject-matter and his literary style for what they are worth, conscious within himself of having thought as clearly, and of having written as intelligently, as he could.

It is no wonder, therefore, that his contemporaries should have found in Osborn's work much of interest, even purely for the sake of the information it contained. He knew things about his times and could present them in a substantial, matter-of-fact way; men were looking for just such sound advice as he was giving. More significant, however, is the fact that Osborn was competent to state the problem of his age. Beneath all his submission to governmental and ecclesiastical forces, as beneath all the cautious adjustments that he advises his son to make, lies the feeling that fundamentally such compromise is only a makeshift.

Yet both his concern with the problem of leading a safe life in a dangerous age, and his neglect of all that was not to be formulated immediately in contemporary terms and for a contemporary purpose, resulted in his work's having as its outstanding literary character pertinence without perspective, so that the same qualities which made Osborn a centre of interest in the seventeenth century were not sufficient to sustain his reputation with people of a different epoch. The incidents in terms of which he develops his ideas ceased to have other than merely historical interest. Men not of the seventeenth century could not trace in Osborn's ideas the problems of that century, simply because Osborn had limited his background to one period. He wrote, it might be said, for a single generation. The power of his intellect and the deep interest he took in contemporary life made him sensitive to being influenced; but the limitation of his method and purpose left him almost powerless to influence. Therefore he characterizes, rather than contributes to, the temper of the age.

Osborn's predominant importance in the advice *genre,* then, is due to his representing and expressing so clearly the temperament and conditions that lead to the development of the *genre.* And within the *genre* it is not too much to claim for him the setting of a fashion and the suggesting of ideas. The Marquess of Halifax's *Advice to a Daughter* has already been mentioned as an example of Osbornian influence. And the Marquis of Argyle, in his *Instructions to a Son,* published originally in Edinburgh and reprinted in an English edition at London in 1661, speaks of "several books in Print, written Prudently, Politickly, and Piously of this very title of late years."[19]

The advice *genre,* of course, continued as a literary type, and the characteristic thought of the earlier books did not disappear, although seventeenth-century individualism ebbed. Chesterfield, it will be remembered, though his ideas approximate Osborn's in

[19] P. 1.

many ways, is after all a conformer to conventions. An interesting phenomenon towards the end of the seventeenth century is the interpenetration of the religious and the worldly kind of advice in books like Stephen Penton's *The Guardian's Instruction, Or, The Gentleman's Romance* (London, 1688), and his *New Instructions to the Guardian* (London, 1694). In these works there survives the idea, though not the form, of the earlier advice books, and the writer is indeed conscious of being part of a tradition; but the older characteristic divisions of subject-matter, and the apophthegmatic expression of thought are gone. The day of smooth Ciceronian English prose was on its way, and Penton's advice, or rather, his suggestions for educational procedures, though they have a charm all their own, lack the strength and force of Osborn's cruder wit. In J. Barecroft's *Advice to a Son in the University* (third edition, London, 1713) as in Penton's books, there is a trace of the worldliness of the older books in the appreciation of the difficulties that honesty has in preserving itself in a rather generally wicked world; usually, however, this book has a calmness and assurance of the value of piety and study that is in marked contrast to the bitter tenseness of Osborn's thought.

In its older and more characteristic form the advice book appears as a stronger literary type, since, like every significant literary *genre,* it fulfils a need that calls for a definite kind of expression. Just as tragedy sets forth man's heroic stability in the face of ill fortune, just as lyric poetry expresses the mutable but important passions of the individual, just as the novel expresses man's attempt to study society by recreating it in fiction, so does the advice *genre* represent the need for individual advice when tradition seems to fail, and the desire to condense the whole problem of conduct into a few expedient rules when a well-rounded philosophical wisdom is difficult of attainment. And of the many books of the type that English literature has produced none, very probably, is so thoroughly suggestive of the literary affiliations and philosophical implications of the *genre* as Francis Osborn's *Advice to a Son,* in which there is expressed so much that even today sharpens the zeal or exasperates the soul of intelligent men.

DRYDEN'S PLAYS: A STUDY IN IDEAS

By MILDRED E. HARTSOCK, PH.D.

FORMERLY CINCINNATI WESLEYAN FELLOW IN ENGLISH
UNIVERSITY OF CINCINNATI
ASSISTANT PROFESSOR OF ENGLISH
LYNCHBURG COLLEGE

DRYDEN'S PLAYS: A STUDY IN IDEAS

I. DRYDEN AND HIS CENTURY

THE literary achievement of John Dryden long since has been judged at the bar of informed opinion and accorded what is doubtless its proper sentence. His work possesses a manifold significance: historical importance in the development of prose style; skill unequalled, perhaps, except by Pope, in satirical and didactic verse; and a peculiar interest with respect both to the evanescent type of the heroic play and to the *genre* of Restoration comedy. This is impressive, even though it has to be recognized that nothing of Dryden's arises from the most profound inspiration. Lowell was right when he said that one feels "the whole of him" to be better than "any random specimens."[1] He occupied a unique position as the foremost man of letters in his times; he experimented in a variety of literary types, with some degree of success in all; he left his mark upon the political and religious speculation of the day. And, however justifiably it may be concluded that Dryden is not a second Shakespeare or Milton, both his intrinsic merit and his eminence among his contemporaries provide ample reason for inquiring into the intellectual background of his work.

Few critical problems have been attacked more often or more inconclusively than this: the question whether or not Dryden's poetry and prose had any sound or consistent intellectual basis. "As to his opinions," A. W. Verrall writes, "he had no profound or coherent theory in politics, in religion, or even in criticism. . . . His logic made him clear and his controversial tone increased his vigour, but the logic is of the moment; arguments for a given position are readily found and well put, but there is no system, not even in the matter of literary criticism."[2] Several incidents in the poet's life—especially his tribute to Cromwell followed by exul-

---

[1] *Among My Books,* New York, 1898, p. 8.
[2] *Lectures on Dryden,* Cambridge, 1914, p. 18.

tation at the return of Charles, and his conversion to Rome upon the accession of the Catholic James—have fostered the conviction that he was a time-server, a man of no deep-lying ideas or loyalties. Mr. Mark Van Doren, calling him a "turn-coat" and a "flatterer," asserts that the sensible view "seems latterly to be that there is little reason to be sorrowful over the behavior of a canny man of letters who never at any time pretended to be equipped with principles worth dying or becoming a pauper for."[3] Macaulay, dean of the virulent critics of Dryden, admitting that the poet had to a preëminent degree the power of reasoning in verse, avers that "the theological and political questions which he undertook to treat . . . were precisely those which he understood least."[4] Samuel Johnson, Walter Scott, and Edmond Malone, on the other hand, regard his so-called apostasies as legitimate and in accordance with a single *direction* of thought; and Scott, in particular, is inclined to attribute to him a profoundly, if not a systematically, philosophic mind.[5] Most of the critics, friendly or unfriendly, stress the fact that the poetry of Dryden is primarily intellectual rather than emotional and that his mind displays something of the delight of the scholastic in juggling ideas; but, except for the attempt of Scott to unify those ideas, the critics have been content, until recent years, to generalize about the poet without specifically analyzing the thought-content of his varied work. And to none of them had it seemed worthwhile to study Dryden in relation to his age: to determine what attitudes widely prevalent in the seventeenth century are most often expressed by him.

Macaulay says, with much truth, that no man exercised so much influence on the age as Dryden, for the reason that "on no man did the age exercise so much influence."[6] Professor Louis I. Bredvold[7] is one of the first of modern scholars, recognizing this

[3] *The Poetry of John Dryden,* New York, 1920, p. 321.

[4] *The Works of Lord Macaulay,* London, 1866, Vol. V, p. 116.

[5] *The Works of John Dryden,* illustrated with notes, historical, critical, and explanatory, and a life of the author, by Sir Walter Scott. Revised and corrected by George Saintsbury. Edinburgh, 1882-1883, Vol. I, pp. 420-1.

[6] *Op. cit.,* p. 104.

[7] Miss Kathleen Lynch, Mr. Claude White, Professor Merritt Hughes, and Mr. Ned Bliss Allen are others who have contributed much to recent study of Dryden.

interplay of influences, to maintain that the ideas of Dryden should be evaluated and linked with the currents of thought amidst which he lived and wrote. The purpose of his book, *The Intellectual Milieu of John Dryden*,[8] is to establish the poet, not as an opportunist who changed his opinions with his coat, not as a man of no serious convictions, but as a thinker who, after a short period of indetermination, followed a clear path of religious, political, and philosophic belief. Admitting that in the early work there are suggestions of Hobbism and Cartesianism, he discounts them as passing phases—if they deserve even that name—and affirms, as his major contention, that from the writing of *Religio Laici*[9] to the end Dryden was a Pyrrhonist:[10] that his scepticism produced in religious thought a fideism which guided him logically to the Roman church, and in politics a Toryism which made zeal and revolution repugnant to him. A large part of his treatise is devoted to a discussion of Roman Catholic apologetics in England: the presence of fideism even within the Mother Church, the contacts which Dryden had with fideistic writers, and the evidences of them in *Religio Laici*. His study, which contributes many hitherto uncompiled facts about Pyrrhonism in England and on the Continent, and which succinctly reviews the scientific movement of the times, is focused upon the *milieu* in which the poet lived, and upon the problem of determining his real opinions from what he wrote. Although Mr. Bredvold quotes passages from the plays which seem to him at least to indicate the scope of the dramatist's intellectual curiosity, he minimizes their importance as reliable bases for deducing seriously held ideas, on the ground that the exigencies of character and situation affect the nature of the views expressed and render it dangerous to assume that the writer ever is speaking in his own person.

The present study of the dramatic works of Dryden has been undertaken with full awareness of the hazard of attempting to translate fictional writing into intellectual autobiography, and, moreover, if one may say so, with complete cognizance of Dryden's

[8] University of Michigan Press, 1934.
[9] He does not suggest a sudden change at this time, but merely points to *Religio Laici* as providing the first definite evidence of Pyrrhonism.
[10] *Cf.* pp. 13, 14, 15.

extensive indebtedness to French sources and to theatrical conventions of his day. The primary aim of this analysis, however,
is not the positing of dogmatic assertions regarding the dramatist's
personal philosophy: not to pull a line from *The Spanish Friar*
or a motive from *Love Triumphant* and confidently to exclaim:
"Eureka! Here is the *real* Dryden." It is, rather, to study important intellectual trends of the seventeenth century which are
reflected in the plays of Dryden; to discover in which of these the
poet was most apparently interested; and, finally, through comparison of the serious and comic plays and through reference to
the non-dramatic works, to secure what evidence there is of the
writer's own probable beliefs. This study, then, will be in one
sense an extension, and in another sense a criticism, of Professor
Bredvold's investigation. Emphasis will be placed upon those
plays which were most wholly Dryden's own: the heroic dramas
and the serious plots of the tragi-comedies. The recent findings
of Mr. Ned Bliss Allen with respect to the sources of the comedies
leave them a useful field for speculation only as deviations from
models and choice of models tend to bear out evidence supplied
by the more original plays and the non-dramatic works.

The century in which Dryden wrote was one of absorption in
ideas: logical expansion of the thought of the Renaissance; persistent efforts to synthesize the naturalism of the new era with the
religiosity of the Middle Ages; the beginnings of reaction against
the confident optimism of man's intellectual re-birth;—all united
to produce a philosophical diversity well calculated to challenge
the minds of literary men. The humanism of the sixteenth century,
Janus-faced, looking with equal interest into the well of the past
and the crystal of the mundane future, resulted, on the one hand, in
the recrudescence of such ancient systems of thought as Platonism,
Stoicism, and Epicureanism, and, on the other, in the development
of the natural sciences and the technique of inductive experimentation. As Nature tended to supersede Heaven and Hell,
metaphysical abstractions began to lose their compelling force for
many men, and materialists like Thomas Hobbes affirmed the
adequacy of philosophic monism to explain the universe. Materialism did not reign undisputed, however, any more than science
progressed unopposed, for groups like the Cambridge Platonists

and certain rational theologians tried to effect a compromise between the free play of reason and the dogmas of faith. Members of the Cambridge circle, for example, became the chief exponents in England of Cartesianism, which took its starting point from the immaterial, reasoning ego and from that derived certainty of God and the existence of the objective world; the dualism of Descartes, they perceived, was not incompatible with that of their own Platonism, and some such division was necessary to preserve the integrity of both reason and faith. Neither materialist nor scientist nor Cambridge Platonist had lost the assurance that man can cope successfully with the problems of life through the functioning of reason; but alongside of them arose still another school of thought, sceptical in character, which countered their positive assertions with the intellectual nihilism of complete doubt.

William James has said that every world-philosophy is merely an expression of the temperament of its creator; and, similarly, it is a truism that a writer will be influenced by those trends of thought to which his personal character is especially receptive. In the preface to *Religio Laici,* Dryden states that he is "naturally inclined to skepticism in philosophy"; and this declaration is corroborated by the discovery that, in so far as the plays provide evidence, he was touched very little by the pure rationalism of Descartes, the idealism of the Neo-Platonists, or the dogma of the Stoics; whereas he unmistakably was affected by those systems which at that time appeared to put less strain upon credulity— the materialism of Hobbes and the Pyrrhonism of Montaigne.

In 1591 Galileo had discovered the laws of motion and affirmed that physical phenomena may be explained by them; and on the mechanistic conception of the universe suggested by that belief Hobbes founded his philosophy. His world-view is based upon a monism which posits sense and the passions as fundamental in human behaviour :

> . . . the *universe,* that is, the whole mass of all things that are, is corporeal, that is to say, body ; and hath the dimensions of magnitude, namely, length, breadth, and depth : also every part of body, is likewise body, and hath the like dimensions ; and consequently every part of the universe, is body, and that which is not body, is no part of the universe : and because

the universe is all, that which is no part of it, is *nothing;* and consequently *no where.*[11]

All mental processes are derived from sensations, which are merely aspects of motion caused by bodies pressing upon the organs of sense:

> . . . for there is no conception in a man's mind, which hath not at first, totally, or by parts, been begotten upon the organs of sense.[12]

In motions towards or away from an object originate the passions, and they are the source of all voluntary action on the part of man. The man who has no passions, Hobbes says more than once, is dead; and thoughts only serve as spies or scouts for the desires, "to range abroad, and find the way to the things desired . . . for as to have no desire, is to be dead: so to have weak passions, is dullness."[13] Reason is nothing more than "*reckoning,* that is adding and subtracting, of the consequences of general names agreed upon for the *marking* and *signifying* of our thoughts. . . ."[14] Truth is an attribute not of things but of speech; for things are as they are, and only what is said about them is subject to error. The purpose of ratiocination, moreover, is not to arrive at truth absolutely conceived, but to secure for the individual whatever he wants.

The ethics of Hobbes is wholly individualistic and nominalistic. Passions in themselves, he affirms, are neither good nor bad: they simply exist.

> But whatsoever is the object of any man's appetite or desire, that is it which he for his part calleth *good*: and the object of his hate and aversion, *evil;* and of his contempt, *vile* and *inconsiderable.* For these words of good, evil, and contemptible, are ever used with relation to the person that useth them: there being nothing simply and absolutely so; nor any common rule of good and evil, to be taken from the nature of the objects themselves.[15]

[11] Thomas Hobbes, *Leviathan.* In *The Complete English Works of Thomas Hobbes,* edited by Sir William Molesworth, London, 1839, Vol. III, p. 672.
[12] *Ibid.,* p. 1.
[13] *Ibid.,* pp. 61-2.
[14] *Ibid.,* p. 30.
[15] *Ibid.,* p. 41.

The constitution of a man's body is in constant mutation, and it is consequently impossible that the same things should always cause in him the same reactions, or that he should be capable of consistent behaviour. For Hobbes man is entirely self-regarding and cannot act from, or be appealed to by, any motive extraneous to his own best interests. In a natural condition, every man is in a real or potential state of warfare against his fellows. Competition, desire for glory, and, chiefly, fear lest they be deprived of life cause men to be ever in strife. Fear and a desire for comfortable existence impel them to devise a central power or authority which can maintain peace and guarantee safety. Reason, then, formulates the conditions of a Commonwealth founded upon the basic law of nature "by which we are forbidden to do any thing destructive to our life."[16] Man deliberately chooses to impose upon himself limitations designed ultimately to convert formal freedom into real security.

The life of man, in the view of Hobbes, is a progress from the satisfaction of one desire to that of another. Specifically, it is lived in accordance with a few dominant instincts, chief among which are the instinct for self-preservation and its concomitant, the desire for power; and reason, although it serves a useful purpose in pandering to the Self, is a definitely subordinate force:

. . . for the passions of men are commonly more potent than their Reason.[17]

The philosopher gives the measure of his own materialism and ethical opportunism when he states that the life of natural man is "solitary, poor, nasty, brutish, and short."[18]

Hobbes is related in various ways to the new science, which, since Bacon's exposition of the inductive method, had increasingly allied itself with humanistic interest in the physical aspects of the world. Deriving the content of man's mind wholly from the five senses, Hobbes points towards the empiricism of scientific method at the same time that, actually, he remains a nominalist; rebelling against the formalism of scholastic reasoning, he sug-

[16] *Ibid.*, p. 134.
[17] *Ibid.*, p. 173.
[18] *Ibid.*, p. 113.

gests the claim of science to intellectual emancipation from the strictures of tradition. Yet Hobbes was not a scientist, nor was his philosophy in any sense an outgrowth of the experimental method. That method, however, did receive a tremendous impetus in 1660, nine years after the publication of the *Leviathan,* with the establishment of the Royal Society by a group of men among whom were Roger Boyle, Sir Christopher Wren, and John Evelyn. Thomas Sprat, historian of the Royal Society, defines their aims thus:

> Their Purpose is, in short, to make faithful *Records* of all the Works of *Nature,* or *Art,* which can come within their Reach; that so the present Age, and Posterity, may be able to put a Mark on the Errors, which have been strengthned by long Prescription; to restore the Truths, that have lain long neglected; to push on those, which are already known, to more various Uses; and to make the way more passable, to what remains unreveal'd. . . . And to accomplish this, they have endeavour'd to separate the Knowledge of *Nature,* from the Colours of *Rhetorick,* the Devices of *Fancy,* or the delightful Deceit of *Fables.* . . . They have attempted, to free it from the Artifice, and Humors, and Passions of Sects; to render it an Instrument, whereby Mankind may obtain a Dominion over *Things,* and not only over one another's *Judgments:* And lastly, they have begun to establish these Reformations in Philosophy, not so much, by any solemnity of Laws, or Ostentation of Ceremonies, as by solid Practice and Examples. . . .[19]

Sprat makes it clear that the society did not pretend to encroach upon the domain of religion, but drew a sharp line between things spiritual and the province of science. Nevertheless, the society's historian expresses confidence that the future will erase this line:

> . . . yet, when they shall have made more Progress in *material* Things, they will be in a Condition of pronouncing more boldly on them [spiritual matters] too. For though Man's *Soul* and *Body* are not only one *natural Engine* (as some have thought) of whose Motions of all Sorts, there may

[19] *The History of the Royal Society of London For the Improving of Natural Knowledge,* London, 1722, pp. 61-2.

be as certain an Account given, as of those of a Watch or
Clock; yet by long studying of the *Spirits,* of the *Blood,* of
the *Nourishment,* of the Parts, of the *Diseases,* of the *Advantages,* of the Accidents which belong to *human Bodies*
. . . there may, without Question, be very near Guesses
made, even at the more *exalted* and *immediate* Actions of
the *Soul*; and that too, without destroying its *spiritual* and
immortal Being.[20]

Though less bold than Hobbes's placing of religion among the fairy
tales of the world, this statement points *in the direction* of a
physical interpretation of soul, and is the more significant because
Sprat was an Anglican clergyman who became a bishop.

The theology of the seventeenth century as well as the philosophy, and often through the direct influence of the new philosophy,
proved in many cases to be in accord with the worldliness of
Renaissance humanism and with the individualism of the Protestant revolt against authoritarian Rome. Even Richard Hooker,
the first to give cogent definition to the Anglican position in the
closing years of the sixteenth century, emphasizes the importance
of reason in theology.[21] Unceasingly he deprecates blind zeal, and
he admits, probably without seeing all the implications of the
admission, that even the authority of the *Bible* resides finally in
man's reason, which tells him that Scripture *is* the revelation
of God. Much more definitely the stress upon reason and utility
appears in the sermons of John Tillotson, late-century Archbishop of Canterbury. On two occasions, at least, Dr. Tillotson
was publicly accused of preaching the doctrines of Hobbes from
his pulpit. Religious wisdom, he says, is the best wisdom because
it is for ourselves—whose end is happiness.[22] And he states unequivocally that the goodness of everything, even religion, is
measured by its use.[23] His declaration that God is so necessary to

20 *Ibid.,* pp. 82-3.
21 Of course this in itself was nothing new, and only signifies, on its face,
that Hooker bases himself upon medieval scholasticism. What was new was
the encouragement given by Hooker and, even more, by his immediate successors in England to the extension of reason's field.
22 *The Works of Dr. John Tillotson,* edited by Thomas Birch, London, 1820,
Vol. I, pp. 327-8.
23 *Ibid.,* p. 326.

the welfare and happiness of mankind that it would seem "as if the being of God himself had been purposely designed and contrived for the benefit and advantage of men,"[24] was deemed by contemporaries to be "downright Hobbism." It would be grave error, of course, to assume that materialism and utilitarianism alone represent the philosophy of the late seventeenth and early eighteenth centuries; but their importance in the work of men so prominent as Hobbes and the Archbishop of Canterbury is proof enough that they were seriously to be reckoned with.

Not dissimilar to the ethical implications of Hobbism were those of a second important movement in the thought of the seventeenth century—the revival of Epicureanism. The Renaissance had directed men's eyes to antiquity before the Protestant reformation; and, consequently, when that reformation dealt a blow to the authority behind Christian ethics, many turned to the philosophies of Greece and Rome for a way of life better adapted to this world than that prescribed by Christianity. So, in England, during the last years of the Elizabethan period, the works of such dramatists as Chapman and Massinger are permeated with Stoicism. In France Epicureanism achieved a wide following. Systematic formulation of a modified Epicureanism was made by Pierre Gassendi, a French priest and critic of Aristotle, in two treatises, *De Vita Moribus et Doctrina Epicuri* and *Syntagma*.[25] Like Hobbes, Gassendi urged the necessity of outward conformity to the religion imposed by the state; but, having paid his respects to the conventional religious explanation of the cosmos, he worked out independently his own atomistic explanation based upon Epicurus. Gassendi cannot, according to Professor Brett, be called a materialist, despite his atomism: for, though he does not admit that the step from matter to mind is unique, mind for him is not a mere function of matter.[26]

[24] *The Works of Dr. John Tillotson,* Vol. I, pp. xli, xlii.

[25] The first treatise was published in 1647; the second in 1655, the year of Gassendi's death. He had been at work upon it for twenty years or more, and had begun to exert some real personal influence upon the course of French thought as early as 1624.

[26] G. S. Brett, *The Philosophy of Gassendi,* London, 1908, p. 267.

The emphasis in Gassendi's revival of Epicureanism was upon physics rather than upon ethics; yet it was the latter which produced the most immediate influence upon French thought. With Epicurus, Gassendi pronounced the *summum bonum* to be pleasure and affirmed that the pleasure which is the end of action is not mere self-indulgence, but is in the highest sense moral. Ultimately he relied upon the Aristotelian paradox that the pleasurable good is what gives pleasure to the good man. His real significance to ethical thought is his opposition to the ascetic ideal through his insistence that pleasure and virtue are not mutually exclusive.[27]

It is more immediately relevant to see how Gassendi's restatement of Epicureanism helped to encourage a new free-thinking and free-living group in French literary life. Between the years 1615 and 1625 there sprang up in Paris a coterie of young men known as *libertins,* some of whom repudiated authority both in their thinking and in their conduct, and others of whom insisted merely upon their right to independent belief. The former had come under the sway of the Italian Vanini, who, from 1615 to 1617, carried on a campaign in Paris and was finally burnt for heresy. His doctrine "Live according to Nature"—by which he meant not the universal Nature of the Stoics, but the individual nature of every man—became the ideal of a number of poets who wrote heretical and immoral verses and in their lives practised every conceivable mode of sensuality.[28] Frédéric Lachèvre, who edited the works of the *libertins,* along with the philippics of their Jesuit accuser, Père Garassus, attempts a definition of the type:

> Un libertin est un homme aimant le plaisir, tous les plaisirs, sacrifiant à la bonne chère, le plus souvent de mauvaises moeurs, raillant la religion, n'ayant autre Dieu que la Nature, niant l'immortalité de l'âme et dégagé des erreurs populaires.[29]

Other *libertins,* like La Mothe le Vayer, Molière, and, in his later years, Cyrano de Bergerac, were serious-minded men, honestly intent upon fighting the battle of liberalism. This French

[27] *Ibid.,* pp. 183-95.
[28] Arthur Tilley, *From Montaigne to Molière,* p. 237 ff.
[29] *Le Libertinage au XVII Siècle,* Paris, 1909, Vol. I, p. xxiii.

group is important to the present study only as it represents the extreme consequences of materialistic philosophy and as it exemplifies in actual life a type of thought and conduct often reflected in Restoration drama, and in Dryden.

Although the *libertins* alluded to Gassendi as a wise master, they perhaps owed even more to the naturalism of that earlier wise master, Michel de Montaigne.

> Whoever shall conjure up in his fancy . . . that great form of our mother Nature, in her full majesty . . . he alone estimates things according to their true proportion.[30]

The sceptical and worldly portions of the philosopher's writings found ready ear among these French advocates of free-living and free-thinking; and marks of his influence are abundant in the work of more important writers. Montaigne, however, was not an Epicurean. At the beginning of his career he had been Stoic, and to the last, Stoical elements lingered in his thought; but, between 1570 and 1580, he encountered, through the translation of Henri Stephen (1562), the writings of Sextus Empiricus, and subsequently became allied with the scepticism of ancient Greece. Sextus, who lived in the third century A.D., provides, in *The Pyrrhonic Hypotyposes* and *Against the Mathematicians,* the most important record of the Greek sceptical thought which took its origin from Pyrrho of Elis[31] and continued, in Arcesilaus and Carneades of the New Academy, through Diogenes Laertius to Aenesidemus and Sextus himself. Pyrrho had been led to scepticism by recognizing the variability and unreliability of the sense perceptions. Mental representations of a single object, he pointed out, differ in different animals; two persons may disagree as to whether the air is hot or cold. Nor is there any homogeneity among the impressions made upon the various senses: there is no way to establish the inter-connections, if there are any, among the qualities of roundness and redness and sweetness in an apple; perhaps, even, there are qualities which our senses are not sharpened to perceive. That knowledge is wholly relative is apparent when it is noted to

---

[30] *Essays of Montaigne,* translated by E. J. Trechmann, London, 1927. 2 vols. Vol. I, p. 156.

[31] None of the works of Pyrrho is extant.

what degree external conditions affect the senses : a man's physical state will colour his mental images; or, on the objective side, the nearness or farness of a thing alters the size of the mental reproduction of it. The senses, furthermore, never come directly in contact with things, but are always separated from them by some medium, in which the real attributes of the object may possibly be changed. The values of objects or occurrences may become greater or less in proportion to their rarity or frequency; and the widely varying customs of countries show the impossibility of a single, rigid moral standard. By such arguments, expressed in ten tropes, or propositions, the Pyrrhonists demonstrated the futility of trying to deduce the real world from sense experience.[32] And sense experience, they continued, is man's only source of knowing; hence, since it is fallible and elusive, there can be no criterion of absolute truth. As the Stoics achieved peace of mind by disciplining themselves to desire only the attainable, so the sceptics fixed the positive aspect of their thought upon the achievement of intellectual calm flowing from suspension of judgement :[33]

> The aim of Pyrrhonism was ataraxia in those things which pertain to opinion, and moderation in the things which life imposes. . . . The method, however, by which ataraxia or peace of mind could be reached, was peculiar to the Sceptic. It is a state of psychological equilibrium, which results from the equality of the weight of different arguments that are opposed to each other, and the consequent impossibility of affirming in regard to either one, that it is correct.[34]

Pyrrhonism became, in ethics, religion, and politics, synonymous with conservatism and the preservation of the *status quo*; for if reason cannot validate standards of any kind, there is no logical justification for inviting disturbance and the pains of readjustment by changes in ideas or institutions, the superiority of which cannot be proved.

[32] Mary Mills Patrick, *Sextus Empiricus and Greek Skepticism,* accompanied by a Translation from the Greek of the First Book of the "Pyrrhonic Sketches" by Sextus Empiricus, Cambridge, 1899, Chaps. I and II.
[33] Referred to as *ataraxia.*
[34] M. M. Patrick, *op. cit.,* p. 27.

Although there were elements of sceptical thought in the fideism of Saint Paul and Augustine, Pyrrhonism as a philosophical system was not known in the Middle Ages. With the coming of the Renaissance, however, it reassumed its earlier importance; and in 1562 a Latin translation of the *Hypotyposes* was published, while in 1621 the Greek text of Sextus Empiricus was printed for the first time. Other sceptical treatises appeared at intervals, and by the advent of Montaigne there was a well-established tradition of sceptical thought to arrest his attention.[35]

Montaigne's statement of Pyrrhonic ideas, in the *Apology for Raimond Sébond*, became, as Mr. Bredvold puts it, "the classic and standard exposition of modern skeptical thought," the authority of which extends like a shadow "over the thought and literature of the whole seventeenth century, in England as well as in France."[36] Attempting to show the relativity of standards, Montaigne employs the ninth trope of Sextus Empiricus: evidence provided by the wide divergence in customs and ideas among the peoples of the world. And in a summary and criticism of the philosophies of the ancients, he explains the tenets of Pyrrhonism and points to the advantages which it possesses over other systems of thought. "Is it not better to remain in suspense, than to be entangled in the many errors that the human imagination has brought forth? Is it not better to suspend one's conviction than to get mixed up with those seditious and wrangling divisions?"[37] Concluding with a more positive declaration of allegiance, he states:

> There is no theory invented by man that offers more likeli-
> hood and profit. It presents man naked and empty, confessing
> his natural weakness and ready to receive from on high some
> power not his own; stripped bare of human knowledge . . .
> suppressing his own judgement to leave more room for faith;

[35] Other sceptical works were Thomas Fitzherbert's *Treatise concerning Policy and Religion*, 1606 and 1610; Father Simon's *Histoire critique du Vieux Testament*; and, earlier, Pico della Mirandola's *Examen Vanitatis Doctrinae Gentium*, 1520.

For a general account of the sceptical tradition I have relied upon Professor Bredvold's *The Intellectual Milieu of John Dryden*.

[36] *Op. cit.*, p. 30.

[37] *Montaigne, op. cit.*, Vol. I, p. 500.

neither disbelieving nor setting up any teaching contrary to
the common observances; humble, obedient, docile, zealous,
a sworn enemy to heresy and consequently free from the
vain and irreligious beliefs introduced by the false sects.[38]

He not only clears away the "rubbish" of dogma, but also shows
the way towards that employment of scepticism in the cause of
faith which his successor Pascal was to rely upon in the next
century. Since the reason is impotent and there can be only blind
ignorance and error, the best practical expedient for man is to
throw himself into the arms of God.[39] Pascal evinces the consistent tendency of Pyrrhonism to find its own position unten-
able and to compromise with ideas which, though not demonstrably true, bear the weight of pragmatic necessity.

Pyrrhonism, especially in its fideistic aspects, became a force
in English thought, as well as in French, during the seventeenth
century. Sir Thomas Browne, curious type of the Renaissance
man, with one eye on the "O altitudos" of faith and the other
on reasoned investigation of this world, had no illusions about the
claims of dogmatic philosophy:

> We do but learn to-day, what our better advanced judge-
> ments will unteach to-morrow; and *Aristotle* doth but in-
> struct us, as *Plato* did him; that is, to confute himself. I have
> run through all sorts, yet find no rest in any: though our
> first studies and *junior* endeavours may style us Peripa-
> teticks, Stoicks, or Academicks, yet I perceive the wisest
> heads prove, at last, almost all Scepticks, and stand like
> *Janus* in the field of knowledge.[40]

Like Pascal, however, he subordinated doubt to his religion;
taught "his haggard and unreclaimed reason to stoop unto the
lure of faith."[41]

---

[38] *Ibid.*, p. 502.

[39] *Cf. Thoughts*, translated by Edward Craig, Boston, 1849, p. 109. Other
French writers of the Pyrrhonic school were Charles de Saint-Évremond,
Pierre Charron, and François la Mothe le Vayer, each of whom, after the
manner of Montaigne, depreciates reason and pays homage to the philosophic
soundness of sceptical principles.

[40] Sir Thomas Browne, *Works*, edited by Charles Sayle, Edinburgh, 1912,
Vol. I, p. 99.

[41] Quoted from Basil Willey, *The Seventeenth Century Background*, London,
1934, p. 50.

Though Sir Thomas Browne's scepticism is basic to his thought, he admits no forthright indebtedness to Pyrrho; Joseph Glanvill, on the contrary, shows familiarity with the Greek philosopher, and his book, *The Vanity of Dogmatizing,*

> . . . is levied against *Dogmatizing,* and attempts upon a daring Enemy, *Confidence in Opinions.* The *knowledge* I teach [Glanvill continues], is *ignorance*: and methinks the Theory of our own natures, should be enough to learn it us. We came into the world, and we know not how; we live in't in a self-nescience, and go hence again and are as ignorant of our recess. We grow, we live, we move at first in a *Microcosm,* and can give no more Scientifical account, of the state of our three *quarters* confinement, then if we had never been extant in the greater world, but had expir'd in an *abortion.* . . . We breath, we talk, we move, while we are ignorant of the manner of these vital performances. The *Dogmatist* knows not how he moves his finger; nor by what art or method he turns his tongue in his vocal expressions.[42]

Glanvill treats of the impossibility of understanding the unity between body and soul, of the inadequacy of sense-experience, of the fallacies of the imagination, of the purely speculative nature of causation—in brief, of the *unknowability* of the universe. Yet, like his French contemporaries, he executes a *volte face* from doubt to religious faith:

> Though I confess, that in *Philosophy* I'm a Seeker; yet cannot believe, that a *Sceptick* in *Philosophy* must be one in Divinity.[43]

Mr. Bredvold points out that both Glanvill and Robert Boyle, controversialist of the Royal Society, though they were ardent defenders of the new science, tried to reconcile scepticism and religion by showing the limitations of reason and the prerogatives of faith. Boyle, he explains, attempted to guard against a "materi-

[42] Joseph Glanvill, *The Vanity of Dogmatizing,* with a bibliographical note by M. E. Prior, Columbia University Press, 1931, Preface.

[43] *Ibid,* pp. 186-7.

alistic interpretation of the new science by emphasizing the uncertainty of science itself."[44]

Both the materialism of Hobbes and the scepticism of the new Pyrrhonists were products of the questioning temper of the Renaissance; and both were widely significant in the seventeenth century. It is the purpose of this study to show that Dryden, not possessed of the type of mind which, confronted by disquieting truths and disruptive forces, seeks escape in philosophic idealism, definitely reflects in his plays the attitudes of the searching mind, sometimes expressing itself in materialistic monism, sometimes refusing to go beyond the safe borders of an honest doubt.

[44] *Op. cit.*, p. 62.

II. DRYDEN AND HOBBES

I

THE period of years during which John Dryden wrote plays was a time of widespread concern among members of the Anglican clergy, the Royal Society, and thinking people generally, regarding the materialistic philosophy of Hobbes. We are sufficiently assured that the dramatist knew Hobbes; and it is not surprising, in any case, to find mention of him in Dryden's prose. Although John Aubrey, the over-zealous biographer of Hobbes, affirms that the two were friends,[1] the references to Aubrey's idol in the poet-laureate's prefaces are sometimes deprecatory. He appraises Hobbes's translation of the *Iliad* by saying that he turned to poetry, as to mathematics, "too late";[2] and of Lucretius he states that, like "our poet and philosopher of Malmesbury," he is "every where confident of his own reason" and always bidding his reader "attend, as if he had the rod over him. . . ."[3] These allusions were made late in the poet's life, however, and consequently are not wholly relevant in determining the extent of Hobbes's influence upon the plays of his early and mid-career. The earliest reference to the philosopher, in the *Essay on Heroic Plays,* commends his repudiation of such paradoxes as "incorporeal substances."[4] Aubrey asserts, moreover, that Dryden was not only a friend of Hobbes, but did incorporate his ideas in the plays.[5] And an examination of the speeches, plot situations, and characters in those plays brings to light a considerable number of similarities to the views of Hobbes with respect to human nature, religion, and political theory.

[1] John Aubrey, *Brief Lives,* edited by Andrew Clark, Oxford, 1898, Vol. I, p. 372.
[2] *Preface to Fables* (1700); Vol. XI, p. 216.
[3] *Preface to Second Miscellany* (1685), Vol. XII, pp. 290-1.
[4] *Works,* Vol. IV, p. 24; *Preface to The Conquest of Granada* (1672).
[5] Aubrey, *op. cit.*

In a study of the sources of Dryden's comedies, Mr. Ned Bliss Allen mentions the discrepancy between the *ethos* of the heroic plays and that of the comedies.[6] The present investigation has revealed no essential difference between the two. Characters in Dryden's plays, whether they be heroic or comic, are almost uniformly selfish and morally insensitive. One of the marks of the heroic play, as introduced by Roger Boyle and continued by Davenant, Otway, and Dryden, is the presence of a hero who is grandly oblivious to all but the achievement of his superhuman feats of strength and valour. Were it merely a matter of the presence of such egoists, or were it merely that the comedies show a low plane of morality and complete absence of social responsibility, one could scarcely generalize concerning Dryden's own ethical perceptiveness. But much more is involved. Characters not only *act* as if they used the *Leviathan* as a handbook of philosophy: they frequently—and without any reason connected with the dramatic plan—express views which are close paraphrases of Hobbist utterances. It is impossible, moreover, to allocate such speeches to any particular type of character: heroes, heroines, villains, servants, witty lovers—all find occasion to voice them. The repetition of such views in play after play demands that they receive serious consideration.

Self-preservation, Hobbes declares, is a law of nature; it is the determinant in formulating civic organization, and it even becomes synonymous with right, for it can be no man's duty to do anything that might menace his own existence, nor a moral obligation to keep any agreement which would imperil his safety.[7] Dryden's characters are self-centred and their conceptions of the virtues are selfishly utilitarian. The law of self-preservation is, to many of them, a categorical imperative to which they give voice and according to which they act. Bertran, prince of the blood in *The Spanish Friar*, who proves at the end not to have been a villain, avers that

[6] *The Sources of John Dryden's Comedies*, University of Michigan Press, 1935, p. 102.
[7] Hobbes, *op. cit.*, pp. 134, 204.

> Self-preservation is the first of laws;
> And if, when subjects are oppressed by kings,
> They justify rebellion by that law,
> As well may monarchs turn the edge of right
> To cut for them, when self-defence requires it.[8]

And Montezuma, the Indian emperor, can see no wrong in killing the visitors to his court, because

> . . . each private man
> In his defence may justly do the same. . . .[9]

Duties to parents, as well as to kings, are automatically abrogated by conflict with the instinct for self-preservation; and Alphonso, hero of *Love Triumphant*, says in defence of his rebellion against his supposed father, Veramond:

> When kings and fathers, on their sons and subjects
> Exact intolerable things to bear,
> Nature and self-defence dispense with duty.[10]

Women justify their acts by reasoning similar to that of men; thus Almeyda, strong-minded heroine of *Don Sebastian*, explains her instigation of the murder of Muley-Moloch:

> When force invades the gift of nature, life,
> The eldest law of nature bids defend;
> And if in that defence a tyrant fall,
> His death's his crime, not ours.[11]

King and commoner alike admit to an ethical Narcissism. The beloved of Prince Arthur implores him:

> Believe thyself, thy youth, thy love, and me;
> They, only they, who please themselves, are wise.[12]

And Muley-Moloch would put the whole world on the rack, "so I be safe, I care not."[13] As the threat of death dispenses with filial

[8] IV, ii; Vol. VI, p. 485.
[9] IV, iii; Vol. II, p. 382.
[10] III, i; Vol. VIII, p. 420.
[11] IV, iii; Vol. VII, p. 428.
[12] *King Arthur*, IV, i; Vol. VIII, p. 187.
[13] *Don Sebastian*, II, i; Vol. VII, p. 349. This speech, to be sure, is uttered by a villain; but the speech immediately preceding (above) is uttered by a pure and virtuous heroine, and it is in exactly the same vein.

obligation, so does self-love justify ignoring it in any circumstance: the Emperor in *Aureng-Zebe,* with reference to his son, declares:

> Say, I'm a father, but a lover too;
> Much to my son, more to myself I owe.[14]

Unheroic persons confess that they are moved from "interest," and heroic ones, upon occasion, not only obviously act from it, but also generalize upon its importance as a determinant of conduct. When they speak of "interest," they refer to some form of personal ambition as opposed to unselfish concern for others, and in the comedies the term is usually used to signify a desire for wealth. Whether uttered by the hero or the villain of the piece, the following passages have the ring of Hobbes:

> The best of men
> Some interest in their actions must confess;
> None merit, but in hope they may possess,[15]

declares Arimant, the virtuous, if somewhat spineless creature of the heroine in *Aureng-Zebe*; and Indamora, openly using him to her own ends, reminds him:

> You first betrayed your trust, in loving me;
> And should not I my own advantage see?
> Serving my love, you may my friendship gain.[16]

Mercury, in *Amphitryon,* in more expansive fashion paints a damning picture of men governed by selfish designs:

> Such bargain-loves, as I with Phaedra treat,
> Are all the leagues and friendships of the great;
> All seek their ends, and each would other cheat.
> They only seem to hate, and seem to love;
> But interest is the point on which they move.
> Their friends are foes, and foes are friends again,
> And, in their turns, are knaves, and honest men.
> Our iron age is grown an age of gold:
> 'Tis who bids most; for all men will be sold.[17]

[14] I, i; Vol. V, p. 213. *Cf. Amphitryon,* Vol. VIII, p. 7.

[15] III, i; Vol. V, p. 239.

[16] III, i; Vol. V, p. 238.

[17] IV, i; Vol. VIII, p. 94. Dryden did not borrow these lines from his French source.

He, again, is a comic character from whom one might expect such views; but what is to be said when Melisinda, obviously intended to be an admirable person, promises Indamora that she will dissuade her own husband from pursuing the princess?

> And, if your virtue fail to move his mind,
> I'll use my interest that he may be kind.[18]

Lorenzo, the opportunist friend of Torrismond in *The Spanish Friar,* affirms that "it is interest governs all the world"; and the greed and ambition of the clergy is generalized by Philocles to constitute a law of conduct, when he says that interest "makes all seem reason that leads to it."[19] Almanzor, protesting that he has no "price" and thinks himself above reward, draws from Boabdelin the retort:

> Then sure you are some godhead; and our care
> Must be to come with incense and with prayer.[20]

The devotions which Boabdelin ironically suggests would, indeed, have been misplaced, for a little later Almanzor protests against Almahide's scruples and wishes her to yield to him at once in one "tumultuous minute":

> Praise is the pay of Heaven for doing good;
> But love's the best return for flesh and blood.[21]

Success, for Hobbes, lies in being rewarded with what one wants; for him it could not be a subjective satisfaction from duty done, with no *mark* of achievement. Aureng-Zebe, model of the "heroic," summarizes what seems to be a common view of those characters like himself intended to be essentially noble:

> How vain is virtue, which directs our ways
> Through certain danger to uncertain praise!
> Barren, and airy name! thee Fortune flies,
> With thy lean train, the pious and the wise.
> Heaven takes thee at thy word, without regard,
> And lets thee poorly be thy own reward.
> The world is made for the bold impious man,

[18] *Aureng-Zebe,* III, i; Vol. V, p. 242.
[19] *Secret Love; or The Maiden Queen,* IV, i; Vol. II, p. 480.
[20] *The Conquest of Granada,* Part I, V, ii; Vol. IV, p. 106.
[21] Part II, IV, iii; Vol. IV, p. 194.

Who stops at nothing, seizes all he can.
Justice to merit does weak aid afford;
She trusts her balance, and neglects her sword.
Virtue is nice to take what's not her own;
And, while she long consults, the prize is gone.[22]

Indamora shares her lover's opinion and proceeds to act upon it. She brutally prostitutes Arimant to her own ends: she tells him that he cannot help himself; that interest will compel him to serve her, though there is no chance that he may win her love. Of her Dryden says in the dedication: "The procedure of Indamora and Melisinda seems yet, in my judgment, natural, and not unbecoming of their characters."[23] If it is natural to be selfish and heartless and more than a little cruel, one concludes, then Indamora is natural; yet she is portrayed as the heroine of the drama.

In *Tyrannic Love* Dryden pictures a Christian martyr who chooses to die rather than submit her person to the Emperor Maximin. She proselytizes the heathen philosopher Apollonius by pointing out that the great advantage—and the only advantage—of Christianity is the hope of reward which it proffers to strengthen man's weak virtue.[24] That this idea is not advanced merely for dramatic purposes is made clear by a passage from the *Preface to the Second Miscellany,* in which Dryden discusses the whole problem of immortality:

> I think a future state demonstrable even by natural arguments; at least to take away rewards and punishments is only a pleasing prospect to a man, who resolves beforehand not to live morally. But, on the other side, the thought of being nothing after death is a burthen insupportable to a virtuous man, even though a heathen. We naturally aim at happiness, and cannot bear to have it confined to the shortness of our present being; especially when we consider, that virtue is generally unhappy in this world, and vice fortunate: so that it is hope of futurity alone, that makes this life tolerable, in expectation of a better. *Who would not commit all the excesses, to which he is prompted by his natural inclinations,* if he may do them with security while he is alive, and

22 II, i; Vol. V, p. 236.
23 Vol. V, p. 197.
24 "Virtue grows cold without a recompence." II, iii; Vol. III, p. 404.

> be incapable of punishment after he is dead? . . . and no
> man will be contained within the bounds of duty, when he
> may safely transgress them.[25]

Here, then, is a considered statement to the effect that man is
naturally inclined to unrestrained pursuit of personal ends, and
that he may be diverted from them only by prospect of some
concrete reward. The martyr St. Catherine is undoubtedly intended
to be a paragon, despite the fact that she would sooner sacrifice
her mother than forgo her martyrdom. She would be partially
understandable if fear of losing her immortal soul through sin
had outweighed human sympathy; but fear of losing eternity
is a subsidiary concern: she is reluctant to lose her "crown of
martyrdom." She is, in short, spiritually ambitious. Her mother,
Felicia, is likewise wholly self-centred, for not a moment's reflection does she need to decide that her daughter must yield to
Maximin so that she herself may live.

The protagonists of serious plays, supposed to follow the pattern of heroism laid down by Dryden in the *Essay on Heroic Plays,*
are likely to be blinded to ethical distinctions by egoism. Almanzor,
superman in *The Conquest of Granada,* accosts the chaste Almahide
in the dead of night and insists that she submit to him. With the
irreproachable virtue of the conventional heroine of romance, she
informs him that, if he really loved her, he could not ask "what
honour must forbid." It is not unusual for the heroine of romance
to elevate the less ethereal standards of her lover; but those
standards seldom sink to the level of Almanzor's when he asks:
"And what is honour, but a love well hid?"[26] A short time after,
when he hears that Almahide has yielded to a rival, he reveals that
this interpretation of honour applies only to his own relationship
with her, for he vilifies her and is by no means prepared to justify
her on the supposition that she may actually love another.

A similar absorption in self is apparent in the characters of
Love Triumphant. Celidea, one of the two heroines, is rewarded
and praised for braving her father's wrath to plead for the happiness of Victoria. Her boldness, however, may be motivated by

[25] Vol. XII, p. 292. (The italics are mine.)
[26] Part II, IV, iii; Vol. IV, p. 192.

the fact that only by disposing of Victoria can she herself win
the man whom she loves. It is legitimate to assume that Dryden
intended such a motive in view of her earlier estimate of human
altruism:

> So, helpless friends, when safe themselves ashore,
> Behold a vessel drive against a rock.
> They sigh, they weep, they counsel, and they pray.
> They stretch their unassisting hands in vain;
> But none will plunge into the raging main,
> To save the sinking passenger from death.[27]

When Alphonso, in the same play, is banished with a curse by the
jealous Veramond, he pleads that he may not receive his father's
"dreadful imprecation" and feels that, if only he may be relieved
of it, his exile will be a blessing. Admittedly alarmed as he is on
his own behalf, he is later wholly unable to understand the reluc-
tance of Victoria to hazard a similar malediction by fleeing with
him.

So self-enclosed is the individual in Dryden's plays that bonds
ordinarily thought sacred are as straws before the wind of two
opposing wills. The poet might well have devised some of his
"heroic" personages with the words of Hobbes in mind:

> And therefore if any two men desire the same thing, which
> nevertheless they cannot both enjoy, they become enemies;
> and in the way to their end, which is principally their own
> conservation, and sometimes their delectation only, endeavour
> to destroy, or subdue one another.[28]

Father and son, brothers, eminent warriors of the same court,
and persons with no reason for enmity other than pursuance of
similar ambitions plot against each other, sometimes marvelling
at their own cold-bloodedness and even half regretting it. Abdalla
hates his brother Boabdelin[29] because he wishes to possess the
power of the latter; he detests Abdelmelech because they are rivals
in love. The brothers, Guyomar and Odmar, pass bitter words in

---

[27] IV, i; Vol. VIII, p. 440. (There is a difference, but one is forcibly reminded
of the famous opening lines of Bk. II of Lucretius' *Of the Nature of Things*.)
[28] Hobbes, *op. cit.*, p. 111.
[29] *The Conquest of Granada*, Vol. IV.

their open competition for Alibech, and Odmar threatens to kill his younger brother.[30] Placidius,[31] who ultimately proves to be admirable enough, hates the truly heroic man who has hindered his advancement; Aureng-Zebe and his father war almost to the death over possession of the son's betrothed; bitter hatred exists between Veramond and Alphonso[32] because of a dilemma in love. Jacintha[33] declares that she will kill her father if he withholds consent to her marriage with Wildblood; Oedipus and Adrastus have been enemies because both were kings and "each disdained an equal."[34] Certainly Dryden need not have known Hobbes to associate jealousy and hate with love and ambition; they are common themes of drama and do not necessarily indicate anything with respect to the poet's own ideology. But there is hardly a character in the heroic plays or in the comedies who is not in tempestuous and often ruthless pursuit of a selfish end; and those characters do not experience any change in the course of the play. There is no Lear who is chastened into a broader humanity. That fact, coupled with the many specific passages regarding the selfishness of men, unescapably suggests that Dryden really entertained a Hobbist view of human nature.

As bonds of kinship and of friendship are subordinate to the desires of the self-centred individual, so the virtues in general are defined in terms of their utility to the Self. Hobbes was an ethical pragmatist rather than a teleologist: honour is "the opinion of power"; what man desires is good, what he hates, evil; covetousness is a vice because one man resents another's possession of riches; ill fortune and losses are dishonourable.[35] These definitions reveal the materialistic basis of Hobbist moral philosophy, and they are relevant to an examination of Dryden's plays. The dramatist's seriously-drawn personages very often entertain a conception of the virtues akin to that of Hobbes; often observe the letter, not the spirit of the law; often indulge in moral casuistry to

[30] The Indian Emperor, Vol. II.
[31] Tyrannic Love, Vol. III.
[32] Supposed father and son in Love Triumphant, Vol. VIII.
[33] An Evening's Love, Vol. III.
[34] Oedipus, I, i; Vol. VI, p. 151.
[35] Hobbes, op. cit., Chap. x, pp. 74-84.

rationalize the desires of the senses. Don Manuel, in *The Rival Ladies,* faces the necessity of either surrendering his sister to a bitter enemy or staining his honour by refusal to keep a promise. He neatly evades the issue by the following plan:

> I'll cut this Gordian knot I cannot loose:
> To keep his promise, Rodorick shall have her,
> But I'll return and rescue her by force;
> Then giving back what he so frankly gave,
> At once my honour and his love I'll save.[36]

Rodorick, too, is prevented only by force from killing Manuel when he is helpless and at his mercy; yet Rodorick is rewarded as a hero at the conclusion. Success and boldness of attempt are the criteria of good, rather than motive or inner probity.[37] In the same play, a robber, who undergoes a lightning-change into an humanitarian, asserts, without being contradicted by his captors, that he has been punished enough "in missing of my wicked aim."[38] Honour, virtue, duty are often merely formal. St. Catherine, in *Tyrannic Love,* obviously represents an effort to portray a noble woman, keenly alive to problems of conduct. But spiritual ambition is not her only flaw; her consciousness of self does not end with aspiration to martyrdom. Death she covets as a pathway to immortal remembrance; but she cannot endure the humiliation of being publicly displayed in the market-place. Such an exhibition of nakedness, she affirms, will despoil her chastity. Chastity, for her, seems to be purely external and to bear no relation to an inner awareness of her own virtue. Similar to St. Catherine's understanding of chastity is Berenice's ideal of honour. She steadfastly refuses to yield to Porphyrius or to impair her husband's honour in any way. And yet her speeches show an emphasis on the letter of the law and a disregard of the spirit. "The desires, and other passions of men," Hobbes says, "are in themselves no sin. No more are the actions, that proceed from those passions, till they know

---

[36] IV, iii; Vol. II, p. 199.

[37] It is pointed out that unrestrained boldness is a conventional quality of "heroic" heroes; but *The Rival Ladies* is not an heroic play. I can discern no difference between the *ethos* of Dryden's heroic plays and that of his other serious plays.

[38] I, i; p. 145.

a law that forbids them."[39] Berenice admits her love for Porphyrius; she rejoices when Maximin is dead; spiritually she is unfaithful long before he is dead. In a love-scene[40] between her and Porphyrius she indulges in what amounts to coquetry and moral sophistry. She decries her own charms only to inflame her lover the more. Although she has shown her preference plainly and has admitted that she once had been about to yield, she declares: "I never did accept your love" and "I never did admit your love to me, but only suffered it." She plays with love, granting certain liberties, taking no measures decisively to suppress her, or his, passion, yet refusing to make a final surrender.

The Preface to *Secret Love,* a tragi-comedy little altered in the main plot from its source in Madame Scudéry's *Le Grand Cyrus,* offers an enlightening commentary on Dryden's view of character. He had been accused of making his hero unadmirable. Philocles, after vainly suing for the queen's permission to marry the one he loves, discovers that the queen herself has a fatal passion for him; and thereupon the glory of a crown gleams more brightly than the worth of a mistress. He tries to justify his own vacillation, he alters his behaviour towards his mistress, and he never definitely renounces ambition until matters are taken from his hands by the decision of the queen to remain unmarried. Of him Dryden says: "But neither was the fault of Philocles so great, if the circumstances be considered, which, as moral philosophy assures us, make the essential differences of good and bad."[41] Evidently Dryden would not expect loyalty to a loved one to weigh heavily against the prospect of ascending a throne. A second instance of an enlightening prefatory comment appears in relation to the tragedy *Cleomenes.* The London fops had accused the poet of making his hero inhumanly unresponsive to the passionate suit of Cassandra. Dryden justifies himself, not in terms of dramatic necessity, but in terms of human nature: "A man," he says, "might have pleaded an excuse for himself, if he had been false to an old wife, for the sake of a young mistress; but Cleora was in the flower of her age,

[39] Hobbes, *op. cit.,* p. 114.
[40] III, i; Vol. III.
[41] Vol. II, p. 420.

and it was yet but honeymoon with Cleomenes; and so much for nature."[42]

A more blatant instance of blunted moral sensibilities occurs in *The Spanish Friar*. Torrismond, returning from a brilliant military campaign, secretly marries the usurping queen whom he dearly loves. Later, his foster-father apprises him that his wife has engineered the murder of his father, the deposed king; and the newly-made emperor must choose between love and duty. He wavers between the two until it becomes known that the infamous plot has failed and that the aged man still lives; whereupon the son clasps his wife to his bosom, rejoicing that all has ended happily. The sophistry of separating the intent from the act cannot have been in the least apparent to Dryden. In accordance with the psychology of Hobbes, Torrismond attaches importance only to overt conduct, and satisfies a desire at the expense of moral depth. Almanzor, very type of the heroic, gives the measure of this morality when he says to Almahide:

> The duty of poor honour were too hard,
> In arms all day, at night to mount the guard.
> Let him, in pity, now to rest retire;
> Let these soft hours be watched by warm desire.[43]

Dianet, a minor figure in *Aureng-Zebe*, from whom there is no reason to expect reflection of any sort, has more to say about honour:

> The points of honour poets may produce;
> Trappings of life, for ornament not use:
> Honour, which only does the name advance,
> Is the mere raving madness of romance.[44]

Dryden's conversion to Hobbist psychology is further evidenced by a recurrent theme of inconstancy and emotional vacillation. "And because the constitution of a man's body is in continual mutation," Hobbes writes, "it is impossible that all the same things should always cause in him the same appetites, and aversions.

[42] Vol. VIII, p. 221.
[43] *The Conquest of Granada*, Part II, IV, iii; Vol. IV, p. 192.
[44] II, i; Vol. V, p. 237.

. . ."[45] Ethically, this is significant because such a psychology produces neither a consistent behaviour nor a stable character reacting in a predictable way. The comedies abundantly illustrate the principle of Hobbes; but because the comedy as a form of art is more artificial and conventionalized, it is advisable to analyze, rather, the serious plays, and to note, finally, that there is a remarkable sameness of emotional instability in comic and heroic plays.

It is not surprising when Lyndaraxa, inhumanly cruel and selfish aspirant to power in *The Conquest of Granada,* asserts:

> There's no such thing as constancy you call;
> Faith ties not hearts; 'tis inclination all.[46]

But one cannot pass it by lightly when Almahide, pattern of the virtuous, says:

> All objects lose by too familiar view,
> When that great charm is gone, of being new.[47]

That Dryden believed the human passions to be subject to constant mutation is shown by his characters' frequent shifts of feeling and idea, by occasional statements made by admirable characters, and by the suspicion which even the heroes entertain of the probability of stable attitudes in their loved ones. *Dénouements* depending upon the impulsive bestowal of love by a principal personage upon someone whom he has hardly so much as noticed hitherto are frequent. One does not make conclusions regarding the philosophy of Shakespeare merely because, in *Twelfth Night* or *As You Like It,* love comes suddenly and unexpectedly; but these are frankly romantic fantasies, whereas the plays of Dryden in which such phenomena occur are supposedly serious treatments of deep passion. In *The Rival Ladies,* Gonsalvo has eyes for no one but the scornful Julia. Throughout the play he voices hyperbolical assertions of what he will do to serve her, and of the impossibility of his living without her. Meanwhile, though his page, the disguised Hippolito, serves him faithfully, there is no evidence of his sus-

---

[45] Hobbes, *op. cit.,* pp. 40-1.
[46] Part II, III, iii; Vol. IV, p. 173.
[47] Part II, II, iii; Vol. IV, p. 152.

pecting her identity or of any evolution of attachment for her. Yet, when Hippolito reveals herself, he is instantaneously as assured of the depth and constancy of his love for her as he had previously been of his ardour for Julia. There is no adequate motivation; the language employed is definitely not that of Platonic love-at-first-sight: his passion simply has found a new object. Similar is the conclusion of the tragi-comedy *Love Triumphant*. Garcia, who through four acts has spurned the love of Celidea and schemed to win her sister, perceives the attractions of Celidea in a trice, as she persuades the king to sanction her sister's love. Likewise, in *The Indian Emperor*, Almeria suddenly is seized by a natural, and *not* a Platonic, love for Cortez who has been her bitter enemy. The comedies, of course, quite often conclude with complete reversals of feeling,[48] but the fact of significance is that in them the human nature is the same as it appears to be in the serious dramas with their startling conclusions.

Inconsistencies, moreover, are not limited to love-situations. Unexpected and unmotivated reform of wicked persons and sudden religious conversion sometimes appear. For no good reason Almeria decides to bestow her dying benediction upon her rival for Cortez's love and sentimentally to join their hands. For a reason not made clear Veramond pardons Alphonso. Morat, in *Aureng-Zebe*, changes from a deep-dyed villain without warning: at one moment he declares that he wants

> Renown and fame
> And power, as uncontrolled as is my will.[49]

A moment later he exclaims:

> Renown, and fame, in vain, I courted long, . . .
> Now you [Indamora] have given me virtue for my
> guide;
> And, with true honour, ballasted my pride.
> Unjust dominion I no more pursue.[50]

Yet Indamora has but just repeated what she and others have pointed out to him before—with complete failure. In equally

[48] *Cf.* especially *An Evening's Love* and *Sir Martin Mar-all.*
[49] V, i; Vol. V, p. 281.
[50] *Ibid.*, p. 282.

unceremonious fashion, Apollonius, pagan philosopher to the Emperor Maximin, in the midst of an eloquent defence of paganism, stops short with

> Where truth prevails, all arguments are weak.
> To that convincing power [Christianity] I must give
>   place.[51]

An even more disconcerting change occurs in *The Rival Ladies* when, after Gonsalvo has mercifully spared the life of a robber, the latter not only expresses boundless gratitude and pledge of service, but even dedicates his remaining days to humanitarian pursuits.[52] The precipitancy and irrationality of these transformations not only suggest Hobbes's principle of mutation, but create as well an appearance of automatism which may be related to a mechanistic philosophy of life. In at least two instances Dryden directly attributes such "mutation" to bodily cause. The naïve Hippolito, in *The Tempest,* who at first is sure that he must possess Miranda, declares, once he has been wounded:

> The fault was only in my blood, for now
> 'Tis gone, I find I do not love so many.[53]

Similarly the bold courage of the boy Cleonidas[54] wanes as he is deprived of food. Sosibius, the priest in *Cleomenes,* in more reflective vein phrases the same materialistic basis of change:

> Man is but man; unconstant still, and various;
> There's no to-morrow in him, like to-day.
> Perhaps the atoms rolling in his brain
> Make him think honestly this present hour;
> The next, a swarm of base, ungrateful thoughts
> May mount aloft; and where's our Egypt then?[55]

Heroic characters, as has been said above, customarily expect inconstancy even in those whom they love. When Almanzor is told that Almahide has yielded to Abdelmelech, he publicly denies it,

[51] II, iii; Vol. III, p. 405.
[52] I, i; Vol. II, p. 146.
[53] V, ii; Vol. III, p. 212. This passage is in the portion of the play which Dryden at least suggested.
[54] In *Cleomenes,* Act V; Vol. VIII.
[55] III, i; Vol. VIII, p. 305.

but the moment he is alone, he admits that he has defended what he knows to be false, for

> She was as faithless as her sex could be;
> And, now I am alone, she's so to me.[56]

Alphonso displays the basest suspicions of Victoria's virtue. When she assures him that he can trust her honour, he replies:

> That may be chafed into a warmth, Victoria.
> Talk, seeing, touching, are incendiaries;
> And these may mount your young desires like straw,
> To meet the jet that draws you.[57]

Although Indamora never wavers in her loyalty to her lover, the fact that the Emperor is known to be his rival awakens a consuming jealousy in Aureng-Zebe. He is prepared to believe anything of her, and he tells her frankly that he is equally miserable when he possesses her and when he does not. Later he suspects her of misconduct with Morat; and it is only his weakness, which apprises him that he cannot live without her, that brings him to Indamora's feet. The chief burden of Troilus's anxiety, as Cressida leaves Troy, is the fear that she may not be strong enough to resist the blandishments of Grecian soldiers. Captain Towerson, English hero of *Amboyna,* returns to the Dutch island half expecting to find that his Ysabinda has been untrue. Cydaria, heroine of the sub-plot in *The Indian Emperor,* is ready to believe the worst of Cortez, upon seeing him execute the formality of kissing a lady's hand. Almahide, finally, goes a step farther in voicing the conviction that distrust is necessary to the development of the highest love:

> Distrust in lovers is too warm a sun,
> But yet 'tis night in love when that is gone.[58]

It is true enough that self-preservation conceived of as a basic human instinct was not new with Hobbes; that transferences of loyalty were conventional in French romance; that Dryden probably lacked the artistic genius necessary to gradual and complete characterization and to convincing *dénouements.* But it still must

[56] *The Conquest of Granada,* Part II, V, i; Vol. IV, p. 201.
[57] *Love Triumphant,* III, i; Vol. VIII, p. 419.
[58] *The Conquest of Granada,* Part II, III, i; Vol. IV, p. 158.

be said that the reasoned statements in the serious plays concerning selfishness in man sound extraordinarily like Hobbes, and that the *Dryden character,* even when he declares himself to be otherwise or is declared by the author to be otherwise, bears a striking similarity to Man as he is presented in the psychology of Hobbes.

Analysis of the ethical problems that appear in the plays, giving rise to the question of the extent to which human beings are responsible for their conduct, involves the enigma of Free Will. Theologians have always been disturbed by the paradoxical supposition that divine law and beneficent deity can exist simultaneously with sin and wickedness; they have often pondered over the exact nature of human moral responsibility. Hooker evaded the problem by stating, in *Of the Laws of Ecclesiastical Polity,* that the will is free "to take or refuse any particular object whatsoever being presented unto it"; that God, by virtue of his omniscience, foreknows but does not predestine; that, for some reason not ascertainable by man, God permitted sin in the world and gave man the freedom to choose the right if he so wished.[59] The seventeenth century, with its religio-political problems, its conflicting tendencies of humanism and puritanism, its acquaintance with Descartes and Hobbes, was keenly alive to philosophic questions so basic as that of free will. Free will became a theme for polemic with churchmen, scientist, and philosopher. In *De Cive* Thomas Hobbes had relegated it to the dust-heap of scholastic nominalism, just as he later did in the better-known *Leviathan*:

> And therefore if a man should talk to me of . . . a *free will*; or any *free* but free from being hindered by opposition, I should not say he were in an error, but that his words were without meaning, that is to say, absurd.[60]

More positively, he describes the Will as the "last appetite or aversion, immediately adhering to the action, or to the omission thereof."[61] He continues:

> The definition of the *will,* given commonly by the Schools, that it is a *rational appetite,* is not good. For if it were, then

[59] Keble's edition, revised by Church and Paget, Oxford, 1888, Vol. I, p. 222.
[60] *Op. cit.,* pp. 32-3.
[61] *Ibid.,* p. 48.

could there be no voluntary act against reason. For a *voluntary act* is that, which proceedeth from the *will,* and no other. But if instead of a rational appetite, we shall say an appetite resulting from a precedent deliberation, then the definition is the same that I have given here. *Will* therefore *is the last appetite in deliberating.*[62]

The materialism and determinism of such a definition were despised by the Church and feared by the Royal Society, which was concerned lest atheism and moral irresponsibility be thought adjuncts of the new science. Many replies to Hobbes were forthcoming, notable among which were those of Robert Boyle and Dr. Bramhall, Bishop of Derry. The last-mentioned Hobbes had met in Paris in public discussion; and later, when a reply of his to the bishop's defence of free will had been surreptitiously published, he entered upon a debate concerning "Liberty, Necessity, and Chance." He maintained that obviously man is free *to do* what he wills, but not free *to will.* Every act of man flows from a First Cause; is determined by a chain of causes, each functioning necessarily, in accordance with the Creator's plan. An untold number of influences and forces make a man what he is, and he cannot see all the links in the chain. He can, to be sure, drink water or not drink water; but he cannot will to be thirsty or not to be thirsty. If he is thirsty, yet does not drink, it is because some other force stronger than thirst moves his will. This interpretation of will reduces it to an absolute necessitation and to the Deistic belief that whatever is, is right, since nature, established from the First Cause, "cannot err."[63]

Dryden has almost nothing to say in his prose concerning free will, and there are no reasoned treatments of it in his non-dramatic poetry. In the dedication to *The Rival Ladies,* however, in praising the work of the Earl of Orrery, he announces himself unequivocally a determinist:

> Here is no chance, which you have not foreseen; all your heroes are more than your subjects, they are your creatures;

[62] *Ibid.,* pp. 48-9.
[63] Hobbes, *Liberty, Necessity, and Chance,* Molesworth's ed. of the *English Works,* Vol. V.

and though they seem to move freely in all the sallies of their ρassions, yet you make destinies for them, which they cannot shun. They are moved (if I may dare to say so) like the rational creatures of the Almighty Poet, who walk at liberty, in their own opinion, because their fetters are invisible; when, indeed, the prison of their will is the more sure for being large; and, instead of an absolute power over their actions, they have only a wretched desire of doing that, which they cannot choose but do.[64]

Weight of evidence from the plays, notwithstanding the occasional presence of antithetical statements, leaves little doubt that, for a time at least, the poet was a necessitarian. But the exact nature of his determinism is not easily ascertainable, for there is a curious mingling of references to Heavenly decree, predestination, Fate, Fortune, and blind Chance. Fate often appears as a consciously malignant force, hardly to be identified with beneficent deity; and Fortune and Chance cannot be reconciled with rigid cause-and-effect philosophy, whether it be founded upon divine pre-ordination or upon wholly material factors. All of the long dialectical passages relating to the problem, however, reaffirm the conviction of the previously cited lines from the Dedication. Almanzor paraphrases Hobbes in a discourse on free will:

> O Heaven, how dark a riddle's thy decree,
> Which bounds our wills, yet seems to leave them free!
> Since thy foreknowledge cannot be in vain,
> Our choice must be what thou did'st first ordain.
> Thus, like a captive in an isle confined,
> Man walks at large, a prisoner of the mind:
> Wills all his crimes, while Heaven the indictment draws
> And, pleading guilty, justifies the laws.
> Let fate be fate, the lover and the brave
> Are ranked, at least, above the vulgar slave.[65]

In 1673 Dryden wrote his rhymed version of *Paradise Lost*; and, aside from form, one of the most significant changes made by him was the incorporation of a long debate concerning free will

[64] Vol. II, pp. 132-3.
[65] *The Conquest of Granada*, Part II, IV, iii; Vol. IV, pp. 190-1.

between Adam and the two angels Raphael and Gabriel. After temptation has begun to assail Eve through dreams, God sends six angels down for protection. Among them are Raphael and Gabriel, who, when Adam asks to whom he owes his gratitude for existence, proceed to instruct him in divine philosophy. Raphael assures Adam that God has formed him with will "unbounded as a deity," and freedom to choose good and shun evil; that God neither demands anything of which man is incapable nor compels him to prefer the good. Gabriel adds that, though man is made good by his creator, it is his own mission and responsibility to sustain his natural state of undefilement. Adam is by no means philosophically naïve, and, like Hobbes, he wishes to know how God can bestow a power which would make the created equal to the Creator. Raphael replies that, while, it is true, God cannot give away his boundless power, he can award unlimited liberty of choice:

> So orbs from the first Mover motion take,
> Yet each their proper revolutions make.[66]

But, Adam asks, if certain things and events have been pre-ordained by Heaven, what is to prevent man's free will from rendering these decrees void? Gabriel answers that man alone "boasts an arbitrary state"; that all else in nature follows the pre-conceived divine plan, unchanged by God or man. The recalcitrant Adam, however, resorts to the very language of the Sage of Malmesbury:

> Yet causes their effects necessitate
> In willing agents; Where is freedom then?
> Or who can break the chain which limits men
> To act what is unchangeably forecast,
> Since the first cause gives motion to the last?[67]

Replying to Bishop Bramhall, Hobbes thus expounds the doctrine of cause and effect:

> That which I say necessitateth and determineth every action
> . . . is the sum of all those things, which being now existent,
> conduce and concur to the production of that action here-

[66] *The State of Innocence and Fall of Man* (1674), IV, i; Vol. V, p. 153.
[67] *Ibid.*

after, whereof if any one thing now were wanting, the effect could not be produced. This concourse of causes, whereof every one is determined to be such as it is by a like concourse of former causes, may well be called (in respect they were all set and ordered by the eternal cause of all things, God Almighty) the decree of God.[68]

The creative and intellective powers of God function independently: creation, Adam is told, is the product of power and will, whereas foreknowledge is a product of the intellect and implies no necessity. God *sees* what man's choice will be, but man is not less free, therefore, to complete the chain of cause and effect. Adam reiterates Dryden's logic in the preface to *The Rival Ladies* in pointing out that because the chain of necessity is long, it is not the less binding, and that because man feels himself to be free, he is not, for that reason, free. The divine emissaries rebuke Adam for impiety, but he protests his humility, saying that he argues only to be better taught. Thereupon he again uses the language of Hobbes to state the relation between causality and necessity:

> For whate'er cause can move the will t'elect,
> Must be sufficient to produce the effect;
> And what's sufficient must effectual be
> Then how is man, thus forced by causes, free?[69]

Raphael affirms that very often man will deny his assent when the cause is sufficient; but his pupil agrees with Hobbes that any cause which does not actually produce the effect is not sufficient. The angel concludes his share of the argument by asserting that the causal chain appears necessary only in retrospect when the whole springs into view. What *is* done is necessarily *done,* but it need not have been as it is. Then Adam, turning to the problem of evil, desires to know why Heaven does not prevent the evil it foresees rather than sanction—even will it—by remaining passive? It is better, he thinks, to be "constrained to good, than free to ill." He is informed that, if there were no freedom to sin, there could be no rewards and punishments—which statement is, of course, a side-

[68] *Liberty, Necessity, and Chance,* Vol. V, p. 105.
[69] *The State of Innocence, etc.,* IV, i; Vol. V, p. 154. *Cf.* Hobbes, *Liberty, etc.,* p. 154.

stepping of the issue. Adam, left alone, remains depressed by the conditions of human existence. He has probed all of the vulnerable spots in his opponent's defence, and his is the last word in the debate:

> Hard state of life! since Heaven foreknows my will,
> Why am I not tied up from doing ill?
> Why am I trusted with myself at large,
> When he's more able to sustain the charge?
> Since angels fell, whose strength was more than mine,
> 'Twould show more grace my frailty to confine,
> Foreknowing the success, to leave me free,
> Excuses him, and yet supports not me.[70]

Adam does not here share the attitude of Hobbes towards the problem of evil: he, in dissatisfaction, accuses God of injustice; whereas Hobbes affirms that God's *power* is a sufficient justification of his every move.

Although Lucifer alludes to the free-born soul, both he and Asmoday speak often of Fate and attribute their failure to it. After Eve has succumbed to temptation and Adam has chosen to share her guilt, Adam again questions the justice of God in giving strong appetites which make formal freedom meaningless. "Where appetites are given," he asks, "what sin to taste?"[71] The physical determinism implicit in his words reminds us of Hippolito's discovery that excess blood has caused his passion for Miranda, of Prospero's conviction that it is vain to bridle nature, and of young Cleonidas's loss of courage when hunger assails him. Then Eve echoes Adam's belief that man has not been treated fairly:

> The laws were hard, the power to keep them, weak.
> Did we solicit Heaven to mould our clay?
> From darkness to produce us to the day?
> Did we concur to life, or choose to be?
> Was it our will which formed, or was it he?
> Since 'twas his choice, not ours, which placed us here,
> The laws we did not choose why should we bear?[72]

[70] IV, i; Vol. V, pp. 155-6.
[71] V, i; Vol. V. p. 167.
[72] V, i; Vol. V, p. 173.

Although the concluding lines imply the freedom to disobey, the first lines suggest the bonds of physical necessity.

Other plays provide evidence that Dryden was not only interested in the problem of free will, but was inclined, as well, to be convinced of the insubstantiality of man's freedom. The Prospero of Dryden's revised Shakespeare[73] is, like his prototype, master of the situation in the first acts of the play. But once the lovers have upset his machinations, he concludes that men must ever try in vain to guide their own destinies, destinies established either by inscrutable fate or by incalculable chance:

> . . . Perhaps my art itself is false.—
> On what strange grounds we build our hopes and
>   fears!
> Man's life is all a mist! and in the dark,
> Our fortunes meet us.
> If fate be not, then what can we foresee?
> Or how can we avoid it, if it be?
> If by free will in our own paths we move,
> How are we bounded by decrees above?
> Whether we drive, or whether we are driven,
> If ill, 'tis ours; if good, the act of heaven.[74]

Like Adam, he writhes at the idea that God has looked to his own glory at the expense of man's peace and stability. It is natural to find the theme of fate in Dryden's *Oedipus,* a version of the traditional story based upon Corneille's *Oedipe*; and although it is perhaps hazardous to correlate it with attitudes expressed elsewhere, the words of Tiresias the seer suggest quite definitely the interest of Hobbes in causality, necessity, the limits of reason, and the order of nature in relation to heavenly justice:

> The gods are just;
> But how can finite measure infinite?
> Reason! alas, it does not know itself!
> Yet man, vain man, would with this short-lined
>   plummet,

---

[73] Though it is impossible to tell exactly what Dryden's share was in the revision of the Dryden-Davenant version of *The Tempest,* the passages quoted are strikingly similar to other passages by Dryden concerning freedom of the will.

[74] *The Tempest,* III, v; Vol. III, p. 175.

Fathom the vast abyss of heavenly justice.
Whatever is, is in its causes just;
Since all things are by fate. But purblind man
Sees but a part of the chain; the nearest links;
His eyes not carrying to that equal beam,
That poises all above.[75]

And Alcander reflects the same Hobbist reasoning:

There's a chain of causes
Linked to effects; invincible necessity,
That whate'er is, could not but so have been.[76]

Both Dryden and Hobbes had said earlier that man does not always perceive his own limitations because he does not see the entire chain of causality, but only the "nearest links."[77]

The conviction that whatever is, is just by virtue of its being a decree of Fate is likewise an Hobbesian principle, related to the philosopher's doctrine of power:

Power irresistible justifieth all actions really and properly, in whomsoever it be found. Less power does not. And because such power is in God only, he must needs be just in all his actions.[78]

An amplification of this idea, showing clearly its roots in Hobbism, occurs in one of the few passages in *Amphitryon* in which Dryden diverges from the original. When Jupiter vouchsafes that he loves because it is in the fates that he should, Phoebus replies that by such casuistry every wicked act might be condoned and every sinner freed from moral responsibility. But it is not clear to him what is meant by Fate: is it a series of fortuitous events? is it causal necessity? or is it a power

That orders all things by superior will,
Foresees his work, and works in that foresight?[79]

[75] III, i; Vol. VI, pp. 183-4.
[76] *Ibid.,* I, i; Vol. VI, pp. 138-9.
[77] This is said repeatedly in Hobbes, Vol. V. *Cf.* also Dryden's Preface to *The Rival Ladies.*
[78] *Op. cit.,* Vol. V, p. 116.
[79] I, i; Vol. VIII, p. 18.

Jupiter reminds Phoebus that he, Jupiter, in his omnipotence, has made Fate and that therefore Fate cannot be fortuitous or unjust. It cannot be unjust to him, for he has willed it; it cannot be unjust to men, for he has created them, and they exist only for his will. The closeness of his reasoning to that of Hobbes is at once apparent:

> To those therefore whose power is irresistible, the dominion of all men adhereth naturally by their excellence of power; and consequently it is from that power, that the kingdom over men, and the right of afflicting men at his pleasure, belongeth naturally to God Almighty; not as Creator, and gracious; but as omnipotent. And though punishment be due for sin only, because by that word is understood affliction for sin; yet the right of afflicting, is not always derived from men's sin, but from God's power.[80]

Dryden again echoes Hobbes when Maximin, in *Tyrannic Love,* says:

> Our Gods are Gods, 'cause they have power and will;
> Who can do all things, can do nothing ill.[81]

But the characters by no means always accept in passive fashion the doctrine that whatever is, is right. It has already been observed that Adam boldly questions divine justice; and in lighter vein Mercury, in the pagan *Amphitryon,* does the same:

> Here's omnipotence with a vengeance! to make a man a cuckold, and yet not to do him wrong![82]

In many passages where references to Fate are found, it is conceived of as a definitely malignant force and is spoken of as if it were something quite apart from God. This idea is often expressed in the non-dramatic poetry, which is likewise pervaded by the Fate-theme. In *Religio Laici,* for example, Dryden explains that reason guides men to belief in immortality as the sole refuge "from fortune and from fate";[83] and in *Annus Mirabilis,* he affirms that labyrinthine fate balks man's best efforts at self-direction:

[80] *Leviathan, op. cit.,* Vol. III, p. 346.
[81] V, i; Vol. III, p. 456.
[82] I, i; Vol. VIII, p. 19.
[83] L. 59; Vol. X, p. 40.

> In fortune's empire blindly thus we go,
> And wander after pathless destiny;
> Whose dark resorts since prudence cannot know,
> In vain it would provide for what shall be.[84]

The remaining passages in the plays which pertain significantly to free will are uttered variously by a villain, a heroine, and a hero; and all are characteristically Hobbist in tone. The Emperor Maximin denies man to be free:

> Free-will's a cheat in anyone but me;
> In all but kings, 'tis willing slavery;
> An unseen fate which forces the desire;
> The will of puppets danced upon a wire.[85]

Leonora, the heroine of *The Spanish Friar*, unlike Maximin, makes no exceptions in favour of kingship:

> . . . I would not do this crime,
> And yet, like heaven, permit it to be done.
> The priesthood grossly cheat us with free-will:
> Will to do what—but what heaven first decreed?
> Our actions then are neither good nor ill,
> Since from eternal causes they proceed;
> Our passions,—fear and anger, love and hate,—
> Mere senseless engines that are moved by fate;
> Like ships on stormy seas, without a guide,
> Tossed by the winds, and driven by the tide.[86]

Alphonso speculates upon the unexpected twists of fortune which, though they seem fortuitous, are within the bounds set by heaven upon human life,

> Which none can stop before the appointed limits,
> And none can push beyond.[87]

At times Dryden appears to veer away from rigid causality towards casuality. Although he quite definitely renounces the postulate of a world "from blind atoms wrought,"[88] as inconsistent

---

[84] Stanza CC; Vol. IX, p. 163.

[85] *Tyrannic Love*, IV, i; Vol. III, p. 430.

[86] III, iii; Vol. VI, p. 467.

[87] *Love Triumphant*, I, i; Vol. VIII, p. 385.

[88] *Tyrannic Love*, III, i; Vol. III, p. 410. Cf. also *To My Honor'd Friend Sir Robert Howard, on his Excellent Poems*, Vol. XI, p. 8.

with the prevailing order in the universe, there are numerous allusions in the plays to the capriciousness of destiny and to the "various turns of human fate."[89] Such passages, however, may do nothing more than assert man's inability to perceive causes or to foresee effects, for the weight of evidence unquestionably indicates belief in a Heaven-ordained Fate, often expressing itself in physical determinism. As there are references to Chance, so are there allusions to the influence of the stars;[90] and Dr. Johnson implies that Dryden really placed faith in the pseudo-science of astrology.[91] Scott, moreover, corroborates this statement of Johnson's, asserting that Dryden was a "firm believer" in astrology.[92] No reasoned defence or explanation of astrological influence occurs, however, either in the plays or in the non-dramatic poetry; and consequently there is no basis for deciding whether the references to it signify anything more than literary convention. It may or may not be relevant to point out that astrology is a subject for jest and ridicule in the comedy An Evening's Love.[93]

Constant employment of Fate as a theme in drama was customary among the writers of heroic plays; and Dryden does not use it more extensively than Davenant or Otway. Taken alone, the Fate-theme provides no key to Dryden's thought: it might be merely a corollary of Platonic love-convention or an inheritance from French romance. But it does take on a possible serious meaning when it is seen to amplify and corroborate the determinism we

[89] The following passage is a sample of Dryden's mingling of the ideas of fate, chance, and fortune:

> Fate, now come back; thou canst not further get;
> The bounds of thy libration here are set.
> Thou knowest this place,
> And, like a clock wound up, strik'st here for me;
> Now, Chance, assert thy own inconstancy,
> And, Fortune, fight, that thou mayst Fortune be!

The Conquest of Granada, Part II, III, i; Vol. IV, p. 162.

[90] Hobbes attributes to the stars a minor influence upon man. Liberty, etc., Vol. V, p. 105.

[91] Lives of the Most Eminent English Poets, Vol. I, p. 409. (Oxford, 1905.)

[92] Dryden's Works, Vol. I, p. 384.

[93] The plot of this comedy was not original with Dryden, and if the play is significant in the above regard, it is so merely because the poet was content to make use of such subject-matter.

have noticed both in specific passages and in treatment of character.

What we may safely call Dryden's determinism is apparent in the motivation of his plots as well as in particular passages in which his characters bless or curse the fate that moves them. Necessitarianism may act logically to render moral considerations superfluous and to provide convenient basis for self-justification; and, in fact, there are characters in the plays who seek to evade ethical responsibility by attributing their conduct to Fate. Leonora, after planning the murder of an aged king and thereafter marrying his son with no thought of the equivocal position in which he is placed, disclaims all guilt, because she is a mere "senseless engine" moved by fate.[94] In similar fashion, Torrismond, her lover, finds in the Universe a reason for sentimentalizing his misfortunes:

> 'Tis true, my hopes are vanishing as clouds;
> Lighter than children's bubbles blown by winds:
> My merit's but the rash result of chance;
> My birth unequal; all the stars against me.[95]

So, too, does Porphyrius, supine hero of *Tyrannic Love,* blame his emotional dilemma upon the ill-will of heaven. He loves the wife of the emperor, who will not leave her husband though he would gladly be rid of her. She will not tolerate the proposal of her lover to do away with the king, she will not yield to Porphyrius; yet she encourages the latter's amorous inclinations. The dilemma of the two lovers obviously arises from their own choices, but Porphyrius repeatedly attributes it to extraneous, inimical forces. And Philocles, caught on the horns of a dilemma, perceives that the situation has passed beyond his control:

> Fate shoves me headlong down a rugged way;
> Unsafe to run, and yet too steep to stay.[96]

A significant illustration of a consistently heroic character who attributes to fate a failure patently the result of his own headstrong will and breach of loyalty occurs in *Don Sebastian,* when

[94] *The Spanish Friar,* III, iii; Vol. VI, p. 467.
[95] I, i; Vol. VI, p. 425.
[96] *Secret Love,* IV, ii; Vol. II, p. 487.

Dorax, upon hearing that his rival has died to save Sebastian, exclaims :

> Had I been born with his indulgent stars,
> My fortune had been his, and his been mine.[97]

Maximin, who changes his love as the wind blows, recognizes a dual influence of stars and "nature," and repudiates all responsibility :

> If to new persons I my love apply,
> The stars and nature are in fault, not I.[98]

Dryden's heroic drama presents something of the same paradox to be found in Hobbes's *Leviathan*. The order of nature, for Hobbes, is irrevocably and absolutely determined; yet he constantly assumes that man can guide his own destiny through the formation of a commonwealth and the delegation of power to a king who, though he rules by the right of nature inherent in the law of self-preservation, can himself formulate law and assign reward. It is a convention of heroic drama that the protagonist should arrogate to himself the privileges of Fate. "I alone am king of me," Almanzor exclaims, and Maximin boasts that he is inferior to no god. But although they and others overcome every physical obstacle and enjoy freedom from external restraints in the conventionally superhuman manner of the heroes of French romance, they inevitably fall victims to their own passions : they are guided by emotional determinism. In both Dryden and Hobbes there is a contradiction between the claims of the powerful individual and the actual necessity which conditions his behaviour. And, in Dryden, it is the latter which receives a reasoned defence in more than one long passage.

As determinism tends to make ethics anomalous, so does it provide a rationale for the life of passion. Hobbes, moreover, in addition to nullifying freedom of the will, further deepens the base of passional life by teleologically subordinating reason to the desires. Reason is merely a scout for the desires; and where reason

---

[97] IV, iii; Vol. VII, p. 440.
[98] *Tyrannic Love,* IV, i; Vol. III, p. 433.

is against man, he implies, man will be against reason.[99] With few exceptions the characters in Dryden's plays are in the grip of devastating emotions, the laws of which are categorical, the force of which is irresistible. The predominance of love over other emotions is not, of course, unique to Dryden's plays. The French romances of Madame Scudéry, La Calprenède, and Gomberville inevitably centre about the passion of love. It is an important element in Corneille, who represents the conflict of love and honour; and the heroic drama of Davenant, Orrery, and Otway treats various aspects of it. Dryden, however, differs from his contemporaries in clearly defined ways. In both Dryden and the French romances there is much of the dialectic of love; in both, the characters have no existence apart from their central passion. But Dryden shows much more plainly, using the familiar philosophic terms, the dualism of passion and reason; the vicissitudes of his characters are more inner, their language less *precieuse* than that of their French counterparts. The struggles portrayed by Corneille and usually those represented by the English writers of "heroic" plays show the difficult but certain triumph of honour over love; in only three of Dryden's plays[100] does the struggle thus eventuate, and one of them was lifted bodily from *Le Grand Cyrus.*[101] This persistent omnipotence of the passions, together with the many passages in which that omnipotence is explained and insisted upon, Dryden probably owed to Hobbist materialism, although he may also reflect the Epicureanism of the French sceptical movement by which he was undoubtedly influenced. On the whole the poet-laureate's presentation of love is more "conscious," more reflective, and less thoroughly conventional than that of the French romances or of his English compatriots.

Miss Kathleen Lynch has attempted to show that Dryden's presentation of love is markedly Platonic.[102] In the Platonic plays of the Caroline period, she points out, Fate exercises a "unique

[99] An aphoristic paraphrase of Hobbes made by Jeremy Collier in *Essays upon Several Moral Subjects,* London, 1720; Vol. IV, p. 141.

[100] *Secret Love, Don Sebastian,* and *The Indian Emperor* (sub-plot).

[101] The main plot of *Secret Love* was very little altered from its source.

[102] "Conventions of Platonic Drama in the Heroic Plays of Orrery and Dryden," *Publications of the Modern Language Association,* June, 1929.

authority." The lovers always love by destiny; the passion seizes upon them at first sight, and it is of no avail to deny its demands. An unsuccessful lover is expected to enjoy the lady's friendship if he may not have her love. His love "has such celestial purity that it discredits and subdues, although in many cases it does not wholly extinguish, physical passion." Self-love vanishes, in these Platonic plays, and jealousy "has lost its tragic appeal and has become an intolerable offense." The Platonic lover, moreover, must be a fluent rhetorician and dialectician of love: he must be able to analyze the passion; to tell what it is; to asseverate its laws and decorum. Even at moments of bitter disappointment, he must be able to phrase gracefully figurative compliments to his lady. After she explains that Dryden was extensively influenced by these characteristics of earlier drama, Miss Lynch writes the following appraisal:

> Dryden's heroes prove his contention that men of heroic calibre are not exempt from weaknesses of character. Although excellent Platonic philosophers on occasion, they speak not infrequently the natural language of passion and chafe under the restraints of their servitude. Dryden's heroines are better Platonists, yet they make concessions in love which will not bear the closest Platonic scrutiny.[103]

Miss Lynch thus says much to negate her principal contention, although not so much as the plays really demand. It is true that the characters love by fate, that they love at first sight often,[104] and that they cannot curb their passions. But the Platonic *tone* is wholly lacking. The love is definitely not celestially pure: its object is possession, and there are frequent insistences upon present enjoyment lest Heaven prove not to offer fulfilment. The physical effects of love are often voluptuously described, as when Troilus exclaims:

> I'm giddy; expectation whirls me round:
> The imaginary relish is so sweet,
> That it enchants my sense; what will it be,
> When I shall taste that nectar? . . .
> Just such a passion does heave up my breast!

[103] P. 470.
[104] Often they do not. Almost always they fall in love suddenly, however.

> My heart beats thicker than a feverish pulse:
> I know not where I am, nor what I do;[105]

or when Aureng-Zebe threatens to "devour" Indamora's kisses with "hungry taste."[106] The lovers *usually* speak the *natural,* if somewhat exaggerated, language of passion, voicing clearly the struggle within them and frequently using physical rather than ethereally Platonic similitudes. Self-love, moreover, is not extinguished to the point of eliminating jealousy. Honoria, whom Miss Lynch cites in this connexion, pays verbal respect to self-sacrifice, but she is quick to quarrel with her rival.[107] Aureng-Zebe, Almanzor, Cydaria, Troilus, Placidius, Antony—all are furiously jealous; all, permanently or temporarily, hate successful rivals. There are but few instances of a disappointed lover's remaining faithfully friendly to the lady.[108] The world of Dryden's plays is distinctly that of passion-ridden characters, with almost none of the courtly decorum and preciosity of persons playing the Platonic game of love, and with none of the spiritual implications of the genuine Platonic convention. The use of Fate is not limited to the love-situation, and the prevailing insistence upon it as a force in human life makes it seem unnecessary to suppose the fate-motif to be a mere convention. If love-at-first-sight and love-dialectic are Platonic in origin, at least they are dealt with by Dryden in a spirit so different as to negate the importance of earlier Platonic drama as a source for the treatment of love in the heroic plays.

Whether writing comedies for the avowed purpose of pleasing an unmoral audience or attempting to fashion what he believed to be noble men and women, Dryden portrays human nature as essentially passional. The three principal figures in *The Rival Ladies* are motivated by a single passion which will not be thwarted, despite almost insuperable obstacles in the way of its satisfaction. Gonsalvo, shipwrecked nobleman, whom two disguised maidens serve and secretly love, has seen Julia, already betrothed to

[105] *Troilus and Cressida,* II, ii; Vol. VI, p. 314.
[106] In *Aureng-Zebe,* IV, i; Vol. V, p. 275.
[107] In *The Rival Ladies,* Vol. II.
[108] Placidius, perhaps, in *Tyrannic Love.* A slave-master relationship exists between Arimant and Indamora, whom Miss Lynch cites as examples—certainly nothing that remotely resembles friendship.

Rodorick. Instantly he has become enamoured of her, although she loves the man she is to marry. From the moment of first seeing Julia, Gonsalvo's life is absorbed by his passion. A friend says of him:

> He trusts his passion
> Like him, that ventures all his stock at once
> On an unlucky hand.[109]

Julia tells him, not only that she cannot love him, but that his very presence is distasteful to her; but he merely declares, "Where passion rules, how weak does reason prove!"[110] He loses the last vestige of rationality in imploring her only to *say* she loves him, even though he knows that she does not. His servitors bid him cast from mind this love which destroys his peace; but he replies, "I cannot." Julia herself, no less devoted to the enemy of her brother, recognizes that her love is wholly opposed to reason:

> Too well I know it: for my love to thee
> Is born by inclination, not by judgment;
> And makes my virtue shrink within my heart.[111]

Like most of the other heroes and heroines, she feels that she has not the strength to live once her lover is dead. Hobbes has said that to be without desires is to be dead; Dryden alters this to signify that failure to satisfy one's dominant desire is worse than death.

Love, in almost every instance, paralyzes the will. In *The Indian Emperor,* when Almeria's hand is raised to kill her enemy, she is assailed by a sudden lethargy which stops her stroke. At first she cannot explain it, but she soon realizes that love has come to direct her will. In the same play, Orbellan, confronted by the hero whom he was about to kill, guiltily pleads, "Forgive it, as my passion's fault, not mine."[112] In many cases, the single passion with which Dryden endues a character appears to be adventitious; to be something quite apart from his essential being; to have, in a word, the directive force of an extraneous power akin to Fate.

[109] III, i; Vol. II, p. 176.
[110] II, i; Vol. II, p. 175.
[111] I, ii; Vol. II, p. 157.
[112] III, ii; Vol. II, p. 362.

In Dryden's plays, the dualism between passion and reason is, with few exceptions, purely nominal, for the characters themselves know how the conflict will eventuate. They are always cognizant of their own emotions, and often debate with themselves as to which of the two forces is stronger in them.[113] Abdalla and Abdelmelech, rival suitors in *The Conquest of Granada,* are madly, fatuously in love with the unscrupulous Lyndaraxa. Both understand her true nature, and both are able to stand aside, so to speak, and look at themselves. When Lyndaraxa departs, after planting in Abdalla's mind the idea of usurping his father's throne, he confesses:

> How bold our passions are, and yet how blind!—
> She's gone; and now,
> Methinks, there is less glory in a crown:
> My boiling passions settle, and go down.
> Like amber chafed, when she is near, she acts;
> When further off, inclines, but not attracts.[114]

That he can reflect intelligently upon his state alters not at all his helplessness. Love grips his will "like a lethargy"; his mind can toy with the idea of renunciation, but he is powerless to put it into execution. The distinction suggested between Will and Reason recalls the objection of Hobbes to the scholastic definition of will as a rational appetite. The will, he maintains, is not rational, because, if it were, there could be no voluntary act against reason.[115] Trying to convince himself that reason *may* be paramount, Abdalla debates the matter with Zulema, a frank exponent of complete unrestraint.

> Abdalla: Reason was given to curb our headstrong will.
> Zulema: Reason but shows a weak physician's skill;
> Gives nothing, while the raging fit does last,

[113] In connexion with the general treatment of reason by Dryden, it is relevant to note the following passage:

> Reason's a trick, when it no grant affords;
> It stamps the face of majesty on words.
> *Conquest of Granada,* Part I, III, i; Vol. IV, p. 77.

These lines recall Hobbes's identification of reason with the giving of "names."
[114] Part I, II, i; Vol. IV, p. 55.
[115] *Leviathan,* Vol. III (of Molesworth's ed. of the *English Works*), p. 48.

> But stays to cure it, when the worst is past.
> Reason's a staff for age, when nature's gone;
> But youth is strong enough to walk alone.[116]

Later, when the more mature Abdelmelech, unveiling to Abdalla the depravity of Lyndaraxa, advises him to forget her, lest his infatuation lead him from the path of duty, Abdalla replies:

> Your counsels, noble Abdelmelech, move
> My reason to accept them, not my love.
> Ah, why did heaven leave man so weak defence,
> To trust frail reason with the rule of sense!
> 'Tis overpoised and kicked up in the air,
> While sense weighs down the scale, and keeps it there;
> Or, like a captive king, 'tis borne away,
> And forced to count'nance its own rebels' sway.

But Abdelmelech springs to the defence of Reason:

> No, no; our reason was not vainly lent;
> Nor is a slave, but by its own consent:
> If reason on his subject's triumph wait,
> An easy king deserves no better fate.[117]

This tribute to reason is unintentionally ironical, because Abdelmelech, like Abdalla, remains in the grip of his passion, first encouraged, then repelled by Lyndaraxa, until death at last releases him. Abdalla, in turn, rejects all pretension to rationality:

> I cannot, will not,—nay, I would not fly:
> I'll love, be blind, be cozened till I die;
> And you, who bid me wiser counsel take,
> I'll hate, and, if I can, I'll kill you for her sake.[118]

Almanzor maintains that love is an enchantment by which the reason is bound, and would banish thought from the domain of love. The same determinism appears in *Aureng-Zebe*. While Indamora is in prison, Arimant reveals his love for her; and, once she knows of it, she tells him coldly, frankly, that she intends to use him as a pawn in her game to defeat the Emperor's plans. "You

[116] *The Conquest of Granada*, Part I, II, i; Vol. IV, pp. 55-6.
[117] III, i; p. 61.
[118] *Ibid.*, p. 62.

know," she says assuredly, "you must obey me, soon or late."[119]
And she has understood him aright: he is a bondman to passion,
though his reason apprises him of his folly:

> Why am I thus to slavery designed,
> And yet am cheated with a freeborn mind?
> Or make thy orders with my reason suit,
> Or let me live by sense, a glorious brute.[120]

He is betraying his kind; he is hazarding his position, not to say
his life, but he can only lament that it is so!

> My virtue, prudence, honour, interest, all
> Before this universal monarch fall.
> Beauty, like ice, our footing does betray;
> Who can tread sure on the smooth slippery way?
> Pleased with the passage, we slide swiftly on,
> And see the dangers, which we cannot shun.[121]

Similarly, the Emperor perceives the enormity of his plan to
become the rival of the son who has preserved his kingdom. He is
well aware of the perfidy of it, but he is never able to subordinate
passion to duty or even to his own welfare.

When Aureng-Zebe defies the treacherous Morat, the Emperor
experiences momentary remorse:

> I feel my virtue struggling in my soul,
> But stronger passion does its power control.[122]

He finally renounces Indamora only when his very life depends
upon a reconciliation with Aureng-Zebe. Once Morat's plot to
dispossess him has been revealed, however, the Emperor cries out
in anguish:

> Why was my reason made my passion's slave?
> I see Heaven's justice; thus the powers divine
> Pay crimes with crimes. . . .[123]

In Aureng-Zebe himself, as in Almanzor, there is a disparity between Dryden's intent and the reality which he has created.

[119] III, i; Vol. V, p. 239.
[120] Ibid.
[121] II, i; p. 220.
[122] III, i; p. 247.
[123] IV, i; p. 270.

Aureng-Zebe's heroic qualities are stressed in antithesis to the
recreancy of other male characters; and even the villains of the
piece are ready with acknowledgement of his superiorities. He pays
verbal respect to reason and the principle of control, declaring that
he stands "firm collected in his strength within"; but, actually, a
mad jealousy blinds him to the virtues of Indamora when they are
obvious; and, attributing his misfortune to Nature, he dissipates
his energies in maudlin sentimentality:

> I grow a fool, and show my rage again:
> 'Tis nature's fault; and why should I complain?[124]

> With, or without you, I can have no rest:
> What shall I do? Y'are lodged within my breast:
> Your image never will be thence displaced;
> But there it lies, stabbed, mangled, and defaced.[125]

His speech, moreover, is often characterized by an uncontrol that
bespeaks a predominance of passion:

> Love mounts, and rolls about my stormy mind,
> Like fire, that's borne by a tempestuous wind.
> Oh, I could stifle you, with eager haste!
> Devour your kisses with my hungry taste!
> Rush on you! eat you! wander o'er each part,
> Raving with pleasure, snatch you to my heart!
> Then hold you off, and gaze! then, with new rage,
> Invade you, till my conscious limbs presage
> Torrents of joy, which all their banks o'erflow![126]

The impression created by such an effusion is strengthened by the
paucity of moral courage shown by Aureng-Zebe. He affirms that
he had rather be dead than deprived of his father's love, and later
he expresses the same feeling regarding Indamora's love. The
strain of sentimentalism at times apparent in Dryden is, it may
well be, a logical outgrowth of an individualistic, naturalistic
philosophy which elevates the passions above reason. If man cannot
guide or control himself, but is at the mercy of passion, he may
well feel a little sorry for himself, one might argue.

[124] V, i; p. 295.
[125] *Ibid.*, p. 297.
[126] IV, i; pp. 275-6.

Antony in *All For Love* is, not less than Aureng-Zebe, the man of passion. Aside from alterations in form and degree of unity, perhaps the fundamental difference between Dryden's play and that of Shakespeare lies in Antony. Dryden divests him of his "Roman thoughts" and political stature, and makes him the abject slave of love and its pursuant fury—jealous suspicion. Another basic change arising from the dramatist's conception of human nature marks his version of the Greek story of Oedipus. The stern ethical import of the Sophoclean tragedy is dissipated by the moral wavering of Oedipus, who is prevented only by the intervention of a ghost from returning to Jocasta's arms even after he has been apprised of the incestuous relationship.

The heroic play *Tyrannic Love* offers equal opportunity to study character at the mercy of emotion. Maximin, almost a burlesque-king, with his supreme egoism and wild defiance, admits:

> I can no more make passion come or go,
> Than you can bid your Nilus ebb and flow.[127]

Madly in love with St. Catherine at a moment's notice, in equally short order his love turned to hate, he dictates that she shall die; but, once she is dead, his love resumes its first violence. The only way, in truth, that he can free himself from one passion is to deliver himself unreservedly to another. There is in Maximin no dualism: he sees no duty apart from self-indulgence. He asks:

> How can I help these faults which nature made? . . .
> Who cannot cure, must humour his disease.[128]

Maximin, to be sure, is frankly evil; but his language is, essentially, no different from that of Aureng-Zebe or Almanzor; hero and villain alike agree that reason is a weak play-king over emotion. None of the characters in these pieces ever really frees himself from passion; yet in the long discussion of religious philosophy

---

[127] IV, i; Vol. III, p. 433.

[128] *Ibid.*, pp. 433, 434. Love is often described as being literally a disease—an interpretation clearly in accord with physical determinism. *Cf.* Prospero in *The Tempest* (III, ii; Vol. III, p. 156):

> Poor child! Thy passion, like a lazy ague,
> Has seized thy blood; instead of striving, thou humourest
> And feedest thy languishing disease. . . .

carried on by Maximin, St. Catherine, and the pagan Apollonius, both pagan and Christian agree that the highest nobility is

> To keep the passions in severest awe,
> To live to reason, nature's greatest law.[129]

If that be a seriously entertained opinion of Dryden's, he fails once more in *Love Triumphant* to realize characters intended to be noble. Celidea, whose love for Garcia appears hopeless, is ashamed of her inability to free herself from this unreciprocated feeling; and cries out:

> . . . O heaven unkind!
> That gives us passions strong and unconfined,
> And leaves us reason for a vain defence,
> Too powerful rebels, and too weak a prince.[130]

When the queen, moreover, explains to Garcia the dilemma in which Victoria is placed by her love for the banished Alphonso, he quickly perceives the inadvisability of his becoming involved in the tangle; but he is not, because of that, deterred from trying to win Victoria for himself. "My reason is convinced," he says, "but not my passion."[131] It is interesting, further, to note the efforts of Ximena to vindicate the behaviour of Alphonso on physical grounds:

> And did not you, my lord, observe Alphonso,
> How, though at first he could not rule his passion,—
> Not at the very first, for that's impossible
> To hasty blood, like his . . .
> Yet in the second moment he repented?[132]

Dryden, in the *Dedication* to *Aureng-Zebe,* expresses a belief, here pertinent to Ximena's words, that there is a close relationship between mind and body:

> Our minds are perpetually wrought on by the temperament
> of our bodies, which makes me suspect, they are nearer allied,
> than either our philosophers or school-divines will allow
> them to be.[133]

[129] II, iii; Vol. III, p. 404.
[130] IV, i; Vol. VIII, p. 440.
[131] IV, i; Vol. VIII, p. 438.
[132] I, i; Vol. VIII, pp. 389-90.
[133] P. 199, Vol. V.

This statement shows clearly Dryden's tendency towards some form of determinism; and it should not be overlooked by those who affirm that the dramatist was not influenced by Hobbes.

The characters in the plays are, then, almost uniformly dominated by passion; even the supermen, who own no limitations, bow before its tempests. External Fate is reinforced by an inner determinism; and the demands of the physical are ineluctable, for never is the emotion shown to be deeply rooted in common interests or in spiritual affinity. The dramatist pictures a world dedicated to a naturalistic pursuit of passional ends; and the dwellers therein are especially significant to an understanding of the ideas of their creator, because, even when he states that they are designed to be heroic, they are still slaves to their emotions and self-centred ambitions. Hobbes represents, philosophically, the materialistic and naturalistic trend in the seventeenth century. Dryden knew the work of Hobbes and obviously reflects it in assertions regarding certain fundamental human instincts and in his exegesis of the problem of free will. And all of the pertinent evidence irresistibly suggests that the psychology of Hobbes, basing man's activity upon the passions—recognizing the reason, to be sure, but emphasizing the priority of the emotions—had so permeated Dryden's thought as to condition, whether consciously or not, his creation of dramatic character.

II

A theory of government logically depends upon the opinions which its formulator holds concerning the inherent possibilities of human nature. Democracy presupposes a sufficient degree of basic goodness in men to enable them to live together without the control of a strongly centralized authority; while monarchy allies itself with the supposition that men, in a natural state, are unwilling and, by reason of the character of their deepest instincts, unfit to guide the destiny of their social group in accordance with unselfish principles designed to promote the welfare of all. So, in the eighteenth century, the writings of Rousseau, who was convinced of the nobility of man as he exists prior to the corrupting influences of an artificial civilization, lent impetus to the democratic revolution;

and so in the seventeenth century, Hobbes, with his panoply of selfish instincts and degraded motives, provided a new foundation for absolutist political philosophy. His, it is needless to say, was not the first defence of absolutism, nor was it the only notable expression of it in that period, for James I, in the *Basilikon Doron*,[1] *The Trew Law of Free Monarchies*,[2] the *Speech of 1609*, and elsewhere, had established the Sovereign in what he looked upon as the incontrovertibly secure position of having received his power directly from God:

> . . . Kings are not onely Gods Lieutenants upon earth, and sit upon Gods throne, but even by God himselfe they are called Gods, . . . and so their power after a certaine relation compared to the Divine power.[3]

Hobbes retains the ultimately divine origin of kingship, but bases it more immediately upon the natural laws of self-preservation and the desire for comfort and aggrandizement. These are, to be sure, God's laws; but the head of the Commonwealth derives his prerogatives, not from gracious bestowal by Heaven, but from a compact formed by men to the end that their desires may not be thwarted by wholly unrestrained self-expression. A mere covenant, however, is not enough to suppress the tendencies of men to secure what they want at the expense of others; a common power is needed "to keep them in awe, and to direct their actions to the common benefit."[4] Consequently, they choose[5] to confer all their power and strength upon one man, or upon one assembly of men, "that may reduce all their wills, by plurality of voices, unto one will. . . ."[6] This choice, it must be repeated, springs from fear, fear lest uncurbed individualism menace the safety or even the life of the individual. Starting from natural law, then, Hobbes agrees finally with James that the Sovereign is "God's Lieutenant, who

[1] 1599.

[2] 1598.

[3] *The Political Works of James I*, with an introduction by C. H. McIlwain, Cambridge, 1918, p. 307.

[4] Hobbes, *op. cit.*, Vol. III, p. 157.

[5] The *contract* seems to take the form of a *tacit* agreement.

[6] Hobbes, *op. cit.*, Vol. III, p. 157.

hath the sovereignty under God."[7] Unlike the Stuart king, though, he does not say that monarchy is the only possible kind of government acceptable to God; he recognizes democracy and oligarchy as well, but, on a purely utilitarian basis, concludes that monarchy best satisfies the needs of man and most easily assures a state of peace. Its superiority is chiefly owing to two virtues inherent in it: (1) the private interest of the monarch is always identical with the public interest, because the king's wealth and strength are increased by the wealth and war-strength of his people; (2) the monarch is subject only to the inconsistency of human nature, whereas the size of a governing assembly is conducive to disagreements arising from envy or interest. An all-powerful central government, Hobbes concludes, is based upon the laws of nature emanating from God, and it finds its most practicable form in the absolute dominion of a king.

Dryden was born into a family which was definitely allied with the Cromwellian party against Charles I; and among the poet's early verses were the *Heroic Stanzas,*[8] upon the death of the Protector. Even before the Restoration, however, he had formed bonds, through marriage and friendship, with the noble Howard family, the members of which had been loyal supporters of Charles I; and, when, in 1660, Charles II reclaimed the throne of England, Dryden became a Royalist and remained one to his death. In 1668, he was appointed to the laureateship and soon thereafter to the post of Historiographer Royal. Subsequently, although his pension was not paid promptly and although he was refused various requests for additional pecuniary aid, he wrote for the king's party, and steadfastly refused help from the opposing faction.[9] In 1681, at a time of political crisis, he produced his best satire, *Absalom and Achitophel,* in defence of royal prerogative against the aspirations of the bastard Duke of Monmouth and his adviser, the first Earl of Shaftesbury. After the accession of James II, Dryden was reappointed to his official positions only when he had changed from the Anglican to the Roman faith; but

[7] *Ibid.,* p. 161.

[8] Mr. Bredvold points out (*The Intellectual Milieu of John Dryden,* p. 132) that he avoids eulogy of "Commonwealth principles" even in this early poem.

[9] Bredvold, *The Best of Dryden,* Introduction, p. xx.

that the change was a mere matter of political expediency is made
to seem unlikely both by the fact that, in *The Hind and The
Panther,* the poet censured the religious policy of the king, and by
the fact that when William and Mary assumed control in the
Bloodless Revolution of 1688, he would not take the oath of
allegiance.

Dryden frequently has been called a political time-server of no
fixed opinions; and yet there is a consistent thread of monarchal
sympathy running throughout the work of his middle and late
career. Mr. Bredvold has attempted to show that his position in
politics was deeply rooted in a sceptical temperament which, placing but little confidence in man's ability to deal rationally with his
environment, deemed it wiser to assure social stability by adhering
to a settled and conservative form of governmental organization.[10]
Adequate proof for his hypothesis is available from prose, poems,
and plays; but an examination of the plays as a unit suggests that
Dryden also was deeply imbued with Hobbist ideas which pointed
in the same direction. Mr. Bredvold reminds the source-hunter of
B. J. Pendlebury's statement that "monarchic sentiment and scorn
of the crowd are typical of the heroic play, which was, in its
origin, the expression of an aristocratic ideal";[11] and warns that,
since such a literary tradition existed and since "there is no trace
of Hobbes in *Absalom and Achitophel* and *The Medal,*"[12] the
expression of absolutism in the plays can scarcely be taken as con-
stituting Dryden's own views. The political poems, however, do
voice an unmistakable monarchism and at least contain nothing to
contradict the theories uttered by characters in the heroic plays.
One cannot help wondering, moreover, whether the following
passage from *Absalom and Achitophel,* does not reflect the poet's
mental grappling with the principles of Hobbism, and does not
imply the truth of the chief of them:

> What shall we think? Can people give away,
> Both for themselves and sons, their native sway?
> Then they are left defenceless to the sword

[10] *The Intellectual Milieu of John Dryden,* Chap. v.
[11] Quoted from B. J. Pendlebury, *Dryden's Heroic Plays,* London, 1923, p. 78,
in Bredvold's *Intellectual Milieu,* p. 136.
[12] *Ibid.,* p. 137.

Of each unbounded, arbitrary lord:
And laws are vain, by which we right enjoy,
If kings unquestioned can those laws destroy.
Yet if the crowd be judge of fit and just,
And kings are only officers in trust,
Then this resuming covenant was declared
When kings were made, or is for ever barred.
If those, who gave the sceptre, could not tie,
By their own deed, their own posterity,
How then could Adam bind his future race?

   . . .   .

Then kings are slaves to those whom they command,
And tenants to their people's pleasure stand.
Add, that the power, for property allowed,
Is mischievously seated in the crowd;
For who can be secure of private right,
If sovereign sway may be dissolved by might?
Nor is the people's judgment always true:
The most may err as grossly as the few;
And faultless kings run down by common cry,
For vice, oppression, and for tyranny. . . .
If they may give and take whene'er they please,
Not kings alone, the Godhead's images,
But government itself, at length must fall
To nature's state, where all have right to all.[13]

Herein are many of the problems treated by Hobbes in *Of Commonwealth,* and the crux of his entire position lies in the question:

For who can be secure of private right,
If sovereign sway may be dissolved by might?

None of the heroic plays is without its monarch, the central aspect of whose kingship is power. Montezuma, the most moderate of Dryden's rulers, believes that

Kings and their crowns have but one destiny:
Power is their life; when that expires, they die.[14]

Dryden does not hold with Hobbes or with James to the extent of hesitating to portray evil nature in monarchs, for most of his royal

[13] Vol. IX, pp. 289-90.
[14] *The Indian Emperor,* V, ii; Vol. II, p. 404.

personages are the villains of the plays in which they appear; and
occasionally they regret their arbitrary exercise of power and
even forgo a portion of it.[15] But Hobbist principles are voiced by
the heroes themselves, as well as by the kings; so that, regardless
of the circumstances of their utterance, it is clear that the political
reasoning of Hobbes was a part of Dryden's intellectual store.

Torrismond, hero of *The Spanish Friar,* explains the common
method of securing sovereign power in much the same way as the
philosopher of Malmesbury:

> Kings' titles commonly begin by force,
> Which time wears off, and mellows into right;
> So power, which, in one age, is tyranny,
> Is ripened, in the next, to true succession.[16]

Boabdelin similarly explains the origin of his powers:

> 'Tis true from force the noblest title springs;
> I therefore hold from that, which first made kings.

Hobbist doctrine is not lost sight of when the Spanish ambassador
reminds him of the Janus-faced nature of his argument:

> Since then by force you prove your title true,
> Ours must be just, because we claim from you.[17]

Although Hobbes recognizes the possibility of kingship by "institution," he affirms that force is a customary source of it, and that
power once obtained thus is as legitimate and as binding as that of
any other governing authority.[18] The same idea is expressed by the
despicable Morat, who plots to supplant both his father and his
brother:

> . . . who by force a sceptre does obtain,
> Shows he can govern that, which he could gain.
> Right comes of course, whate'er he was before;
> Murder and usurpation are no more.[19]

[15] *Cf.* Veramond in *Love Triumphant*; Morat in *Aureng-Zebe.*
[16] IV, ii; Vol. VI, p. 493.
[17] *The Conquest of Granada,* Part I, I, i; Vol. IV, p. 47.
[18] Hobbes, *op. cit.,* Vol. III, p. 159.
[19] *Aureng-Zebe,* V, i; Vol. V, p. 280.

And duties, even filial duties, *are no more,* for he tells his father:

> You cancelled duty when you gave me power.
> If your own actions on your will you ground,
> Mine shall hereafter know no other bound.[20]

As Hobbes says that the essence of political sovereignty is power, so he states also that God merits worship, not because of his mercy or benevolence, but because of his omnipotence; and Morat draws the analogy between the earthly and the heavenly monarch:

> What power makes mine, by power I mean to seize,
> Since 'tis to that they their own greatness owe
> Above, why should they question mine below?[21]

The power enjoyed by the ruler, according to the philosopher of Malmesbury, must be indivisible; it must be greater than that of any single subject, and greater than the combined powers of all of them.[22] Montezuma, probably the most intelligent of Dryden's sovereigns and less given to rhodomontade than most of the others, phrases this principle when he says:

> That monarch sits not safely on his throne
> Who bears, within, a power that shocks his own.
> They teach obedience to imperial sway,
> But think it sin if they themselves obey. . . .
> My crown is absolute, and holds of none.
> I cannot in a base subjection live. . . .[23]

Maximin, in similar fashion, inveighs against any division of power, and asserts that when king and assembly both lay claim to power, one or the other must be possessed of only nominal authority:

> That senate's but a name:
> Or they are pageant princes which they make;
> That power they give away, they would partake.
> Two equal powers two different ways will draw,
> While each may check, and give the other law.
> True, they secure propriety and peace;[24]

[20] IV, i; Vol. V, p. 268.
[21] *Ibid.,* p. 270.
[22] Hobbes, Vol. III, pp. 168-9.
[23] *The Indian Emperor,* I, ii; Vol. II, p. 339.
[24] Hobbes says that division of power is a threat to peace. Vol. III, p. 177.

> But are not fit an empire to increase.
> When they should aid their prince, the slaves dispute;
> And fear success should make him absolute.
> They let foes conquer, to secure the state,
> And lend a sword, whose edge themselves rebate.[25]

Such a senate, Hobbes writes, must ultimately surrender its powers—temporarily at least—to one man who, by virtue of unified action, can accomplish results:

> . . . there is no great commonwealth, the sovereignty whereof is in a great assembly, which is not, as to consultations of peace, and war, and making of laws, in the same condition, as if the government were in a child. For as a child wants the judgment to dissent from counsel given him, and is thereby necessitated to take the advice of them, or him, to whom he is committed: so an assembly wanteth the liberty, to dissent from the counsel of the major part, be it good, or bad. And as a child has need of a tutor, or protector, to preserve his person and authority: so also, in great commonwealths, the sovereign assembly, in all great dangers and troubles, have need of . . . dictators . . . which are as much as temporary monarchs, to whom for a time, they may commit the entire exercise of their power.[26]

Employing a figure vaguely reminiscent of the *Leviathan,* Boabdelin characterizes the people and their legislative bodies:

> See what the many-headed beast demands.—
> Cursed is that king, whose honour's in their hands.
> In senates, either they too slowly grant,
> Or saucily refuse to aid my want.[27]

Veramond rivals Maximin as a spirited exponent of absolutism, for he declares that his will is law, and that "kings are not kings, unless they be obeyed."[28] He justifies his own usurpation of Ramirez's throne by the argument of superior power:

> Then, when he lost the power, he lost the claim,
> And marks of sovereign right.[29]

[25] *Tyrannic Love,* I, i; Vol. III, pp. 386-7.
[26] Hobbes, *op. cit.,* Vol. III, p. 177.
[27] *The Conquest of Granada,* Part II, I, ii; Vol. IV, p. 130.
[28] *Love Triumphant,* III, i; Vol. VIII, p. 429.
[29] I, i; Vol. VIII, p. 388.

When Alphonso asks Veramond how his conscience can permit him to enjoy a throne obtained by force, he, implying that human nature generally would find the answer easy, tells the boy to ask that question of himself when he is king.[30] Upon hearing Almanzor boast that he is

> . . . as free as nature first made man,
> Ere the base laws of servitude began,
> When wild in woods the noble savage ran,

Boabdelin, the emperor, summarizes the reasoning by which Hobbes arrived at the decision that an absolute central authority is necessary to individual self-preservation:

> Since, then, no power above your own you know,
> Mankind should use you like a common foe;
> You should be hunted like a beast of prey:
> By your own law I take your life away.[31]

The lodging of power in the ruler to prevent men from hunting each other like beasts of prey, does not, however, give to the ruler the right to indulge in such an occupation himself. Hobbes imposes but few limitations upon the monarch, but his fundamental law of nature compels him to admit that the king cannot justly command a subject to take his own life nor expect passive submission from him when it is jeopardized.[32] Bertran, in *The Spanish Friar*, explains that the law of self-preservation may be used to excuse the attack upon a subject by a king, or, conversely, the rebellion of a subject against his ruler.[33] Self-preservation is the only defensible purpose of rebellion, however, in the state described by Hobbes; and revolt against a ruler for any other reason is injustice on the part of subjects:

> And therefore, they that are subjects to a monarch, cannot without his leave cast off monarchy . . . for they are bound, every man to every man, to own, and be reputed author of all, that he that already is their sovereign, shall do, and judge fit to be done. . . . Besides, if he that attempteth to depose

---

[30] *Ibid.*, p. 387.
[31] *The Conquest of Granada*, Part I, I, i; Vol. IV, p. 43.
[32] Hobbes, *op. cit.*, Vol. III, p. 204.
[33] IV, ii; Vol. VI, p. 485.

his sovereign, be killed, or punished by him for such an
attempt, he is author of his own punishment . . . and because it is injustice for a man to do anything, for which he
may be punished by his own authority, he is also upon that
title, unjust.[34]

When Boabdelin, reasserting the necessity for unlimited control,
says:

> But kings, who rule with limited command,
> Have players' sceptres put into their hand.
> Power has no balance, one side still weighs down,
> And either hoists the commonwealth or crown.[35]

Abenamar agrees:

> While people tug for freedom, kings for power,
> Both sink beneath some foreign conqueror:
> When subjects find too late they were unjust,
> And want that power of kings, they durst not trust.[36]

The subjects, in accordance with Hobbist principles, are unjust
because they have violated the contract upon which all political and
social organization rests: the voluntary yielding of authority to
a central government in return for security. Perhaps the clearest
reflection of Hobbes's State of Nature and the clearest statement
of a need for a central power appear in the conversation between
Ulysses and Agamemnon in *Troilus and Cressida*:

> For, when the general is not like the hive,
> To whom the foragers should all repair,
> What honey can our empty combs expect?
> Or when supremacy of kings is shaken,
> What can succeed? How could communities,
> Or peaceful traffic from divided shores,
> Prerogative of age, crowns, sceptres, laurels,
> But by degree, stand on their solid base?
> Then everything resolves to brutal force,
> And headlong force is led by hoodwinked will.
> For wild ambition, like a ravenous wolf,

---

[34] Hobbes, Vol. III, p. 160.
[35] *The Conquest of Granada,* Part II, I, ii; Vol. IV, p. 130.
[36] *Ibid.,* pp. 130-1.

> Spurred on by will, and seconded by power,
> Must make an universal prey of all,
> And last devour itself.[37]

Both kings and more truly heroic characters in the plays often express the belief that monarchs, because of their arbitrary power, can do no wrong. Hobbes asserts that ". . . they that have sovereign power may commit iniquity; but not injustice, or injury in the proper signification."[38] Dryden's characters expand this to declare that those who have sovereign power can commit neither private sin nor public injustice.

> Who can do all things, can do nothing ill.
> Ill is rebellion 'gainst some higher power:
> The world may sin, but not its emperor.
> My empress then shall die, my princess live;
> If this be sin, I do myself forgive,[39]

Maximin exclaims; and Morat affirms that "Monarchs, unquestioned, move in higher spheres."[40] These two speakers are ignoble; but when Aureng-Zebe proudly boasts

> I own no wrongs; some grievance I confess;
> But kings, like gods, at their own time redress,[41]

and Abdelmelech says that "The majesty of kings we should not blame,"[42] the same sentiments are being voiced by heroic persons. Guyomar, one of Dryden's wholly admirable characters, likewise holds a Nietzschean view of kingly behaviour:

> But kings by free consent their kingdoms take,
> Strict as those sacred ties which nuptials make;
> And whate'er faults in princes time reveal,
> None can be judge where can be no appeal.[43]

---

[37] I, i; Vol. VI, pp. 290-1.

[38] Hobbes, *op. cit.,* Vol. III, p. 163. Hobbes bases this theory upon the social contract whereby all that the ruler does originates in the people themselves. Dryden, however, reverts to Hobbes's statement elsewhere to the effect that God cannot do ill because he is omnipotent; that earthly rulers can do no wrong, merely by virtue of possessing unlimited power.

[39] *Tyrannic Love,* V, i; Vol. III, p. 456.

[40] *Aureng-Zebe,* IV, i; Vol. V, p. 268.

[41] II, i; Vol. V, p. 220.

[42] *The Conquest of Granada,* Part I, III, i; Vol. IV, p. 60.

[43] *The Indian Emperor,* IV, ii; Vol. II, p. 377.

He utters these words in reply to Alibech's assertion that when kings are stubborn or unwise, it is the duty of private subjects to rebel; but as soon as Guyomar has pointed out what he believes to be the fallacy in her argument, she recognizes that he is right and she wrong.

Not only must rulers be unquestioned by subjects, but also no law can be made against them—even by themselves—for it is against reason and the law of nature, Hobbes says, for a man to do anything which is not in his own interests. And Almanzor agrees that "No king against himself a law can make."[44]

There are scattered throughout the heroic plays many incidental references to the superiorities and sacred qualities of kings; and not always are these superiorities merely corollary to possession of power. Dryden veers away from Hobbes's theory of the contract, with its ultimate sanction in God and natural law, towards James's theory of Divine Right. This theory Dryden asseverates in a postscript to the *History of the League*:

> That government, generally considered, is of divine author-ity, will admit of no dispute; for whoever will seriously consider, that no man has naturally a right over his own life, so as to murder himself, will find, by consequence, that he has no right to take away another's life; and that no pact betwixt man and man, or of corporations and individuals, or of sovereigns and subjects, can entitle them to this right; so that no offender can lawfully, and without sin, be punished, unless that power be derived from God. It is He who has commissioned magistrates, and authorised them to prevent future crimes, by punishing offenders, and to redress the injured by distributive justice; subjects therefore are account-able to superiors, and the superior to him alone. For, the sovereign being once invested with lawful authority, the subject has irrevocably given up his power, and the depen-dence of a monarch is alone on God.[45]

Torrismond mentions the "power that guards the sacred lives of kings";[46] Raymond alludes to the murdered Sancho as "Heaven's

---

[44] *The Conquest of Granada,* Part I, I, i; Vol. IV, p. 43.
[45] Vol. XVII, p. 153.
[46] *The Spanish Friar,* III, iii; Vol. VI, p. 470.

image double-stamped, as man and king";[47] Dorax speaks of the monarch as Heaven's image;[48] and Montezuma states:

> But heaven has need of no such viceroy here,
> Itself bestows the crowns that monarchs wear.[49]

If Dryden diverges from Hobbes regarding divine right, he closely echoes him in his often-expressed attitude towards the position of the subject in the commonwealth. In the *Leviathan,* the philosopher makes it clear that freedom of the subject is wholly incompatible with the existence of harmonious social and political order,[50] and describes men in the mass, who have repudiated authority, as being brutish in the extreme. Heroic characters in the plays not infrequently inveigh against the common herd and insist upon the necessity of their absolute obedience to authority. Cortez, who himself is attempting to dispossess Montezuma, is at one with his enemy in decrying popular criticism of kingship:

> Monarchs may err; but should each private breast
> Judge their ill acts, they would dispute their best.[51]

Of the people, Zulema, in *The Conquest of Granada,* says:

> Those kings, who to their wild demands consent,
> Teach others the same way to discontent.
> Freedom in subjects is not, nor can be;
> But still, to please them, we must call them free.
> Propriety, which they their idol make,
> Or law, or law's interpreters, can shake.[52]

Professor Merritt Hughes suggests that "Dryden's use of the term 'law's interpreters' seems to reflect the extreme view of Hobbes that law emanates solely from the sovereign's arbitrary will."[53] Almanzor and the Queen in *Secret Love,* both supposedly exem-

[47] *Ibid.,* V, ii, p. 510.
[48] *Don Sebastian,* III, i; Vol. VII, p. 387.
[49] *The Indian Emperor,* I, ii; Vol. II, p. 338.
[50] See Chap. XXI.
[51] *The Indian Emperor,* II, ii; Vol. II, p. 346.
[52] Part II, I, ii; Vol. IV, p. 130.
[53] "Dryden as Statist," *Philological Quarterly,* 1927, p. 348; *cf.* also Hobbes, Vol. III, Chap. 26.

plary characters, voice the same opinion of the common people in relation to their ruler:

> Hence, you unthinking crowd!—[exclaims Almanzor]
> Empire, thou poor and despicable thing,
> When such as these make or unmake a king![54]

And the Queen scorns to consider the desires of her subjects who are concerned about her prospect of marriage:

> My peoples' fears! who made them statesmen?
> They much mistake their business, if they think
> It is to govern.
> The rights of subjects, and of sovereigns,
> Are things distinct in nature:—Theirs is to
> Enjoy propriety, not empire.[55]

The heroine of *The Spanish Friar* brings to mind the emphasis of Hobbes on the bestial character of man's ungoverned nature, when she describes the people as

> That hot-mouthed beast, that bears against the curb,
> Hard to be broken even by lawful kings.[56]

In the twenty-first chapter of the *Leviathan*, the philosopher points out the fallacies in popular interpretations of liberty and states that very often the masses of men do not comprehend the only possible meaning of the word. One of the statesmen in *The Spanish Friar* regrets that the majority of men are so unintelligently devoted to the shibboleth of "liberty" that they will fight for any cause of which it is the slogan.[57] Their responsiveness to such appeals,

[54] *The Conquest of Granada*, Part I, I, i; Vol. IV, p. 46.

[55] I, iii; Vol. II, p. 434.

[56] III, iii; Vol. VI, p. 466. *Cf.* also Dorax in *Don Sebastian*, Vol. VII, p. 432; and *Troilus* (Vol. VI, p. 342):

> The public is the lees of vulgar slaves;
> Slaves, with the minds of slaves; so born, so bred.
> Yet such as these, united in a herd,
> Are called, the public! Millions of such cyphers
> Make up the public sum. An eagle's life
> Is worth a world of crows. Are princes made
> For such as these; who, were one soul extracted
> From all their beings, could not raise a man?

[57] IV, ii; Vol. VI, p. 489.

which pander to the desire for self-expression, justifies the assertion of Ulysses, in *Troilus and Cressida*:

> Then, since from home-bred factions ruin springs,
> Let subjects learn obedience to their kings.[58]

Occasionally Dryden makes comic or sophistical reference (in the vein of Hobbes) to problems of political theory. The sailors in *The Tempest,* once they are accustomed to the island, decide to set up a commonwealth among themselves; and the dramatist presents a parody on the methods of democratic procedure when a centralizing force is lacking. The men quarrel, half-humorously, over the problem of which shall be the viceroy and which the subjects. All aspire to the highest position, and there is no convenient way of determining who shall be successful.[59]

The curate in *The Duke of Guise* employs the Hobbist principle of power for his own ends:

> Rebellion is an insurrection against the government; but they
> that have the power are actually the government; therefore,
> if the people have the power, the rebellion is in the king.[60]

Here, obviously, since the play represents the righteous failure of the plotters, of whom the curate is one, Dryden is controverting this perversion of Hobbes. Again, in *Albion and Albanius,* Zeal says:

> And when 'tis for the nation's peace,
> A king is but a king on trial.[61]

But Zeal, together with Democracy, is portrayed as having an infernal origin and as being a vicious influence upon society; and consequently what she says must be taken to be exactly contrary to the author's point of view; these two plays, *The Duke of Guise* and *Albion and Albanius,* were occasional pieces, inspired by crises in the political situation in England. Shortly after the passage of the Exclusion Bill of 1680, an association was formed for the defence of the Protestant religion and of the king's person. Such a league immediately suggested the similar body organized

[58] V, ii; Vol. VI, p. 390.
[59] II, i; Vol. III, pp. 131-2.
[60] I, i; Vol. VII, p. 25.
[61] II, ii; Vol. VII, p. 262.

in France during the reign of Henry II, and the attempted plot of
the Duke of Guise to supplant him. Dryden, in 1683, was asked to
collaborate with Nathaniel Lee in the writing of a tragedy entitled
The Duke of Guise; and he contributed the opening scene, the
whole of the fourth act, and the first part of the fifth. *Albion and
Albanius,* an opera, centres about the same period of time, and
recounts the events of Charles II's reign, celebrating particularly
the return from exile of the Duke of York and paying homage to
Charles himself. Both plays are distinctly royalist in purpose and
tone; but neither, aside from the passages quoted, is especially
suggestive of Hobbist political philosophy.

In accord with the general disapproval of a division of power,
the characters in the plays express disillusioned and cynical attitudes towards statesmen and political assemblies of one kind or
another. It is probable that Dryden's views were at least partly the
result of his having witnessed the *Sturm und Drang* of the period
during and after the Interregnum: the unceasing cabals, the religious instability, the lack of consistent and constructive direction on
the part of the nation's politicians. But occasionally they definitely
echo the writings of Hobbes. In the *Leviathan,* the philosopher,
pointing out the advantages of monarchy, comments upon the too-
frequent perfidy of assemblies, the tendencies of ministers to
pander to favourites, and the likelihood of statesmen's flattering
each other and serving each other's covetousness and ambition.[62]
A minor character in *Aureng-Zebe* voices much the same doubt
regarding statecraft:

> The ministers of state, who gave us law,
> In corners, with selected friends, withdraw:
> There, in deaf murmurs, solemnly are wise;
> Whispering, like winds, ere hurricanes arise.
> The most corrupt are most obsequious grown,
> And those they scorned, officiously they own.[63]

[62] Vol. III, pp. 174-5.
[63] I, i; Vol. V, p. 205.

Statesmen are looked upon by heroes and kings alike as being essentially hypocritical, unintelligent, and given to indulgence in meaningless formalities.[64]

It cannot be said with the same assurance that Dryden was, politically, a Hobbist as that, philosophically, he was a determinist. Although the sentiments in the plays are predominantly royalist, distinctly anti-Hobbist ideas are occasionally expressed by characters, as when Alphonso asks:

> What have the people done, the sheep of princes,
> That they should perish for the shepherd's fault?
> They bring their yearly wool, to clothe their owners;
> And yet, when bare themselves, are culled for
>   slaughter;[65]

or again, when Bertran states that "The just applause of godlike senates is the stamp of virtue";[66] or, still again, when it is said, in *Aureng-Zebe,* that "nature's laws are by the state's destroyed."[67] But, nevertheless, the passages cited as relevant to the origin of kingship in force and the instinct for preservation; to the importance of power as the essential aspect of government; to the necessity for the absolute obedience of the people; to the conviction that omnipotence determines justice and injustice; to the Machiavellian tendencies of statesmen;—all these combine to indicate that Dryden was familiar with the writings of one of the foremost political theorists of his time, and that he at least found nothing basically incompatible between the opinions of Hobbes and his own ideas. The ultimate source of his beliefs no doubt lay in his own experience and observations, but the language in which they are expressed often unmistakably echoes that of his contemporary, Hobbes.

[64] Cf. *Don Sebastian,* Vol. VII, p. 350; *Cleomenes,* Vol. VIII, p. 296; *Aureng-Zebe,* Vol. V, p. 256.
[65] *Love Triumphant,* IV, i; Vol. VIII, p. 446.
[66] *The Spanish Friar,* I, i; Vol. VI, p. 423.
[67] I, i; Vol. V, p. 204.

III. DRYDEN AND MONTAIGNE

STUDY of Dryden's political views, as they appear in the plays, leads naturally to French scepticism, the second body of thought which contributed to the poet's ideas and which oftentimes produced conclusions regarding statecraft, religion, and human nature identical with, or akin to, those of Hobbes. At some points where the English philosopher and the French sceptics tend to converge, it is possible to ally the dramatist more definitely with one than with the other; but at other points, it must simply be admitted that either may have influenced Dryden, and that probably, since he knew both, they reinforced each other in his thinking.

Montaigne, basing his principles upon those of Sextus Empiricus, believed, as did his intellectual forbears, the Pyrrhonists, in the maintenance of the political and religious *status quo*. By processes of negative reasoning, he—and they—reached the conviction that the epistemological problem can be solved only in terms of zero: man can know nothing, can say nothing with certainty about the fundamental nature of human life, its purposes, its motives, or its institutions. But men, he recognized, must live in some degree of security and social harmony; consequently, in order to avoid the complete intellectual and moral anarchy that would result from a complete nihilism based upon sound sceptical thought, human beings ought passively to accept things as they are. Why, after all, should a man change an opinion or a way of life when his reason is totally incapable either of proving to him that his present views are erroneous and hurtful, or of illuminating for him a sure path to improvement? Montaigne asserts that he dislikes "innovation in any disguise whatever";[1] and repeatedly warns of the dangers of change, especially political change:

[1] *Essays,* Vol. I, p. 115.

It is much to be doubted whether the manifest advantage of changing an established law, be it ever so bad, outweighs the evil involved in the removing of it, inasmuch as a government is a structure of various parts so closely joined together, that it is impossible to shake one part without the whole body feeling the concussion.[2]

And he further says:

Nothing presses so hard upon a state as innovation; mere change gives scope to injustice and tyranny.[3]

Dryden's deeply-rooted distrust of the unreasoned zeal of the masses, which has been noted and shown to spring from a conservative loyalty to absolutist principles, may be related to the sceptic's defence of things as they exist. There is, the poet believes, a virtue in adhering to what is old and tried, and a danger in failing to do so:

The silly crowd, by factious teachers brought
To think that faith untrue, their youth was taught,
Run on in new opinions, blindly bold,
Neglect, contemn, and then assault the old.
The infectious madness seizes every part,
And from the head distils upon the heart.
And first they think their prince's faith not true,
And then proceed to offer him a new;
Which if refused, all duty from them cast,
To their new faith they make new kings at last.[4]

While such a passage—and similar ones, inveighing against zeal and change—is, in tone, like passages in Montaigne, there is no direct evidence that Dryden's political *statism* rests upon a foundation of general philosophic doubt, although the presence of other sceptical elements in his thought tends to add weight to that supposition. The reflections of Hobbism are much clearer and less debatable. Dryden's religious thought, on the contrary, shows a much closer similarity to that of Montaigne than to that of Hobbes.

[2] *Ibid.*
[3] *Ibid.*, Vol. II, p. 422.
[4] *Tyrannic Love,* II, iii; Vol. III, p. 402.

It is not always possible fully to disentangle the threads of seventeenth-century ideas which enter into the patchwork of Dryden's religious concepts, for not infrequently an attitude expressed by one of his characters may be traced either to the materialism of Hobbes or to the scepticism of Montaigne. What his beliefs were up to the writing of *Religio Laici* in 1682 has been a not less fertile subject for controversy than his reasons for becoming a Catholic in 1685, or the more general question of his religious sincerity. A. W. Verrall,[5] Josef Wild,[6] and others, have called him a Deist; George Saintsbury[7] fails to find any evidence of Deism; while Sir Walter Scott[8] and Professor Bredvold[9] detect a continuous development, from the first writings to the last, of a Fideism which posits reliance upon faith, adherence to the established forms of religion, and complete abnegation of reason. There can be no question that in 1682 the poet was established in the tradition of Montaigne, who alleges that human powers are in no way capable of apprehending Truth:

> Reason ever goes astray in all matters, but especially when she meddles with divine things. . . . For, although we have given her certain and infallible principles, although we illumine her steps with the sacred lamp of Truth which it has pleased God to communicate to us, we daily see, nevertheless, how, if she stray ever so little from the ordinary path, if she turn aside and wander out of the way marked and trodden by the Church, she immediately loses her way, becomes embarrassed and entangled, whirling around and floating, aimless and unchecked, in that vast, turbulent and undulating sea of human opinions.[10]

Dryden's introduction to *Religio Laici* is the poetic counterpart of this passage:

> Dim as the borrowed beams of moon and stars
> To lonely, weary, wandering travellers,

[5] *Lectures on Dryden*, p. 150.
[6] *Dryden und die römische Kirche*, Leipzig, 1928, p. 13 ff.
[7] *Dryden*, in "English Men of Letters Series," New York, 1881.
[8] Dryden's *Works*, Vol. I, pp. 262-3.
[9] *The Intellectual Milieu of John Dryden*.
[10] *Op. cit.*, Vol. I, p. 518.

> Is reason to the soul: and as, on high,
> Those rolling fires discover but the sky,
> Not light us here; so reason's glimmering ray
> Was lent, not to assure our doubtful way,
> But guide us upward to a better day.[11]

Dryden's *Religio Laici,* the title of which is borrowed from Herbert of Cherbury's exposition of Deism, opposes natural religion which assumes that the few, bare essentials of Christianity can be arrived at by the reason.[12] The truths comprehended by the Deists, he reminds them, are not the products of their own minds:

> Revealed religion first informed thy sight,
> And reason saw not till faith sprung the light.
> Hence all thy natural worship takes the source;
> 'Tis revelation what thou think'st discourse.
> Else how com'st thou to see these truths so clear,
> Which so obscure to heathens did appear?
> Not Plato these, nor Aristotle found. . . .[13]

In the *Preface,* moreover, he writes:

> . . . our modern philosophers, nay, and some of our philosophising divines have too much exalted the faculties of our souls, when they have maintained that, by their force, mankind has been able to find out that there is one Supreme Agent, or intellectual Being, which we call God.[14]

An examination of the plays written between 1668 and 1682 leads to the conclusion that, although there is a strain of rationalism, and more than one of Hobbism in them, the religious philosophy voiced by the characters is predominantly Pyrrhonist. The

[11] Ll. 1-7; Vol. X, p. 38.

[12] The principles of religion as set down by Lord Herbert were five in number, as follows: 1. That there is one supreme God; 2. That he is to be worshipped; 3. That piety and virtue are the principal part of his worship; 4. That we must repent of our sins; and that if we do, God will pardon them; 5. That there are rewards for good men, and punishments for bad men, in a future state.—John Leland, *A View of the Principal Deistical Writers that have appeared in England in the Last and Present Century,* with observations upon them and some account of the answers that have been published against them. In *Several Letters to a Friend,* 1754, p. 3.

[13] Ll. 68-74; Vol. X, p. 40.

[14] P. 13.

evidence to be culled from specific passages points much more clearly to Montaigne than to Lord Herbert and his successors.

A passage often cited to show Dryden's deistic beliefs is the dialogue, in *Tyrannic Love,* between St. Catherine, the Christian martyr, and Apollonius, the pagan priest, in which, by explaining the rational advantages of Christianity, the saint converts her opponent. When the Emperor, Maximin, granting that belief is necessary, doubts man's ability to discern anything specific of the *way* to heaven, St. Catherine asseverates the two guides by which such knowledge may be obtained: 1)' the light of natural reason; and 2) faith in the unseen. And she affirms that her faith in Christianity is more acceptable to reason than his paganism, because, since it is monotheistic, it evades the antinomy of "many infinites." Apollonius rests his defence upon an ethical basis and discounts the need for supernaturalism or a system of rewards:

> And what more noble can your doctrine preach,
> Than virtue, which philosophy does teach?
> To keep the passions in severest awe,
> To live to reason, nature's greatest law;
> To follow virtue, as its own reward;
> And good and ill, as things without regard.[15]

The saint then explains the superiority of the Christian over other religions to be that it recognizes the frailty of human nature by offering the reward of Heaven to those who practise good and the pain of Hell to those who do not, and provides adequate motivation for the virtues exalted by the pagan:

> Yet few could follow those strict rules they gave; ·
> For human life will human frailties have;
> And love of virtue is but barren praise,
> Airy as fame; nor strong enough to raise
> The actions of the soul above the sense.
> Virtue grows cold without a recompence.
> We virtuous acts as duty do regard;
> Yet are permitted to expect reward.[16]

[15] II, iii; Vol. III, p. 404.

[16] *Ibid.*; *cf.* Tillotson, *Works,* 1820, Vol. IV, p. 247: he says that assurance of "a glorious and eternal reward" is the peculiar discovery of Christianity.

She admits that there is nothing unique about the virtues themselves, but insists only that the means of their enforcement is
unique. She concludes by showing that Christianity makes virtue
more "inner," stressing the intention as well as the act. Apollonius
is at once convinced purely on the basis of reason and perception
of the practical advantage of the new faith. As Mr. Bredvold notes,
he has heard nothing of divine revelation or of the teachings of
Christ. These passages, without question, lack the prevailing tone
of anti-rationalism characteristic of Dryden's religious philosophy;
but there is nothing in them, either, to identify them beyond doubt
with Deism. The two-fold force of Reason and Faith is a part of
the Anglican tradition as expounded by Hooker; and the emphasis
upon the utilitarian purpose of reward and punishment, while it
does appear likewise in Herbert's tenets of Deism, also figures
importantly in liberal-minded theologians generally, like Hooker
and Tillotson, who, in keeping with the trend of Renaissance
thought, endeavoured to link Christianity more closely and more
reasonably to human nature than it had been in the Middle Ages.
The absence of allusion to Christ or the revelation may not be
significant of Deism, in view of the curtailment of such allusions
on the stage of the period. The dialogue, as a whole, shows much
of the spirit of Hobbes, who makes religion subservient to the
needs of the *self,* and of Montaigne, who, keenly aware of human
frailty, asserts that men do not willingly lend to devotion any
services that do not gratify their own passions.[17] An echo of
Hobbes's "tales publicly allowed," moreover, appears in the recognition of the pagan that "pleasing fable" comprises a large element
in any religion. Montaigne also remarks: "It is likely that miracles,
visions, enchantments, and the like extraordinary phenomena derive their credit chiefly from the power of imagination, acting
principally on the more impressionable minds of the common people."[18] There are other passages, in addition to the dialogue of the
saint and the pagan, which hint at Deism without being sufficiently
developed to prove any definite connexion with it. Almanzor, in

[17] *Essays,* I, p. 434.
[18] *Op. cit.,* Vol. I, p. 93.

The Conquest of Granada, suggests Deistic rationalism when he says:

> By Reason, man a godhead may discern,
> But how he would be worshipped cannot learn.[19]

And in *Tyrannic Love,* Dryden employs reason to deduce the existence of God by an argument also used by Descartes: St. Catherine declares that the order in the Universe bespeaks the immediate oversight of a superior being:

> But such an order in each chance we see,
> (Chained to its cause, as that to its decree,)
> That none can think a workmanship so rare
> Was built, or kept, without a workman's care.[20]

Quoted by Mr. Bredvold and pointed to as a sympathetic treatment of Deism is the long debate, in *The Indian Emperor,* between the Christian priest and the pagan Montezuma. When the Christian implores the ruler to change his faith, he avers that he sees no reason for changing without more certain guarantee than he has yet had of Christianity's being the true Light. The true religion, he says, must claim the belief of all men;[21] and, until such a one appears, the wise procedure is to hold only to such essentials of faith as trust in God and pursuit of virtue. The Christian priest concurs in the belief that nature "teaches whom we should adore," but declares that it must be supplemented by divine revelation. Montezuma, however, repeats that nature, of which all men are a part, rather than the "heavenly beams" which shine only upon a chosen few, must be the guide. The priest turns to concrete example, pointing out that Christians gladly become martyrs for their cause; but the Emperor has the advantage of being at the very moment in a position to prove his steadfastness:

[19] Part II, IV, iii; Vol. IV, p. 190.

[20] III, i; Vol. III, p. 410.

[21] *Cf.* the French *libertin,* Gabriel de Foigny. In his *La Terre Australe,* the Utopian man asks: "Mais comment croire . . . que le Haab [God] a plutôt parlé aux uns qu'aux autres? Et d'où peut provenir cette acception de personnes, qu'il préfère plutôt les uns que les autres pour les favoriser de ses lumières?" He points out the injustice and unreason of special and limited revelation. Lachèvre, *op. cit.,* Vol. X, p. 113.

You do no more than I for ours do now.
To prove religion true—
If either wit or sufferings would suffice,
All faiths afford the constant and the wise.[22]

As a final appeal, the churchman exhorts him to refer himself to the unerring head of the Catholic polity; but Montezuma exclaims:

Man, and not err! what reason can you give? . . .
The light of nature should I thus betray,
'Twere to wink hard, that I might see the day.[23]

Just as Adam remains unconvinced of free will and has the last word after the departure of the angels, so the Indian Emperor stoutly adheres to his principles. He closely approaches Deism, but at the same time he voices characteristically sceptical ideas. He is by no means dogmatic about his own theology, for he is not convinced that any religion has yet proved wholly satisfactory:

. . . all religions with each other fight,
While only one can lead us in the right.
But till that one hath some more certain mark,
Poor human-kind must wander in the dark;
And suffer pain eternally below,
For that, which here we cannot come to know.[24]

Nor does he trust implicitly in the rational powers of man to pronounce, without error, upon such questions. He is admittedly following a middle way between the few principles of which reason seems to assure him and the possibility that at some future time, he may have "more certain mark" of religious truth; he is exactly in the Pyrrhonists' position of adhering to what is established so long as complete certitude is lacking.

The so-called deistical passages in the play are few in number; and when they do occur, they may be traced just as convincingly to other sources of influence. St. Catherine, for example, in saying that "Faith's necessary rules are plain and few," echoes not only the Deist but Hobbes as well, for the latter narrows the requisites

22 V, ii; Vol. II, p. 398.
23 *Ibid.*
24 *Ibid.*, p. 397.

of religion to "faith in Christ" and "obedience to laws."[25] There is, it may be concluded, no sound evidence in the plays that Dryden, before 1682, was a Deist.

Both early and late plays, on the other hand, suggest the influence of Pyrrhonism upon Dryden. Montaigne's *Apology for Raimond Sébond,* written ostensibly to defend Sébond's book on natural theology, but in reality to assail Christian dogmatism, attacks man's vain pretension to knowledge, especially to religious certainty, which, like every other intellectual conviction, must rest upon faith:

> . . . if this little portion of reason we possess has been allotted to us by heaven, how can reason make us the equal of heaven? How can it [heaven] subject its essence and conditions to our knowledge?[26]

And again:

> . . . what can be more fruitless than to try to divine God by our analogies and conjectures, to measure him and the world according to our capacity and our laws?[27]

Dryden's serious drama contains frequent poetic paraphrases of these passages from Montaigne. Oedipus, in the play of the same name, asks:

> If that the glow-worm light of human reason
> Might dare to offer at immortal knowledge,
> And cope with gods, why all this storm of nature?[28]

And when Eurydice asks whether there are no friendly gods, the seer, Tiresias, reproves her for futile questioning:

> The gods are just;
> But how can finite measure infinite?
> Reason! alas, it does not know itself!
> Yet man, vain man, would with this short-lined plummet,
> Fathom the vast abyss of heavenly justice.[29]

[25] Hobbes, *Leviathan,* Vol. III of *English Works,* p. 585.
[26] Montaigne, *op. cit.,* Vol. I, pp. 442-3.
[27] *Ibid.,* pp. 509-10.
[28] II, i; Vol. VI, p. 160; cf. *Religio Laici,* "And reason saw not, till faith sprung the light." Vol. X, p. 40, l. 69.
[29] III, i; Vol. VI, p. 183.

In almost identical language, St. Catherine censures her persecutors for writing "glosses" on heaven's will:

> Thus with short plummets heaven's deep will we
>   sound,
> That vast abyss where human wit is drowned!
> In our small skiff we must not launch too far;
> We here but coasters, not discoverers, are.[30]

Almanzor, too, affirms that the will of heaven must ever be a dark riddle; and the Queen, in *Secret Love,* protests that it is bold to search for, or to find, too much concerning heaven's intent. The preface to *Religio Laici* leaves no doubt that these passages quoted from the plays sincerely indicate Dryden's acceptance of Montaigne's attitude towards religion:

> Being naturally inclined to scepticism in philosophy, I have no reason to impose my opinions in a subject which is above it. . . . And indeed it is very improbable that we, who, by the strength of our faculties, cannot enter into the knowledge of any being, not so much as of our own, should be able to find out, by them, that supreme nature. . . . They, who would prove religion by reason, do but weaken the cause which they endeavour to support: it is to take away the pillars from our faith, and to prop it only with a twig.[31]

With reason undermined, only the alternatives of complete atheism or reliance upon faith remain; and Dryden makes the choice which Montaigne and Pascal made in earlier years.

Agreed that faith is the cornerstone of religion, the sceptics were willing to make pragmatic compromise with ideas which, though not demonstrably true, could contribute to the ease or happiness of life. Dorax, in *Don Sebastian,* who has not much belief in life after death, justifies faith in immortality on a Pyrrhonist or pragmatic basis. When his friend, having drawn the fatal lot, is about to die, Dorax realizes that the faith of that friend, however dubiously founded, will sustain him:

> Religion bears him out; a thing taught young,
> In age ill-practised, yet his prop in death.

[30] IV, i; Vol. III, p. 439.
[31] Vol. X, pp. 11, 13, 14.

> . . . Now if there be hereafter,
> He's blest; if not, well cheated, and dies pleased.[32]

Pascal, showing the utilitarian advantages of faith, uses the same kind of reasoning:

> . . . not to wager that God is, is to wager that he is not. Which side then do you take? . . . Your reason is not more annoyed in choosing one than the other, since you cannot but choose. . . . But your happiness? Let us balance the gain and the loss; upon taking the risk that God is, if you win, you win everything; if you lose, you lose nothing. Believe then if you can.[33]

And, as there is no reason to disbelieve since it is more comfortable to believe, so it is fruitless and pointless to affirm the superiority of one kind of faith over another:

> All faiths are to their own believers just;
> For none believe, because they will, but must.[34]

Pragmatic acceptance of religious faith, however, is not so much stressed in the plays as agnosticism; and doubt is particularly manifest when the characters reflect upon immortality. It would be inaccurate to say that the characters are always sceptical of a future state, for not infrequently they make brief but unequivocal affirmations of certainty about it, as when the proselytized Apollonius exclaims: "A life eternal I by death obtain";[35] or when Eurydice assures Adrastus that death shall not divide them. More often, although they declare a belief in immortality, it is not strong enough to eradicate fear of death;[36] and occasionally they admit an honest doubt about the after-life. Dryden's women are especially unheroic in the face of death; and in the preface to *Aureng-Zebe*, he explains that he has made them so in order to make them seem *real*.

Cydaria, Julia, Felicia, Nourmahal, Indamora, Berenice—all, in fact (except St. Catherine) who speculate upon it, are given to

[32] I, i; Vol. VII, pp. 333-4.
[33] *Thoughts*, Boston, 1849, p. 200.
[34] *Tyrannic Love*, IV, i; Vol. III, p. 441.
[35] *Ibid.*, II, iii; p. 406.
[36] *Cf.* Montaigne, Vol. I, Chap. xx.

Hamlet-like musings upon its terrors, and all agree with Cydaria
—and Hobbes—that death is "that which naturally we shun."[37]
They are not convinced, however, that there definitely is *not* a
future life: they are merely in a state of scepticism or agnosticism
as to its probability. Indamora traces her fear to uncertainty about
the nature of death:

> Distrust, and darkness of a future state,
> Make poor mankind so fearful of their fate.
> Death, in itself, is nothing; but we fear,
> To be we know not what, we know not where.[38]

Her death imminent, she confesses:

> . . . feeble nature now, I find
> Shrinks back in danger, and forsakes my mind.
> I wish to die, yet dare not death endure; . . .
> Oh, had I courage but to meet my fate,
> That short dark passage to a future state,
> That melancholy riddle of a breath![39]

St. Catherine, though she woos immortality herself, recognizes that
weak man does not commonly share her optimism:

> Here we stand shivering on the bank, and cry,
> When we should plunge into eternity.
> One moment ends our pain;
> And yet the shock of death we dare not stand. . . .
> 'Tis but because the living death ne'er knew,
> They fear to prove it as a thing that's new.[40]

Using the same figure of the river, Berenice admits that her fear
has almost routed her faith:

> As some faint pilgrim, standing on the shore,
> First views the torrent he would venture o'er;
> And then his inn upon the farther ground,
> Loth to wade through, and lother to go round; . . .
> So I at once

[37] *The Indian Emperor*, IV, iv; Vol. II, p. 386.
[38] *Aureng-Zebe*, IV, i; Vol. V, p. 257.
[39] *Ibid.*, V, i; pp. 285, 288.
[40] *Tyrannic Love*, V, i; Vol. III, pp. 451, 452.

> Both heavenly faith and human fear obey,
> And feel before me in an unknown way.[41]

These passages on death do not necessarily imply a disbelief in immortality, but only a sufficient lack of certainty to render the prospect of dying unendurable. Other characters, however, openly challenge the probability of the life eternal. When Almeyda, heroine of *Don Sebastian,* is appalled by her reverses of fortune, she asks:

> But is there Heaven? For I begin to doubt.[42]

And little Cleonidas, dying of starvation in an Egyptian prison, interrogates his father:

> But are you sure
> Our souls shall be immortal?

When Cleomenes wishes to know the reason for his question, he replies:

> Because I find, that, now my body starves,
> My soul decays. I think not as I did;
> My head goes round; and now you swim before me.
> Methinks my soul is like a flame unfed
> With oil, that dances up and down the lamp,
> But must expire ere long.[43]

Although the father elsewhere evinces piety, he passes by without a word this excellent opportunity for combining parental reassurance with religious instruction. A notable contemporary of Dryden, Jeremy Collier, had no doubt that the poet disbelieved in immortality. In *A Short View of the Profaneness and Immorality of the English Stage,* he quotes Dryden and comments upon him:

> *Our minds* (says he) *are perpetually wrought on by the Temperament of our Bodies, which makes me suspect they are nearer allied than either our Philosophers, or School-Divines will allow them to be.* The meaning is, he suspects our Souls are nothing but organiz'd Matter; Or, in plain *English,* our *Souls* are nothing but our Bodies; and then

[41] *Tyrannic Love,* IV, i; Vol. III, p. 437. Cf. also *The Spanish Friar,* III, iii; Vol. VI, p. 463 ff.

[42] III, i; Vol. VII, p. 383.

[43] V, ii; Vol. VIII, pp. 341-2.

when the Body dies, you may guess what becomes of them! Thus the Authorities of Religion are weaken'd, and the Prospect of the other World almost shut up.[44]

There are, moreover, a few passages in the plays which unequivocally interpret death to be merely a cessation of being. Hippolito tells Dorinda that it is

> . . . to dream, a kind of breathless sleep,
> When once the soul's gone out.[45]

And Cortez calms the perturbation of Cydaria by pointing out the chief virtue of dying:

> For in the grave no passions fill the breast,
> 'Tis all we gain by death, to be at rest.[46]

The allusions to death and immortality, on the whole, suggest that Dryden maintained the suspension of judgement which was a principle of the followers of Sextus Empiricus; in the plays he does not irretrievably commit himself on these problems, and no attitude beyond one of uncertainty can definitely be assigned to him. In portraying characters whom death terrifies and who cannot fortify themselves against it, he seems, however, rather to ally himself with Hobbes than with Montaigne, for in Chapter XX of the *Essays* Montaigne assumes a position similar to that of the Stoics or of the Epicurean Lucretius, arguing that fear of death, which frightens only because of its trappings, may be allayed by recognition that to be rid of life is no evil. Dryden's personages are often of the opinion that life is an evil to be escaped; but self-preservation is an instinct so deeply rooted in them that they cannot undertake the discipline recommended by Montaigne.

When heaven is accepted by characters as a certainty, it is always pictured in wholly physical terms, many of which descriptions are conventional literary expressions that do not indicate seriously-held ideas: heaven is adorned with crystal walk and battlemented towers; souls retain powers of sensory enjoyment; and activities differ but little from those on earth. But occasionally appears a

[44] *A Short View of the Profaneness and Immorality of the English Stage*, London, 1738, pp. 44-5.
[45] *The Tempest*, V, ii; Vol. III, p. 211.
[46] *The Indian Emperor*, II, iv; Vol. II, p. 354.

detail so grossly material that it points either to a lamentable lapse of artistic taste or to a materialistic bias that precludes any real understanding of the spiritual implications of immortality:

> If I die first [Berenice promises], I will
> Stop short of heaven, and wait you in a cloud;
> For fear we lose each other in the crowd.[47]

When she consoles her lover with the hope that they may enjoy each other in life to come, he protests that those who prove niggardly here, may prove no more generous in heaven: therefore they had better, he thinks, take advantage of present opportunity. The chief function of immortality in the serious plays is to offer the enjoyment of love impossible of fulfilment in this life. The conception of immortality, moreover, is sometimes employed comically, with a marked lack of reverence and good taste.[48]

The unwillingness of the sceptics to take a dogmatic stand on ultimate religious truth is a part of their general policy of pursuing the middle way in a life, moderate, conservative, and free from intellectual error. It is not surprising, therefore, to find them looking askance at zeal of any kind. Both Montaigne and Hobbes attribute faction and dispute to over-zealous defence of a belief. This attitude, too, is characteristic of Dryden. Montezuma urbanely repulses the proselytizing zeal of the Christian missionary and advocates a calm reservation of final judgement. In *Albion and Albanius,* Zealota, or feigned zeal, shares the position of villain with Democracy: both together conspire to murder the noble Albion, who represents King Charles. Misdirected Zeal is portrayed as the bitter foe of good government, and she herself admits her connexion with hell. Of herself and Democracy she says:

> Our mother bore us at a birth,
> Her name was Zeal before she fell;
> No fairer nymph in heaven or earth,
> Till saintship taught her to rebel:
> But losing fame,
> And changing name,
> She's now the Good Old Cause in hell.[49]

---

[47] *Tyrannic Love,* V, i; Vol. III, p. 460.
[48] *Cf. The Tempest,* IV, ii; Vol. III, p. 185; also *An Evening's Love,* Vol. III.
[49] II, i; Vol. VII, p. 258.

Dryden means to point out that a pious zeal may very easily be converted into a vicious misapplication of enthusiasm through ambition and through undue acquisition of power and prestige on the part of its possessor. Mustapha, the far from admirable priests' aide in *The Indian Emperor,* is of the opinion that

> . . . mankind is grown wiser at this time of day than to cut one another's throats about religion.[50]

Although Montaigne and Hobbes are at one with Dryden in distrust of Zeal, it is not necessary to suppose that he was especially influenced by them, for the same attitude was held by liberal English theologians, like Hooker and Archbishop Tillotson. The latter, for example, writes:

> . . . even when it [zeal] is a virtue, it is a nice and dangerous one: for the wisest men are apt to mingle their own passions and interests with their zeal for God and religion.[51]

The plays of Dryden suggest, at least, most of the fundamental problems of religion, presenting either a definite uncertainty or alternating certainty and scepticism in juxtaposition. The allusions to the goodness of heaven are numerous; yet in not a few reflective lines do the characters question the justice of God. It has already been noted that both Adam and Eve hold God responsible for their misfortune; and, like that of Job, the faith of Cleonidas wavers as he sees good men suffer. Cleomenes hesitates to say "hard things of heaven" when he is starving, but Cleonidas asks:

> But what if heaven
> Will do hard things, must not hard things be said?[52]

Montaigne recognizes the problem of evil suffered by good men, but asserts that, God's ways being impenetrable, it must be assumed that there is just reason for it. Hobbes also recognizes the problem, but solves it rather speciously, from the ethical point of view, by saying that God's omnipotence destroys all question of right and wrong in relation to his acts. Dryden's questioning of

50 IV, iii; Vol. VII, p. 430.
51 *Works,* 1820, Vol. IV, p. 513.
52 V, ii; Vol. VIII, p. 341.

divine providence, however, is not demonstrably related in its details to either Hobbes or Montaigne.

From the disparate allusions in the plays to faith, immortality, and death it is possible to conclude that the religious position of Dryden was, like that of the Pyrrhonists, one of suspended judgement, bordering perhaps more closely upon disbelief than upon solid conviction. The influence of the French sceptics and of Hobbes may well have come together at a focal point upon the problem of religious doubt; for, though agnosticism is the prevailing state of mind, the materialism of Hobbes lifts its head whenever the poet attempts to present a spiritual concept, like that of heaven, and when, occasionally, he implies that soul may be a mere function of matter. There is something of the same paradox in Dryden's mingling of assured statements regarding heaven's justice and the promise of immortality with lengthily expressed doubts about both, that there is in Hobbes's erection of a conventional religious system upon a foundation which logically admits of no such structure. And this paradox is not very different from the Pyrrhonist's compromise between profound philosophic doubt and a pragmatic acceptance of faith.

Whatever doubt may remain concerning the state of the poet's religious beliefs generally during the time he was writing plays, there can be none regarding his opinions of the clergy, and particularly of the Catholic priesthood. Satire on the foibles of churchmen is older than the *fabliaux,* and it is not lacking in other Restoration drama; but in frequency and virulence of censure, there is nothing in contemporary English plays which is analogous. The source of Dryden's distrust and contempt is again probably not single. Josef Wild traces his feeling to the formative influences of childhood:

> Um diesen eingewurzelten Hass recht zu erklären, dürfen wir annehmen, dass er auf jugenderlebnisse zurückgeht. Wir hörten oben, wie sich seine Verwändten unter Cromwell als Verfolger der Geistlichkeit hervortaten, und Christie nimmt an, dass Drydens Vater als Friedensrichter in Northamptonshire auch Enteignungskommissär (Committee-Man) gewesen sei, der Geistliche aus ihren Ämtern vertrieb und Güter von Geächteten einzog. Er dürfte Sich deshalb den Hass

vieler zugezogen haben und auch unser Dichter musste
darunter leiden, denn öfters wurde ihm vorgeworfen.[53]

These experiences, added to his later observation of priestly cabals
and Romish plots, time and again menacing the stability of government, unquestionably formed the groundwork of his opinions; but
in entertaining them, he was following once more the two chief
trends of thought to which he was intellectually akin, Hobbism and
scepticism. Hobbes not only subordinates the churchman to the
statesman, but attacks as well the specific evils of the clergy:

> . . . who does not see, to whose profit redound the fees of
> private masses, and vales of purgatory; with other signs of
> private interest, enough to mortify the most lively faith, if,
> as I said, the civil magistrate, and custom did not more sus-
> tain it, than any opinion they have of the sanctity, wisdom,
> or probity of their teachers? So that I may attribute all the
> changes of religion in the world, to one and the same cause;
> and that is, unpleasing priests; and those not only amongst
> Catholics, but even in that church that hath presumed most
> of reformation.[54]

The group of "libertine" poets and dramatists in France, who
developed what loosely may be called the Epicureanism of Montaigne's philosophy, were similarly antipathetic towards churchmen. They were violently attacked by the clergy for their views (by
the Jesuits particularly); and they, in turn, retaliated with satire
on, and forthright criticism of, their persecutors. Théophile de
Viau and other less prominent poets of his *coterie* were imprisoned
for heretical allusion to the church and its acolytes; and in their
poems and letters, the personal characters of the priests were black-
ened and their intellectual bigotry exposed. As an instance, in
Cyrano de Bergerac's *Les États de la Lune,* the priests, along with
almost every other aspect of contemporary civilization, are sati-
rized for the narrowness of their scruples of conscience.[55] Théophile
writes of his enemies:

> Si le Ciel m'avoit fait un de ces gros prélats
> De tous les fils du Ciel on me croiroit l'Atlas,

---

[53] *Dryden und die römische Kirche,* p. 19.
[54] Hobbes, *Leviathan,* Vol. III of *English Works,* p. 109.
[55] Lachèvre, Vol. VIII, Part I, p. 60.

> Si j'estois Cardinal et fusse une beste
> Mon chapeau couvriroit les défauts de ma teste. . . .[56]

In one of his *Lèttres Satiriques,* Cyrano expresses the common notion of "clergy-covetousness":

> . . . le plus grand signe de réprobation auquel un malheureux puisse être sûjet en cette vie, c'est de ne pas donner de bonnes dîmes à son Curé. Regardez Caïn : qu'est-ce qui le fit damner? Ce ne fut pas pour avoir tué son frère, ce fut bien pour autre chose. Ce fut, mes chers Parroissiens, pour avoir éscorniffé les gerbes des Dîmes qu'il devoit à Dieu. . . .[57]

Some of the bolder libertines, like Claude de Chauvigny, attributed to the priesthood every sort of indecency and grossness and depravity. The libertine group, through its connexion with Montaigne and Gassendi and through the notoriety attached to its debauchery and to its feud with the Jesuits, was widely known; and it may be assumed, though he makes no mention of it,[58] that Dryden, in the light of his extensive acquaintance with French literature, at least knew for what it stood.

The plays of Dryden are filled with assaults upon the personal character of the priesthood, as well as upon its undue prominence in secular affairs. He portrays a whole series of clergymen who, totally unaware of the spiritual function of their office, continually prostitute the people and the church to a desire for power and gain. Self-seeking churchmen play an important part in the serious plays as well as in the comedies; and heroic personages evince a frank contempt for them.[59]

Another source of annoyance to Dryden, in which he is more akin to Hobbes than to the sceptics, was the prominence of the church in political activities. Montezuma, upon being told that the Pope has given his kingdom to Spain, disclaims the secular prerogatives of the church:

---

[56] Lachèvre, Vol. III, p. 112.

[57] *Ibid.,* Vol. VIII, Part II, p. 299.

[58] Dryden uses the word *libertine* in the preface to *An Evening's Love*; and the word was not, then, in wide use.

[59] There are manifold disparaging allusions to the clergy in *The Spanish Friar, Troilus and Cressida, Don Sebastian,* and others.

> Ill does he represent the powers above,
> Who nourishes debate, not preaches love;
> Besides, what greater folly can be shown?
> He gives another what is not his own. . . .
> Empires in heaven he with more ease can give,
> And you, perhaps, would with less thanks receive:
> But heaven has need of no such viceroy here,
> Itself bestows the crowns that monarchs wear.[60]

Montezuma not only voices Hobbes's general views on the secular-minded clergy, but he also echoes a specific passage from the *Leviathan,* having to do with the exact situation which calls forth the Indian Emperor's words:

> This right of the heathen kings cannot be thought taken from them by their conversion to the faith of Christ; who never ordained that kings, for believing in him, should be deposed, that is, subjected to any but himself, or, which is all one, be deprived of the power necessary for the conservation of peace amongst their subjects, and for their defence against foreign enemies.[61]

The most complete and scathing indictment of the worldly interests of churchmen occurs in *Don Sebastian,* in one of the longest single speeches to appear in any of the plays. Dorax asks:

> Why, then, these foreign thoughts of state-employ-
>   ments,
> Abhorrent to your function and your breedings?
> Poor droning truants of unpractised cells,
> Bred in the fellowship of bearded boys,
> What wonder is it if you know not men?
> Yet there you live demure, with downcast eyes,
> And humble as your discipline requires;
> But, when let loose from thence to live at large,
> Your little tincture of devotion dies:
> Then luxury succeeds, and, set agog
> With a new scene of yet untasted joys,
> You fall with greedy hunger to the feast.
> Of all your college virtues, nothing now

---

[60] *The Indian Emperor,* I, ii; Vol. II, pp. 337-8.
[61] *English Works,* Vol. III, p. 538.

> But your original ignorance remains;
> Bloated with pride, ambition, avarice,
> You swell to counsel kings, and govern king-
>   doms. . . .
> Content you with monopolising heaven,
> And let this little hanging ball alone:
> For, but give you a foot of conscience there,
> And you, like Archimedes, toss the globe.
> We know your thoughts of us that laymen are,
> Lag souls, and rubbish of remaining clay,
> Which heaven, grown weary of more perfect work,
> Set upright with a little puff of breath,
> And bid us pass for men.[62]

By reason of their ascetic training, churchmen have not the state-
men's subtlety in dissembling, and make "silly, woful, awkward
politicians," whose "interest is not finely drawn, and hid . . ."
Care of souls should be quite enough to occupy their whole time.
Dorax repeats a Hobbist precept to the Emperor, who, he feels, has
trusted his priest too far:

> Sir, let me bluntly say, you went too far,
> To trust the preaching power on state affairs
> To him, or any heavenly demagogue:
> 'Tis a limb lopt from your prerogative,
> And so much of heaven's image blotted from you.[63]

More than once it is implied that the clergy deliberately falsify and
make use of feigned miracles and prophecies. Troilus, learning of
Cassandra's vision of Hector's death, exclaims:

> By heaven, 'twas never well, since saucy priests
> Grew to be masters of the listening herd,
> And into mitres cleft the regal crown;
> Then, as the earth were scanty for their power,
> They drew the pomp of heaven to wait on them.
> Shall I go publish, Hector dares not fight,
> Because a madman dreamt he talked with Jove?[64]

[62] II, i; Vol. VII, pp. 352-3.
[63] III, i; Vol. VII, pp. 386-7.
[64] *Troilus and Cressida*, V, i; Vol. VI, p. 375.

To be sure, Dryden's animus against the clergy might well have been wholly personal in origin; on the other hand, it is certainly in the tradition of, and probably was influenced by, Hobbism, if not also by the French *libertinage* movement.

Hatred and suspicion of priestcraft is but one of the attitudes common to Dryden and the continental free-thinkers. It is impossible to establish any direct relationship between the poet-laureate and the school of Théophile de Viau; and the libertinism and popular Epicureanism that pervade his comedies may be only a reflection of the court life of his day. Alexandre Beljame gives a trenchant summary of the spirit prevalent among the classes for whom Dryden was writing comedies, with the avowed intention of pleasing:

> L'unique but de cette cour, c'est le plaisir. "Notre sphère d'action dans cette vie, dit Rochester, est le bonheur." Et il ajoute élégamment: "Quiconque regarde au delà est un âne." Le Puritanisme faisait de l'existence humaine une vallée de larmes, un chemin semé de luttes et d'épreuves par lesquelles on achète la vie éternelle. Ses successeurs se contentent de la vie présente. Mais pour jouir comme il faut . . . pour faire gaiement le chemin de la vie, il faut n'être embarrassé par rien: on supprime donc tous les *impedimenta*. D'où venons-nous? Où allons-nous? Qu'importe! Nous sommes, et c'est assez. La vertu, la pudeur, mensonges! La pitié, l'honneur, le courage, préjugés de petites gens![65]

To prove, consequently, that the libertinism—the contempt of marriage, the obscenity, the copious allusion to sexual precocity and looseness—of the comedies[66] came to Dryden from the writings and example of the French *libertins* would be to prove that the libertinism generally rampant in England came from them. And even if it were possible to prove that, such a task is not within the compass of the present study. There are certain specific aspects of Dryden's work, however, which suggest that he very well may

[65] *Le Public et les Hommes de Lèttres in Angleterre au 18 Siècle,* Paris, 1881, p. 8.

[66] *Cf.* Allardyce Nicoll's discussion of the difference between Dryden's comedies, and those of the other dramatists of the period. *A History of Restoration Drama, 1660-1700,* Cambridge, 1928, p. 214.

have been influenced by the French perversions of Montaigne's "free-thinking" philosophy, though such an hypothesis is by no means verifiable. A part of the freedom-cult of the *libertins* was complete disrespect for parental authority; and many of Dryden's plays echo that disrespect. Sons not only rival fathers in love and attempt to extort money from them, but also make slighting remarks about parents and, in reasoned passages, question their prerogatives. Ozmyn, in *The Conquest of Granada,* avers:

> Nature, that bids us parents to obey,
> Bids parents their commands by reason weigh.[67]

And Aureng-Zebe reminds his father:

> Sons may have rights which they can never quit.
> Yourself first made that title which I claim.[68]

Julia, in more clearly rebellious mood ruminates upon parental restrictions:

> If I durst question it, methinks 'tis hard!
> What right have parents over children, more
> Than birds have o'er their young? yet they impose
> No rich-plumed mistress on their feathered sons;
> But leave their love, more open yet and free
> Than all the fields of air, their spacious birthright.[69]

Indeed, Montaigne himself has no high conviction that the bond between parent and child is strong by nature:

> . . . it is easily seen by experience that this natural affection,
> to which we give so much authority, has very slender roots.[70]

Another way in which Dryden is like the French *libertins* is in his light use of religious terminology with relation to the experiences of love. It is not unusual, in both lyrical and dramatic poetry, to find effective employment of the imagery of religion to describe some aspect of love. When Romeo stands, his lips two blushing pilgrims, ready to pay obeisance at the shrine of Juliet, one thinks

[67] Part I, V, i; Vol. IV, p. 102.
[68] II, i; Vol. V, p. 234.
[69] *The Rival Ladies,* II, i; Vol. II, p. 174. *Cf.* also *Don Sebastian*; *An Evening's Love.*
[70] *Essays,* Vol. I, p. 389.

it no irreverence: by such a figure the purity and sincerity of the love are made manifest. In Dryden and Viau's school, however, love becomes a substitute for religion and makes the latter trivial. Viau, entering a temple, is struck by the beauty of Philis:

> Tandis qu'à mon secours tous les Dieux se reclame,
> Je voy venir Philis; quand j'apperceus ses yeux,
> Je m'escriay tout haut: Ce sont icy mes Dieux,
> Ce Temple et cet Autel appartient à ma Dame.[71]

And again:

> Tout seul dedans ma chambre, où j'ay faict ton
> Église,
> Ton image est mon Dieu, mes passions, ma foy....[72]

Ptolemy, in *Cleomenes,* cries out:

> . . . to the temple,—
> Come, my fair Cassandra,
> That I may have an object worth my worship.[73]

And Cassandra is equally devout:

> The god that I adore is in my breast;
> This is the temple; this the sacrifice.
> But to the powers divine we make appeal,
> With great devotion, and with little zeal.[74]

Serious subordination of religion to love is less common, however, than flippant assertion that religious faith should be changed or feigned if necessary—to facilitate the progress of passion. The juxtaposition of love and religion in such plays as *Cleomenes* and *An Evening's Love* definitely suggests the peculiar lightness of the same juxtaposition in the writings of Viau and his followers.

The *libertins,* both in practice and theory, were much given to exalting sexual perversions; and it is a possibility, at least, that Dryden's rather extensive use of incest as a dramatic theme reflects a popular interest which that group had aroused in such subjects.

[71] Lachèvre, Vol. III, p. 88.
[72] *Ibid.,* p. 78.
[73] III, i; Vol. VIII, p. 308.
[74] *Ibid.*

Incest, actual or imminent, appears in eight of Dryden's plays[75]—
an employment of the theme to an unprecedented degree among
Restoration playwrights. It is true, however, that incest appears in
a few later Elizabethan plays,[76] and these may have guided the
poet's choice.

In one way, Dryden is quite definitely allied with the French
Epicureans against Montaigne who was his master in many ways.
It is obvious that he has little regard for the pretensions of Stoicism; whereas Montaigne took refuge from his own Pyrrhonism
in the philosophy of the Romans. Whenever Dryden refers by
name to Stoicism, he criticizes it adversely. It is contemptuously
alluded to in one place as "the self-denying cant"; and Woodall,
devil-may-care opportunist in *Limberham,* thumbing his nose at
the moral preachment of his servant, exclaims:

> Away, old Epictetus, about your business, and leave your
> musty morals.[77]

Philocles, in *Secret Love,* given the opportunity to marry the
Queen if he will renounce the woman he loves, rationalizes his
impulse to foster his ambition:

> Greatness lies ready in some shape to tempt me.
> The royal furniture in every room. . . .
> Now tell me, Stoic!
> If all these with a wish might be made thine,
> Would'st thou not truck thy ragged virtue for 'em?
> If glory was a bait, that angels swallow'd,
> How then should souls allied to sense resist it?[78]

And, finally, in the *Dedication* to *Don Sebastian,* Dryden, in his
own person, summarizes his estimate of stoical philosophy:

> For stiffness of opinion is the effect of pride, and not of
> philosophy; it is a miserable presumption of that knowledge
> which human nature is too narrow to contain; and the rug-
> gedness of a stoic is only a silly affectation of being a

---

[75] *The Rival Ladies, The Spanish Friar, Marriage à la Mode, The Tempest,
Love Triumphant, Oedipus, Don Sebastian, Aureng-Zebe.*
[76] *Cf.* also Rochester's *Valentinian* and Howard's *The Usurper.*
[77] IV, i; Vol. VI, p. 79.
[78] V, i; Vol. II, pp. 493-4.

god,—to wind himself up by pulleys to an insensibility of suffering, and, at the same time, to give the lie to his own experience, by saying he suffers not what he knows he feels.[79]

This commentary closely echoes Montaigne's suspicion of stoical indifference. The French philosopher, in his essay *Of Cruelty*, suggests that Stoicism is too negative to be wholly noble, and is of the opinion that the members of the sect, like Cato, who apparently died with unbelievable contempt of suffering, really took a sensuous delight in their own conduct.[80] And elsewhere he writes in the exact vein of Dryden:

> Moreover, I have always regarded as affectation that precept that so sternly and precisely tells us to put on a good face, a disdainful and indifferent mien, when suffering pain.[81]

But his essays as a whole more than once ring out in Stoic accents.

[79] Vol. VII, pp. 302-3. *Cf.* also "To My Honor'd Friend Sir Robert Howard, on His Excellent Poems," ". . . your art hides art, as Stoics feign then least to feel, when most they suffer pain," ll. 19-20, Vol. XI, p. 7.

[80] Vol. I, p. 412 ff.

[81] Vol. II, p. 211.

IV. CONCLUSION

IT is difficult, and perhaps impossible, to decide the exact measure in which the plays of Dryden reflect the ideas of Hobbes and of Montaigne. The inconsistency of human nature, the strength of the instinct for self-preservation, the distrust of zeal, the relative powers of reason and passion, the generally pessimistic view of humankind—all are similarly treated, but with varying emphasis, in the writing of the two men; and the religious doubts freely voiced by the characters oscillate between the materialism of the English philosopher and the suspended judgement of the Pyrrhonists. Notwithstanding, satisfactorily definite conclusions may be reached concerning the dominant trends of thought which manifest themselves in the dramatic works, and tentative decisions made regarding the intellectual history of the poet himself.

Dryden's preoccupation with the nature of causation and the problem of Free Will unquestionably owes much to the theories contributed by Hobbes to the contemporary discussions of the extent of human freedom. The reasoning of Adam, particularly, in the new version of *Paradise Lost,* the reflective speeches of heroic personages, the consistent inability of characters to act as their reason tells them to act, and the prevalence of allusions to fate can scarcely be explained on any ground other than that the poet was a determinist. And, moreover, in 1664 when he wrote the preface to *The Rival Ladies,* Dryden was nearer to Hobbes than to Pyrrhonism, for he therein definitely accepts the *dogma* of determinism. Chronology may or may not be significant in this connexion: there are fewer references to the subject in the last half-dozen plays than in the earlier ones, although they still occasionally appear, and although Fate is still a recurring motif. The last of the long, reasoned discussions of free-will occurs in *The Spanish Friar* (1681); and in such late plays as *Don Sebastian* (1690) and *Cleomenes* (1692) the characters are less at the mercy of the irrational part of their own natures. In *Love Triumphant*, however, which is the last dramatic piece, elements of Hobbism are to be seen in the treatment of character.

In addition to Hobbist determinism, Dryden clearly reflects, in his portrayals, the materialistic motives of interest and of selfishness, and occasionally suggests a philosophic monism in making the mind wholly dependent upon the body. The implication of monism in Cleonidas's doubt of the independence of soul,[1] and the outright admission of such doubt in the *Dedication* to *Aureng-Zebe* may also owe something to Montaigne, for in the same dedication, the poet refers to Montaigne's assertion that "when the body is out of order, its companion is seldom at his ease."[2]

The completely insensitive attitudes of heroes and heroines towards fine moral distinctions are unquestionably the product of the same ethical conceptions which dictated the nominalistic definitions of the virtues given by Hobbes. The prefaces, it has been noted, nullify the theory that degraded motive and ethical blindness in characters arise simply from artistic insufficiency, for in them Dryden himself reveals the same moral obtuseness.[3] Although the predominance of passion over reason may have a French as well as an English parallel, and though it owes something to "heroic" convention, it is probable that it, too, has its roots in materialism. Montaigne, like Hobbes, admits the commonly superior strength of the passions; but, at the same time, he provides for the disciplining of the emotions, and by no means is of the opinion that man is wholly helpless in their toils. The majority of persons do not, perhaps, exercise this discipline; but nevertheless a certain degree of Stoicism is possible, and he recommends moderation with the assurance that he is not mouthing vain exhortations.[4] Hobbes, on the contrary, allows for no curtailment of the passional life other than that which the force of an external power can validate. The "Dryden character," cognizant of his weakness, has none of the elements of inner strength which Montaigne holds out as, ideally, to be attained, but is, rather, more fully in accord with the

[1] In *Cleomenes*.
[2] Vol. V, p. 199.
[3] *Cf.* Prefaces to *Cleomenes* and *Secret Love*, especially.
[4] *Cf. Essays*, Bk. I, Chap. xx.

complete inner determinism of the "Hobbist Man." And, finally, the frequent passages which declare the supremacy of the passions suggest that Dryden is presenting a well-defined view of human nature, and not merely aping the conventions of the French romance.

In religious and political ideas, too, Dryden and Hobbes are akin. The characters in the plays often veer away from suspended judgement, towards a materialist's view of heaven, or an atheist's view of the probability of an after-life. Politically, they are monarchists; and echoes of Hobbes come from the emphasis on force in governing, upon the dangers of relying on subsidiary councils or of dividing power in any way, upon the hazards of zeal, and on the evils of the state of nature. The conservatism of the poet is also in the tradition of the French Pyrrhonist; and in the dedication to the *Aeneis,* Dryden agrees with Montaigne that an honest man ought to be contented with that form of government which he received from his ancestors, and under which he was born. Conservative hatred of change and of zeal was common to both the French and the English philosopher, but the stress upon power and force is a definite reflection of the latter.

Evidences of Hobbism in the early non-dramatic works are sparse, but so also, before 1683, are proofs for Pyrrhonism or Deism or any of the ideas often attributed to Dryden. The central reasoning in *Absalom and Achitophel,* however, particularly the allusion to the state of nature,[5] suggests the *Leviathan*; and in both the same poem and *The Medal,*[6] the motives of self-interest are emphasized, and the conclusion reached that "power is ever wise." In the light of a minute study of the plays, Professor Bredvold's summary dismissal of the influence of Hobbes as being relatively unimportant—of no more significance, in fact, than that of Descartes—turns out to be ill advised.[7]

[5] *Cf.* above, pp. 130-131.

[6] Vol. IX, p. 447, l. 90.

[7] I have failed to find any real evidence of Cartesianism other than the single instance of Adam's reasoning about the *I* in *The State of Innocence,* and one similar instance in *Amphitryon* which Dryden took from the French source. Cartesianism may be suggested by the few so-called deistical passages.

Of Dryden's affinity with the sceptical trend of his age there is incontrovertible proof in the prefaces. Accused of trying to dictate the laws for dramatic poesy, he repudiates the charge in *Defence of An Essay,* and indicates his familiarity with the history of sceptical thought:

> . . . I must crave leave to say, that my whole discourse was sceptical, according to that way of reasoning which was used by Socrates, Plato, and all the academics of old, which Tully and the best of the ancients followed, and which is imitated by the modest inquisitions of the Royal Society.[8]

In the *Preface* to *An Evening's Love,* written during the same year, he shows an unwillingness to form categorical judgements either in art or in philosophy: "Why," he asks, "should there be any *ipse dixit* in our poetry, any more than there is in our philosophy?"[9] Four years later (1682), he disavows the intention of imposing his religious views upon the Mother Church, with this admission:

> Being naturally inclined to scepticism in philosophy, I have no reason to impose my opinions in a subject which is above it.[10]

Commenting, in the *Preface to the Second Miscellany,* upon the tone of finality in Lucretius—and in Hobbes—he states that, in translating the Roman poet, he has laid by his "natural diffidence and scepticism for a while, to take up that dogmatical way of his. . . ."[11] No less assured than his doubting mind is Dryden's thorough acquaintance with the writings of Michel de Montaigne, and his admiration for them. The prefaces to *Don Sebastian* and *All For Love* contain allusions to the wisdom and honesty of Montaigne; and it has been noted that the dramatist justifies his characterization of Dorax by reference to the essayist's reflection on Inconstancy. These sympathies with scepticism and its pre-eminent French exponent make it doubly safe to state that certain ideas in the plays bear the stamp of Montaigne and his followers in the Pyrrhonist school. The exact independent indebtedness of

[8] (1668); Vol. II, p. 307.
[9] Vol. III, p. 243.
[10] *Preface* to *Religio Laici,* Vol. X, p. 11.
[11] Vol. XII, p. 292.

Dryden to French scepticism is, on the basis of the dramatic work alone, difficult to determine. Qualities of human nature, like self-interest and strength of passion, are stressed by Montaigne, but they loom larger in the writings of Hobbes. The surest link between Dryden and the continental free-thinkers appears in the religious views of the dramatic characters. Unquestionably there is, in the plays, the strain of fideism which Mr. Bredvold posits as the unifying factor in the poet's thought. Wherever there is a prolonged discussion of religion, the inadequacies of reason and the compelling necessity of faith are expounded. Passages suggesting rationalism or Cartesianism are very rare; deprecation of reason is frequent, and the relativity of religious standards, perceived by a study of the practices of different countries, is recognized in several places. The prevailing tone in speeches pertaining to the after-life, its character or its reality, is one of doubt, although at times, it has been observed, the doubt verges dangerously upon disbelief. There is no mention of Pyrrho in the plays or their prefaces; and from what Dryden himself says of his doubts, there is no proof that his scepticism was of the Pyrrhonic cast;[12] that it was philosophically thoroughgoing. But the fideism, taken with the known connexion with Montaigne, shows definitely enough that he was in that tradition.[13]

There is, in one sense, a unity of tone throughout the plays. They show no significant concern with the more idealistic currents of thought in the seventeenth century; Platonism or Stoicism may creep in at rare intervals as literary adornment or, in the former case, as a conscious borrowing from French romance; but the prevailing spirit is worldly, sceptical, even materialistic. There is no reason to doubt that Dryden characterized himself aright when he alluded to his naturally sceptical temperament; and that temperament undoubtedly accounts for the type of ideas which he

[12] In Chap. 1 of his *Intellectual Milieu,* Mr. Bredvold speaks of the *protean* nature of scepticism in the century, and of the impossibility of narrowing it to the exact principles of Pyrrho.

[13] Dryden knew the fideistic writings of Father Simon, for *Religio Laici* was dedicated to the English translator of Simon's *Histoire critique du Vieux Testament,* a work sceptical in purport, which attempts to show the unreliability of Biblical text. *Cf.* Bredvold, p. 101.

commonly reflects, as well as for the course of his own intellectual history. It has been affirmed repeatedly by defenders of the faith, especially during the conflict in the nineteenth century between religion and science, that to remain an agnostic is, practically, to lean more definitely towards the presumptions and the ethical consequences of materialism. And so Dryden does. Although at bottom the dogma of sense and motion and the dogma of the curative powers of political order are as incompatible with Pyrrhonism as is the dogma of metaphysics, Hobbism might naturally appeal to one of sceptical inclination, who had not plumbed the depths of doubting, as a philosophy of commonsense, properly enough exhibiting cynicism about human nature, figuring as distrust of that which is not to be seen or felt or heard. To minds not hardened to a world without discernible purpose, the ethical result of being cut apart from the eternal by a physical monism and the result of denying the validity of the reason in formulating standards are the same. Either is likely to produce the Hobbist conception of man's life as nasty, brutish, and short; to foster the abandonment of all serious aim. Even in a relatively high type of character either may eventuate in the elevation of the passions; on a lower plane, either is a passport to libertinism. Which of these ultimately exerted the greater influence upon the ideas in Dryden's plays no one can say. It is evident that, for a time at least, the dramatist was profoundly touched by the philosophy of Hobbes; and, from the recurrence of such ideas after 1683, it seems probable that what was no doubt an unconscious bias towards materialism lingered after the poet had come definitely under the sway of French scepticism. It may well be that a general discontent regarding human knowledge and institutions, attributable to both sources, accounts for the unexpected frequency in the plays of the theme of romantic escape. The heroine of *Marriage à la Mode,* thwarted in love, would return to the

> . . . woods, and plains, where first my love began,
> There would I live, retired from faithless man:
> I'd sit all day within some lonely shade,
> Or that close arbour which your hands have made:

> I'd search the groves, and every tree, to find
> Where you had carved our names upon the rind. . . .
> Thus would I live. . . .[14]

Similarly, Jocasta wishes to seek out some barren island

> Where print of human feet was never seen;[15]

and Sebastian goes to live where ". . . from the purling streams and savage fruits," he may "have wholesome beverage, and unbloody feast." Almanzor, perhaps, utters the most familiar of the romantic passages when he says that he is as free as Nature first made man,

> When wild in woods the noble savage ran.[16]

Scepticism and materialism, and their offspring disillusion, may have worked hand in hand to bring Dryden, finally, to the Mother Church, in which was all sorrow and all peace.

[14] II, i; Vol. IV, p. 295.
[15] *Oedipus,* IV, i; Vol. VI, p. 210.
[16] *The Conquest of Granada,* Part I, I, i; Vol. IV, p. 43.

JEREMY COLLIER'S ESSAYS

By KATHLEEN RESSLER, PH.D.

FORMERLY ARMSTRONG-HUNTER SCHOLAR IN ENGLISH
UNIVERSITY OF CINCINNATI
ASSISTANT TO THE DEAN OF MEN
UNIVERSITY OF CINCINNATI

JEREMY COLLIER'S ESSAYS

I. INFALLIBILITIES AND METAPHYSICS

WHEN Henry More wrote of his "inordinate Desire after the Knowledge of things" he was but voicing the insatiable curiosity of the seventeenth-century intellectual. He and Whichcote and others of the Cambridge group were setting students "much on reading the ancient philosophers, chiefly Plato, Tully, and Plotin"; Glanvill exulted because through the ingenuity of his age the "more excellent *Hypotheses* of *Democritus* and *Epicurus*" had been disinterred; in another direction, Hobbes and Locke were dissipating long-cherished "chimeras." Writers of this century rested secure in their belief that intellectually "the world was all before them, where to choose."[1] But whatever their ultimate destination, first they inescapably had to grope their way "with wandring steps and slow" through the wood of metaphysics and theology. Not the easiest problem left to solve was that of harmonizing the traditional doctrines of theology with the newer philosophy of reason and all that it entailed. With increasing readiness they began to utilize the now-revived "light of nature," an oracle the interpretation of which rose so peculiarly from a subjective source that its decrees quite naturally depended for effectiveness upon individual intensity and clarity of vision. It is not surprizing that more than one thinker traversed his circle of puzzled thought back to his starting-point, having collected on the way certain relics of genuine scholasticism.

Among the alert, receptive minds of the age, Jeremy Collier, recognizing that one's beliefs must come from within, not without, that somehow the thinking man can travel as he will, spares his reader painful wanderings through a labyrinth of doubts, vacillating notions, seekings after authority. He erects his beliefs upon a

[1] *Paradise Lost*, XII, 646.

rationalistic basis; if he founders and intuition fails, then he finds the path surely marked·by divine law. He sets down his idea in the scholastic vein of a St. Thomas and yet with the intellectual justification of the Platonists. It is equally reasonable, he observes, to suppose the visible world coëxistent with God from the beginning, or produced by him from nothing. The latter is preferable: it reflects more to the credit of a God who thereby becomes the creator of all things. This Deity in whom the universe finds its beginning and end is a self-sufficient and independent God, omnipotent and omniscient: " 'Twas his Power which made his *Ideas* fruitful, and struck the World out of his Thought. 'Twas this which answer'd the Model of the Creation, gave Birth to Time and Nature, and brought them forth at his first Call. . . ."[2] Collier goes on to postulate an endlessly good Deity from the order and beauty of the universe, and from the mirroring in the human soul of such divine attributes as reason and free will. We find this intellection among the Platonists: John Smith arrives at his conclusions concerning the Nature and Existence of God by way of observing the clear imprint of divinity on the soul and in the providential workings in the physical world.[3] For both writers the attaining and sharing of the Goodness of God constitutes the *summum bonum*.

In this Goodness the reasons for creation have their being; from the "inexhaustible Fullness in the Divine Nature the Benignity of it" may be inferred. "God could never have any need of any thing without him":

[2] *Of Power,* pp. 64, 65. Collier's essays and dialogues were published as *Essays upon several Moral Subjects,* Parts I and II, in 1697; other editions, 2nd, 3rd, 1697; 4th, 1700; 5th, 1703; 6th, 1708, 1722. Vol. II, or Part III, 1705, 1720; Vol. III, or Part IV, 1709. *Essay on Gaming,* 1713. Collected edition, 1722. Editions used in this study: Vol. I, 6th, 1722, corrected and enlarged; Vol. II, 3rd, 1722, with large additions; Vol. III, 2nd, 1725.

[3] *Select Discourses,* London, 1821, pp. 133-78. Smith remarks that "the whole fabric of this visible universe [is] whispering out the notions of a Deity," and quotes, as does Collier: "The heavens declare the glory of God; and the firmament sheweth his handywork." (*Psalms* xix:1.) Smith is concerned more with that "copy within ourselves" than with externals; he adds, "The schoolmen have well compared sensible and intelligible beings in reference to the Deity, when they tell us that the one do only represent *vestigia Dei,* the other *faciem Dei.*" (p. 136.)

He was always happy in himself; Infinite admits of no Addition; he wanted no World to entertain him, no Subjects to support his Greatness . . . : Besides, the Plan of Nature was always before him; the whole Creation lay in his mind; he saw the Properties and Scales of Things from all Eternity; for nothing could have any Form or Force but what he intended to give it; for 'twas his Wisdom which *design'd,* his Will which order'd, and his Power which produc'd the World.[4]

The act of creation grew, then, out of a supreme goodness overflowing in order that others might partake thereof:

Now since God has no empty Spaces, no unsatisfied Desires, nothing to project for himself; what could dispose him to create the *Universe*? Must it not be for foreign Advantage? And is not this the Property of goodness? Why were conscious Beings struck out of the *Idea,* and Thought and Perception thrown into Spirits? Did not God do this to make a new Seat of Pleasure, and give the Creatures a share in his own Happiness?[5]

This is essentially the conception presented in the *Timaeus*[6] of Plato, who had borrowed it from ancient Pythagorean doctrine. Here again appears resemblance between the ideas of Collier and the Cambridge Platonists. In pointing certain "inferences which naturally flow from the true Knowledge of the divine nature and attributes" John Smith says:

And the *first* is this, That all *divine productions or operations that terminate in something without him, are nothing else but the free effluxes of his own omnipotent love and goodness,* which always moves along with them, and never willingly departs from them. When God made the world, it was not out of a piece of self-interest, as if he had had any design to advance himself, or to enlarge his own stock of glory and happiness; for what beauty or perfection can be in this whole

[4] *Of Goodness,* pp. 7, 8.
[5] *Ibid.,* p. 8.
[6] The creator framed this universe because "He was good, and the good can never have any jealousy of anything. And being free from jealousy, he desired that all things should be as like himself as they could be." *Timaeus,* Jowett's translation, Oxford, 1924, Vol. III, p. 450.

creation which was not before contained in himself as the
free fountain of all? or what could he see out of himself that
could add any thing to his own stature, which he found not
already in himself? . . . "It was not for any need, or that he
might gain some honour to himself from men, archangels or
angels, as the tribute or rent to be paid to him from his
creation," as Clemens Alexandrinus observes out of Plato.[7]

Ralph Cudworth of the Cambridge school likewise reflects that
"the reason why God made the world, was from his own overflowing and communicative goodness, that there might be other
beings also happy besides him. . . .[8]

Nor does the Divine Goodness, once spilled over in creation,
withdraw as an anthropomorphic being to celestial heights to look
down upon struggling creatures. Throughout the universe there is
a divine emanation that even in its vastness descends to the
"diurnal course" of material renewings:

'Tis the Divine Power which is the basis of all Things; which
continues the Vigour of Second Causes, and keeps the Sun and
Moon in repair. This holds every thing constant to Appointment, and true to the first Plan. Thus the Revolutions of
Seasons, the Support of Animals, the Perpetuity of Species
is carried on and maintained. Without this, things would soon
run Riot and ramble out of Distinction, the Succours of Life
would be cut off, and Nature drop into Decay.[9]

If in lesser matters divine benevolence is withheld, it is because
God does not intend every desire to be satisfied, else "the Schemes
of *Providence* might be disturb'd";[10] nor does he "think fit to alter

---

[7] *Select Discourses,* pp. 151, 152.

[8] Cudworth, *The True Intellectual System of the Universe* (first edition
1678), London, 1845, Vol. III, p. 486. *Cf.* p. 487, n. 1, for editor's thorough treatment of the idea; he traces the Platonic concept to the version of creation
presented by the Pythagorean Timaeus Locrus in his *De Anima Mundi.* The
occurrence of this belief in St. Augustine's *Confessions* and *De Civitate Dei* is
suggestive of another source of contact for Collier.

[9] *Of Power,* pp. 64, 65. Hooker has expounded the same argument: the
obedience of creatures to the law of nature is the stay of the world, and the "rule
of natural agents that work by simple necessity, is the determination of the
wisdom of God. . . ." (*Ecclesiastical Polity,* seventh edition, Oxford, 1888,
Bk. I, p. 228.)

[10] *Of Power,* p. 63.

the Coarse of Nature, and break through a Chain of Causes, to punish every Mismanagement."[11]

Collier's speculation upon the working of physical laws through second causes inevitably leads him into the matter of duality and ideas of motion and extension. And it becomes obvious that he, like the Platonists, utilized the Cartesian rational basis to effect a metaphysical approach to understanding.

To the seventeenth-century theologian the problem of duality was one fraught with fine anxieties. Mere acceptance was not sufficient; its implications had to be faced and met. The notion of Hobbes that thought and consciousness were phantasms due to atomic action in the brain was, of course, worse than unacceptable. The Platonists recognized that, in the words of an historian of science, "a theory which made extension and its modes the only properties of bodies could not explain life and thought, and tried to reconcile religion and mechanical philosophy by an apotheosis of space. This process was carried further by Malebranche, who identified Infinite Space with God Himself, a substitute for the Aristotelian Pure Form or Absolute Actuality. . . . God is thus the immanent cause of a pantheistic Universe, and the Cartesian dualism of mind and matter is resolved in a higher unity when viewed *sub specie aeternitatis*."[12] Most notable among the occasionalists who developed the spiritualistic side of Cartesianism, Nicholas Malebranche,[13] combining observation and mystical interpretation, held that spiritual and physical phenomena proceed directly from God, with no casual force operating between the two aspects of being. It is this view that Collier embraces, rather than the Cartesian separateness of *res extensa* and *res cogitans,* each subject to its own set of laws.

Collier concurs largely in Malebranchian theory in his ideas of matter and extension. Matter is "nothing but extension variously figured," and it is not impossible for spirit to move matter, else

[11] *Of Pleasure,* p. 187.

[12] William C. D. Dampier-Whetham, *A History of Science and Its Relations with Philosophy and Religion,* New York, 1931, p. 151.

[13] A French priest (1638-1715), aptly characterized as an able exponent of "the mystical or Augustinian factor in Cartesian philosophy." *Cf.* Brett, *A History of Psychology,* Vol. II, 1921, p. 226 ff.

motion would not exist. Extension "implies no Necessity of being moved: It supposes no more than a bare Capacity for such an Event."[14] All matter is the same, none is sensible. In short, "That the full notion of *Corporeity* is comprized within the three *Dimensions,* is as clear as that Two and Two makes Four."[15] Since insensible matter cannot act, the power of motion lies in a supernatural agency: it is "either an incommunicable Perfection of the Supreme *Being,* or else a sort of Prerogative Royal, which he is pleased to keep in his Hands, that we may be the more sensible of our Dependance."[16] Generally, Collier concludes,

> The Regularity of Motion, visible in the great Variety and Curiosity of Bodies, and the constant and even Revolutions of some of them, is a Demonstration that the whole Mass of *Matter* is under the Conduct of a mighty Intelligence.[17]

Thus for Collier a materialistic explanation does not account for forces illimitable, hence incomprehensible to the human mind. What man, he asks, is "so vain as to pretend to know the Extent of Nature, and the Stretch of Possibility, and the Force of the Powers invisible?" "No Conclusions can exceed the Evidence of their Principles; you may as well build a Castle in the Air, as raise a Demonstration upon a Bottom of Uncertainty."[18]

Collier finds the attributes of man to fit into the large metaphysi-

[14] *Of Thought,* p. 84.

[15] *Ibid.,* p. 80.

[16] *Ibid.,* p. 85.

[17] *Ibid.,* p. 84. It is a ridiculous solution of the problem of how matter and spirit cohere, declares Collier, to say that the greater fragments of matter are connected with hooked particles.

Another Greek concept reappearing in seventeenth-century speculation was that of an "inter-planetary aether," used for one by Kepler to explain movements of other planets by the sun. (Dampier-Whetham, *History of Science,* p. 161.) Collier speaks of the belief of the stoics and Church Fathers in animation of the sun and stars; if this were true, he says, the sun would fully perceive itself. "And supposing the Union not *Vital,* yet if there is an *Intelligence* seated in the Centre of these luminous Bodies; if there is a *Regent* Spirit posted in the Sun to govern his Motion, to recruit the Consumptions, and keep the Balance even: If the Matter stands thus, such a Superintendent must be pleased with the Dignity of the Charge, and the glorious Effects consequent upon 't." (*Of Goodness,* p. 8.)

[18] *A Short View of the Immorality and Profaneness of the English Stage* . . . (first ed. 1698), fourth ed. 1738, p. 124.

We find reflection of a Cartesian principle when Collier explains that "all Motion is perform'd by Resistance, and Resistance supposes Contact, and Contact

cal scheme of things no less neatly than does the mysterious "pre-rogative-royal" of motion. Here again he is amazingly close to Malebranche. His belief that correspondence between body and soul depends upon "the Laws of the Union" finds an exact counter-part in Malebranche's "Laws of Conjunction of soul and body."[19] These the French philosopher interprets particularly in his *Twelfth Dialogue on Metaphysics* and as well in his *Treatise of Morality* and in his *Recherche*. The *Seventh Dialogue* presents a résumé of "the inefficacy of natural causes," and an exposition of the lack of union of body and soul except through God, to whom each of us is directly united. Here, as in Collier's similar dialogue *Of Thought,* the argument in part revolves about the potentialities of matter, and the possible interaction of mind and body. God, in creating man, immediately bestowed upon him mental powers issuing so directly from the Deity that "we are nearer related to the Supreme Being than to Father or Mother." This belief has of course ethical as well as metaphysical significance to Collier. What of man's exact relation to his Maker? Is he determined in all respects? It is Collier's intense interest in the moral life of man that partially leads him to assert roundly the doctrine of Free Will at the same time that he recognizes chance as a second cause effecting the larger ends of the Deified Free Will (the only Will that enjoys complete liberty). When man, then, exercises his faculty for rational conduct he is exemplifying the fact that he is not a toy in the hands of fate—he is a being divinely endowed with the power of intelligent choice. We are, Collier declares, "to be commended or discommended for nothing but the right Use or Misemployment of this Freedom" because

> nothing is properly our own, except the Government of our own Wills; . . . Now when a Man . . . finds in him-

requires a Superficies, and this implies Extension; so that where Extension is absent, the other Requisites must fail of course." (*A Thought,* p. 83.) Such comment is indicative of the current interest in theories of motion.

[19] *Dialogues on Metaphysics and on Religion* (1688), translated by Morris Ginsberg, New York, 1923. *De la Recherche de la Vérité* (1674-1675) was brought out in Latin translation in 1685; in English by R. Sault, in 1692; and by T. Taylor, in English, in 1694; the *Traité de Morale* (1683) was translated into English by Sir J. Shipton, 1699.

> self a sincere and steady Resolution of doing that always,
> which his Conscience is assured ought to be done . . . this
> makes him reckon nothing valuable but what is in his own
> Power. This Opinion, together with a suitable Practice, as
> it's the greatest Privilege of Human Nature, so it lies within
> the Power of all Persons, of what Rank or Condition soever.[20]

God has so condescended as to "appeal to our Reason, and make our
own Consciences the Judge. . . . He will not over-rule our Plea by
his irresistible Sovereignty, nor resolve our Fate into any absolute
and irrespective Decrees."[21] Will, which is stronger than reason, is
impelled to direct motion; plus understanding, it intensifies the
power of the soul which is determined towards good: "the Appearance of Good moves the Will by natural Necessity."[22] When both
will and reason combine to embrace God, man approaches nearest
earthly happiness, and that is through conscious loss of himself.
Collier holds the words of St. Paul, "in Him we live, and move,
and have our being,"[23] to bear more literal interpretation than is
usually conceded. John Smith points to "*One Infinite* source of all
that *Reason* and *Understanding*" which our minds "partake of"
and "in which they live, move, and have their Being."[24] Similarly
Malebranche believed that

> as it is He who makes them [our souls] feel Pleasure and
> Pain, and all the other Sensations, by the Natural Union He
> has instituted between them and their Bodies, which is no
> other than His Decree and General Will: So it is He, who by
> Means of the Natural Union he has plac'd between the Will
> of Man, and the Representation of Ideas, included in the

[20] *Sermon VI*, p. 212. This and other sermons are quoted in this study from
the second edition of *Several Discourses upon Practical Subjects*, London, 1726.
[21] *Sermon II*, p. 47.
[22] To Malebranche, will is the divinely inspired inclination towards good, its
freedom the power by which the soul checks this inclination towards good in
general, and fixes it upon a particular object. *Cf. A Treatise of Morality,* translated by James Shipton, London, 1699, p. 93. *Cf.* Hooker: "Goodness doth not
move by being, but by being apparent"; and reason discovers good, and teaches
the "possibility" of it to the will. (*Ecclesiastical Polity,* Bk. I, pp. 222-4.)
[23] *Acts* xvii:28.
[24] *Select Discourses,* p. 168.

immensity of the Divine Essence, gives them to know all that they know: Nor is this Natural Union anything but his General Will. . . . Let us believe with St. Paul, that He is not far from every one of us, and that in Him we live, and move, and have our Being.[25]

So strong is the essence of divinity infused into men that there results a "community of being": "We are all cast in the same *Mould,* allied in our Passions, and in our Faculties. . . . All Mankind is as it were one great *Being,* divided into several Parts; and every Part having the same Properties and Affections with Another."[26] However much we are connected, or discover in man the *faciem Dei,* "no finite or derived Excellency" can deify him. "Independency is the only sovereign and distinguishing Prerogative, and the Line which cuts between God and a Creature."[27] No perfection "not unalterably fix'd in its Subject, and absolutely *sui iuris* can be divine."[28] Here Collier echoes a Platonic idea:

All created Goodness is but Copy, and Communication: 'Tis originally in the Supreme Being; there 'tis possessed in a Sovereign Degree, without Limits or Alloy, without Variableness.[29]

[25] *Recherche,* Vol. I, Bk. III, Part II, Chap. VI, pp. 121, 122.

[26] *Of General Kindness,* pp. 149-50. Collier repeats this conception in his dialogue *Of Honesty:* the same attributes "run thro' the whole Mass of Mankind," and if there is no natural affinity felt it is because "they are so much one Being, that they can be no more related, than a Man can be of Kin to himself" (p. 69). "So much alike they are," he continues, "that, it may be, 'tis not easy to assign the Reason why one Man is not another: or to speak more strictly, how the whole human Nature, can make any more than one Person: Motion often travels a great Way, and drives thro' a long Extent of Matter, now Thinking is as quick as Lightning; how comes it about then, that the Communication of Spirits is more enlarg'd; that Consciousness should be confin'd to a single Body, that Thoughts should not pass from Man to Man, and like Flames catch upon each other? If there was such mutual Penetration among human Minds, all Mortals would be like several Pieces of the same Cloth tack'd together. This would be an *incorporating Union* with a Witness, and one Soul would be as it were the Limb of another. But God who has thought fit to multiply Spirits, has bounded their Activity, stop'd the Progress of *Sentiment;* and not suffer'd Parts of the same Nature to run into each other" (p. 69).

[27] *Sermon IX,* p. 304.

[28] *Ibid.*

[29] *Of Goodness,* p. 5.

In asking the source of Collier's religious certainties we encounter the problem of Scriptural interpretation, a matter of basic importance to the seventeenth-century mind. On this score he shifts in opinion with a facility that need neither disturb nor alarm; rather does it mark healthy growth in the theologian earnestly searching after truth and living at a time when traditions were beginning to sound a hollow note. Characteristic of John Smith's *Discourses* are Collier's calm disregard of any need to distinguish between "natural" and "revealed" religion as values, and his assumption that the "revealed" is "natural." Like the average Anglican of his day he holds the Scriptures to be indisputably the Word of God; divine laws "are the grand Rule" and may be known from *"the Inspir'd Writings"* or "discover'd by natural Light."[30] Clearly reflected in the dialogue *Of Honesty* is this current attitude. Here one speaker queries: "if I must after all try the Lawfulness of my Desires by a higher Rule . . . to what purpose should I enquire into them? Why am I bidden to consult my self?" Collier's spokesman explains that

> tho' the Law of God is the only warrantable Direction . . . it does not follow from hence, that the subordinate Rule is of no Use. For the *Scriptures* speak often in general Terms: They don't descend to every Case, nor point upon every Circumstance. Thus in some Emergencies a Man must determine for himself, and be left to the *Guidance* of his own Reason. 'Tis true, we are bound to follow the *Scriptures* where they declare themselves, and decide upon the Question. But when the Holy *Oracle* is silent, when the Voice of Heaven cannot be heard, we must look to the Light within us, and make the most of our Understandings.[31]

But people dislike the trouble involved in "searching for unprofitable Truth": "It must shine with a strong Light, and come full upon their Understandings; otherwise 'tis odds if they take any Notice of it."[32] Collier concludes:

[30] *Of Honesty*, p. 61.
[31] *Ibid.*, p. 80.
[32] *Ibid.*, p. 81. *Cf.* Hooker's similar comment on the general disinterestedness in finding truth. (*Ecclesiastical Polity*, p. 198.)

Tho' the *Scripture* ought to be the Measure of our Practice, when it decides the Question; yet we can't always consult this Rule: Our Occasions are sometimes sudden; Business won't stay, and we are oblig'd to resolve upon the Spot. This Case may frequently happen in Journeys, in Company, in Commerce. But tho' a Man does not always carry a *Bible* about with him, he is never without his Thoughts: Tho' his Memory may fail him; tho' he can't recover the *Text,* to clear his Doubt; yet he may read his own Mind. And here, if he'll take any Pains, he may spell out his Duty, and find the *Work of the Law written in his Heart.*[33]

Why, then, if every man "has a full Idea of Justice in Himself . . . what need is there of a *Revelation?*" The Laws of Nature proclaimed on Mt. Sinai have been handed down to refresh the memory, direct conscience, "preserve the Notion of Virtue clear and uncounterfeited"; should ignorance mislead, "this infallible *System* will set us right."[34]

Collier clearly implies here the infallibility of the Bible in fundamentals; but he likewise reflects Anglican liberalism and accepts the theory of accommodation in conceding that scriptural interpretation remains open to the discretion of the reader. "To doubt the Meaning of some part of the Bible may," he declares, "be done without a Fault"; but "to question any Facts in Scripture would be to renounce Christianity."[35] He holds to be true "the facts of Christ's life" because they are based upon written evidence; further, the account of the life, death, and works of Christ constitutes for us an infallible guide. Therein lies a truth the "admirable simplicity" of which Chillingworth remarked, a truth which became a primary tenet of seventeenth-century Anglicanism.

There remains much of Scripture that is to be held as corollary, and to be interpreted figuratively and personally. Here, in the more flexible business of disputation and decision, man often cannot stand alone; for "bare Nature is very insufficient to conduct us to Truth and Virtue," to accept truths that conflict with inclination.

[33] *Ibid.,* p. 86.
[34] *Ibid.,* p. 88.
[35] *A Short View of the Immorality and Profaneness of the English Stage,* p. 264.

Now the Doctrines of *Christianity* pressing hard against favourite Vices, makes Men not willing to allow it a fair Examination; and to catch at any shadow of a Reason for a Disproof . . . We should be in great Danger to forget the other [World] . . . unless we were often admonish'd of our duty by a more vigilant Reason, and aided in the Performance by a greater Strength than our own. From whence it follows, that a bare Proposal of the Reasons of *Christianity,* are not sufficient for Practice, unless they are fortify'd, and the Weight of Things press'd by a supernatural Power . . . This animates our Resolutions, regulates our Choice, and sublimates our Pleasures. By this Assistance, Reason stands upon its guard, and the Affections are call'd off from Folly. Without this inward Teaching, the World, the Flesh, and the Devil, would be much an Over-match for the best Instructions: Without this, written Revelation would fall short, and the Ministrations of Men prove ineffectual. . . . Nothing but a supernatural Force can overbear the Prejudices of Flesh and Blood; nothing can reform the Will, and mollify the Heart, but he that made it.[36]

Here is essentially the attitude of the Cambridge Platonists. Revelation, not confined to the written Word, emanates directly from God—that is, for those hearkening to the clear voice of Reason and "the light of Nature." This dependence upon an "inner certitude" strengthened by God found full development in such rationalists as Ralph Cudworth, John Smith, and Herbert of Cherbury, who, in embracing the Platonic primacy of ideas, grounded their mysticism and vindicated their rejection of those theological elements they could not intellectually justify. Traditional reliance upon the subjective assurance to be gained from an inner-engraved "work of the law" is exemplified by Hooker: in "moral actions, divine law helpeth exceedingly the law of reason to guide man's life; but in supernatural it alone guideth."[37] The law of reason is universally written in men's hearts. Collier's position is that of Milton who wrote that "Every believer has a right to interpret the Scriptures for himself, inasmuch as he has the Spirit for his guide, and the

36 *Sermon XI,* pp. 367-70.
37 *Ecclesiastical Polity,* p. 281.

mind of Christ is in him"; that Scripture is twofold—"one external, which is the written word, and the other internal, which is the Holy Spirit, written in the hearts of believers." Both are certain that "the Spirit which leads to truth cannot be corrupted," that "the Spirit which is given to us is a more certain guide than Scripture, whom therefore it is our duty to follow."[38]

To Collier, then, revelation often means, as it does to the Platonists, a personal experience, an inflowing that strengthens natural reason. Obviously he believes in a complementary fusing of these two processes of enlightenment, the one to validate the other. Awareness of his connexion with Pascal recalls the latter's declaration that the mind of man is too weak to arrive alone at the true principles of theology, which "are above nature and above reason" and are to be grasped only through supernatural guidance.[39]

Collier is characteristically a divine of his day when he recognizes that the Scriptures were written by men for men and that accordingly, to meet "vulgar apprehension" precepts must be clothed in sensuous imagery. Hence the gorgeous trappings of such scenes as depict a brilliant setting for the hereafter; only strong, pure intellects can evolve from cold ideology concepts of an immortal life. The unimaginative "generality" must utilize scriptural teaching, because they cannot rely upon reason.[40] Recognition of both this fact and the value of emotion in maintaining traditional doctrines is seen in Collier's treatment of the Judgement.[41] This belief, he explains, may largely be made from the "Remorse and Applauses of Conscience, and has gain'd Ground where there was

---

[38] *The Christian Doctrine,* Chap. xxx. (Patterson edition, pp. 1040, 1041.)

[39] Blaise Pascal, *Thoughts,* translated by E. Craig, Boston, 1849. Part I, Chap. I, p. 40.

[40] "The Vulgar," writes Collier, "have but a strait Notion of Infinity. Their Philosophy is most likely to conclude, that he who knows all the Concerns of our World, may know all Things: So extensive a Perfection as this looks like the Ocean to them; they cannot see over it, and therefore are apt to imagine it has no Bounds. So that 'tis most convenient for them to believe, that such transcendant Degrees of Knowledge belong to none but God himself." *Sermon IX, p.* 305. This attitude towards the "vulgar" understanding and the need to "doctor" presentation for it is seen in John Smith's *Discourses.*

[41] Its certainty he finds universally agreed upon among Jews and Gentiles, "Greeks and Barbarians"; and authority for certitude in Josephus, Plato, Cicero, Justin Martyr, and Tertullian.

nothing but natural Reason, and the Attributes of God to prove it." Since the entire race of man is to be judged, the decree "should be either discoverable by the Light of Nature, or reveal'd to our first Parents, and so kept up by a general and uninterrupted Tradition."[42] In picturing the complete ruin of the Last Day when foundations are literally shattered, he paints a scene vivid enough to smite with terror the "vulgar apprehension." He is purposely mindful that the "greatest Part of Mankind must have remote Truths . . . conveyed by sensible objects."[43] Thus he not only agrees with Sir Thomas Browne that "unspeakable mysteries in the Scriptures are often delivered in a vulgar and illustrative way"[44] but justifies his turning literalist in offering up theology to the uninitiate. This need to clothe ideas in the language of mundane experience accounts partially, perhaps, for his version of immortality.

The doctrine of Resurrection Collier characterizes as one "of pure Revelation" that "natural Light and human Reason could never reach."[45] While he rejects the idea of pre-existence of the soul he retains the Platonic elements that have been infused into Christian theology: the spirit is corrupted by the flesh during its earthly sojourn; from the dark prison of the body, a "twilight," the captive soul is ultimately freed and refined; and there is in Collier's implication of degrees in the process of soul-refinement a suggestion of the elaborate scheme of purification found in the *Timaeus*. In the new state both mind and the senses will enjoy

[42] *Sermon I*, p. 9.

[43] *Sermon IX*, p. 289. He narrates, pp. 12-28, *Sermon I,* the events of Judgement Day, with all things unravelling into their first chaos and finally to be wiped out by fire, when the heavens will kindle, springs of fire will burst from the earth, and whole countries will be rent. Collier suggests something of a Dantesque notion for the punishment of sins, the intemperate to be punished in those senses abused, the impostor to have his lot with deceivers, and so on.

[44] *Religio Medici,* I, XXXIV.

[45] *Of the Resurrection,* p. 391. This dialogue is expanded from an earlier sermon, *The Difference Between the Present and Future State of Our Bodies,* licensed 23 April, 1686, London. The dialogue stands last in Part IV of the *Moral Essays,* 1709. To avoid the repetitions in the conversation of the dialogue, quotations have here been drawn from the sermon unless the expanded later piece offers new ideas.

God; according to Scripture "the senses are plainly invited." Why not?

> Unless the Soul can reach some Satisfaction through the Senses . . . Capacity must sleep, Happiness be maim'd, and the Body rais'd to no Effect. Abstracted Notions and Spiritual Delights, all subtiliz'd and sublimated to Thought, are apt to fly over the Understandings of the Generality. Such a nice Happiness, without a mixture of sensible Advantage, might possibly be too fine for the Affections to take hold of at present. For this Reason, 'tis probable, Heaven is describ'd by a state of Pleasure suited to our Apprehensions, and by Images of Greatness we are acquainted with. Thus in *Holy Scripture,* 'tis call'd *Paradise,* and a *Kingdom; Crowns, Thrones, Splendid Solemnities,* are Part of the Representation. And as these Expressions are not to be strain'd to a literal Accomplishment, so neither are they to be expounded out of all affinity and Resemblance. For since the Soul has suffer'd in the Body, why should it not be pleas'd under something of the same Circumstances? Since *Matter* has been instrumental to Virtue, why should it not be productive of Delight?[46]

After death the soul is disunited from the body for a period preceding paradise, but its method of conveyance is unknown:

> Whether the Soul in the State of Separation acts independently of Matter, purely by the Strength of her own powers, or whether in order to the better understanding her self and other Beings, she makes use of a Body of Air shaped out into such Limbs and Sences as she hath occasional employment for; whether or no the want of her old companion is supplied this way, is uncertain. But whatever abatements of happiness the pious Soul may suffer for want of a suitable Body between the time of Death, and the General Judgment, then we are sure this inconvenience will be removed, and it will be repossessed of its antient Seat out of which Violence or Nature had forced it.[47]

This doctrine "helps the meanest understanding to conceive the Nature of Happiness of the other World": the "generality,"

---

[46] *Of Religious Temper,* pp. 111, 112.
[47] *Sermon of the Difference Between the Present and Future State of Our Bodies,* p. 1.

always "used to dwell in these houses of clay, . . . would not have been so well able to apprehend the happiness of pure and uncompounded Spirits." *And as we have born the Image of the earthy, so we shall also bear the Image of the heavenly*; hence what "can we more rationally infer" than that our visible selves shall be quitted but for a time and then restored? Collier outlines in detail the inconveniences of our present bodies as contrasted with advantages of "glorified bodies." He speculates curiously, for example, on our future liability to pain and concludes that when "the Soul is disengaged from the oppression and soil of the Body, it will act upon itself with greater vigour, and make the Springs of Thought go much smarter than they do now."[48] The refined "glorified body" will have assumed an "exalted and vigorous condition":

> All grossness and feculency which adheres to it now, shall be purged off; all unevenness and roughness of parts will then be filed into an exact serviceableness, and the Soul will no longer labour under the disorders of an unwieldy and uncompliant constitution.[49]

The parts of the body "will be rang'd in a Figure, and agitated with a Motion, exactly fitted to Activity and Ease" and "refin'd to a nearer Resemblance with the Ambient Air; the Activity of the Spirits will be improv'd; and the Soul, in all Likelihood, have greater Force to set them at work."[50] The senses will be more comprehensive and quicker, for "whatever Notices they convey to the Mind, will be more intimately and vigorously communicated."[51] The organs of sight and hearing will continue to function, "probably that of Smelling too," and perhaps new senses will be formed. Celestial bodies will be graceful and august, and fortified against disease and accidents. How this metamorphosis will come about is open to speculation:

[48] *Sermon of the Difference, etc.*, pp. 11, 12. God, he adds, has mercifully "bound the Soul so gently to the Body" that a short struggle will loose it. Collier here cites the maxim of Epicurus: "It is impossible for that pain which is violent to continue long." (*Morals*, London, 1670, p. 131.)

[49] *Ibid.*

[50] *Of the Resurrection*, p. 426.

[51] *Ibid.*, pp. 426, 427.

Possibly the Bodies of the *Saints* may have such an advantagious change from the Laws of Motion, from the Figure of their Parts, or the Temperature of the climate, as may preserve them from suffering any Alteration, or Loss of Parts: Or if the Parts fly off, as they do now, 'tis easie with God to furnish a Supply, without the preparatory Use of Eating, or Concoction. . . . Whether this Privilege will result from new *Mechanism,* or Supernatural Succour, from settled Providence or Miracle, is neither material to dispute, nor possible to determine. That glorified Bodies will continue thus everlastingly undecay'd, we are sure.[52]

This concept of immortality grows partly out of the conviction that matter instead of perishing reverts to the use of the First Cause.[53] Ralph Cudworth similarly ponders the state of the soul after death and, like Collier, asks: does it not continue to use a "vehicle"? The belief that the soul is not stripped of bodily shape Cudworth holds "to be plainly the teaching of the 'old philosophic Cabala'"; the "gross, earthy part" is shed, but a vestment remains "to give to the departed soul locality and capacity of motion."[54] This doctrine he harmonizes with that of the Christian Resurrection on two points: "that the supreme happiness of the soul is not to be found in disjunction from all body"; and "that its future bodily investment cannot be of a gross, earthy nature." He believes that "The spiritual resurrection-doctrine of St. Paul is an inspired affirmation of the Neo-Platonic dream of a 'luciform' and 'celestial' vehicle for the purified soul," and that certain corollary ideas closely parallel those of the Cabbala. The change in the habiliments of the soul "will consist not in merely 'gilding and varnishing over of the outside,' but in a spiritual transformation, whereby we shall be

---

[52] *Of the Resurrection,* p. 433.

[53] One speaker in the dialogue asks, "Don't you consider, when a man is dead, the Parts unclasp and fly off, the Atomes remove to great Distances, run into several Forms, and make part of the Bodies of other creatures?" The answer is that "there will be old *Matter* enough reserv'd for the Business of Identity" (p. 392).

[54] *Cf.* John Tulloch, *Rational Theology and Christian Philosophy in England in the Seventeenth Century,* London, 1874. Vol. II, p. 280. He has here summed up admirably the winding, expansive discussion in the *Intellectual System,* Vol. III, p. 310 ff.

fashioned in the likeness of Christ's glorious body."[55] This scriptural inference[56] Collier magnifies to build up his vision of the new bodies—Christlike, though perhaps faintly imaged—with "no Marks of Age or Imperfection, of Obscurity or Meanness . . . no disfiguring Blemish, no Scars remaining, excepting those of wounds receiv'd in their Master's Cause, which may then shine out with a more orient, and distinguishable Lustre."[57] Although Collier reveals an acquaintance with Pythagorean doctrines, he makes no mention of Cudworth or of any current interest in the theory he expounds; and he gives no sign of knowing that in 1654 Henry More had published his work on the Cabbala. Citations in *Of the Resurrection* he draws from Tertullian's *De resurrectione carnis,* and from Minucius Felix.[58] The Cabbalistic philosophy seen in Milton constitutes a barely possible seventeenth-century influence; several signs, however, point to the conclusion that this is not to be considered a "source" for Collier but rather a parallel instance of an interest in a renascent vein of thought.[59]

On another side, Collier's tendency towards a less literal and more modern attitude is evinced in the noticeable lack of violence in his treatment of the Fall and the Devil—always fruitful grist for the ecclesiastical mill. True, acceptance of the "curse" is implicit in the concession that our first parents "before the Fall, were much higher, and more happy, than the biggest of their posterity."[59a] But

[55] Tulloch, *Rational Theology and Christian Philosophy, etc.,* II, p. 281.

[56] *Philippians* iii:21. Christ "shall change our vile body, that it may be fashioned like unto his glorious body. . . ."

[57] *Of the Resurrection,* p. 431.

[58] The earliest Latin apologist for Christ. Nothing is known of him, except that his book dates *c.* 160.

[59] *Cf.* Denis Saurat's treatment of Milton as a Cabbalist in his *Milton, Man and Thinker* (New York, 1925), and as well his *Literature and Occult Tradition* (London, 1930).

Voicing of belief in the future expansion of "earthy" faculties is seen in Timothy Nourse: When the soul soars to God, "Fruition will not exclude Appetite, because the Faculty will still be enlarg'd to receive greater Measures of untasted Joys . . . and so by an infinite Progress and Succession of New Beauties, 'twill ever advance itself into Perfection. . . ." (*A Discourse Upon the Nature and Faculties of Man, in Several Essayes: With some Considerations upon the Occurrances of Humane Life,* London, 1686, p. 180.)

[59a] *Of the Resurrection,* p. 419.

was Adam "expell'd Eden" into a wretched state? No. "He found a comfortable Banishment":

> He was not thrown into a Dungeon, condemn'd to Darkness, and exposed to Starving and Stench. 'Tis granted, He was sadly reduced; the Communication with *Heaven* was cut off; He lost the honour of conversing with his *Maker*; He was not supply'd as formerly without Trouble; He was under a necessity of Labour; He was obnoxious to Pain, brought under the Force of Time, and Death and Diseases were let loose upon Him. But after all, this was rather an Abatement of Happiness, than a State of Misery: The Divine Bounty was far from being withdrawn. . . .[60]

Here is added proof of God's goodness. Collier, rising to defend his Creator, points a scornful finger at moral weaklings who would lay "the Blame of their Disobedience on the Defect of their Nature." Men err in imagining themselves secure by an act of God; but "that no Man might fix himself in a wicked Life by such a fatal Mistake, and aggravate his Crimes by accusing God Almighty; the Apostle expressly affirms, that God is far from placing us in an unavoidable state of Sin. . . ."[61] Man's temptation to evil is not a snare to satisfy the idle curiosity of God, but opportunity to prove his integrity. His sins rest on his own head— not in his possession of a physical nature. The body, says Collier, "is a senseless inanimate Thing, without any manner of Thought or Apprehension; and therefore can't be under the Direction . . . of a Law. But Sin is seated in the rational Part, and supposes Judgment and Consent."[62]

Thus Collier considers the problem of sin not a determined dogma but an ethical question to be solved intellectually. Here again he aligns himself with the Platonists, who were unable to reconcile with their concept of Reason a picture of man bereft of "natural light," and who of course ran counter to this implication of the orthodox Fall doctrine. This represents on the whole the rationalistic tolerance of the day for "innocence of error" that we find so ably defended in Jeremy Taylor. Again, Collier quite probably

[60] *Of Goodness*, p. 12.
[61] *Sermon XI*, pp. 378, 379.
[62] *Ibid.*, pp. 382, 383.

was rejecting a theological tradition repellent to his primary interest in morality.

The doctrines of the Fall and of Original Sin are corollary to a belief in the importance of Satan as a living force. Collier's few references to the Devil he lifts in their literal sense out of common scriptural usage; or else he employs catch-terms that drop from a pen facile in Biblical phraseology. Never does he utilize the traditional devil-machinery that contemporary divines exulted to drag into the pulpit. The idea that Satan works his ends by lying and stratagem is to be rationalized and treated dispassionately. The absence of pyrotechnics against the "prince of darkness" suggests Collier's approach towards a lack of sustained "Satan-consciousness," an attitude indicative of the vanishing importance of that mythological figure: for the influence of Satan in theology weakened more and more as the century waned. Generally Collier tends to remain unimpressed by demonology; to give credence to superstitious beliefs would be to outrage the God-given "light of nature." Mr. Basil Willey aptly remarks, "The idea that to abandon belief in witches was to begin on the slippery slope to atheism was a common one at this time"; and adds that many felt "they must cling to Satan in order to keep God."[63] That "the vulgar" were not alone in fearing that to reject one was to reject the other is seen by reading in men like Glanvill, Smith, More, and Browne.

Collier's concept of the Church as a society with Christ at the head is that tradit.or one found in Hooker, and in Milton; and, like Hooker,[64] Collier distinguishes between legitimate grounds for the operation of civil and of ecclesiastical authority: the origin of the Church is divine, its authority immediately vested by God and consisting in the right to preach the Word, to persuade men to embrace it, and to exclude from the Church those persons not professing true faith. The Church likewise has an authority derived

[63] *The Seventeenth Century Background*, London, 1934, p. 55. *Cf.* p. 54, however, for a contradictory notion of "Satan's prestige"; Mr. Willey uses the term "Satan-consciousness."

[64] According to Hooker, the Church has for its basis "the natural inclination which all men have ur to ciable life, and consent to some certain band of association," that belonging to the Church of God being "a law supernatural, which God himself hath revealed concerning that kind of worship which his people shall do unto him." (*Ecclesiastical Polity*, I, p. 274.)

from civil law, which concerns any ecclesiast only in so far as he is a member of a state and "does not in the least affect his Spiritual Capacity."

> The Power which results from that, flows from another Fountain; and is given by our Saviour himself; and therefore can not be weakened, or recalled, by any State Constitution whatever. . . . Neither was this Power to expire with the Apostles, but to be conveyed by Succession, through all the Ages of the World; there being the same Cause for its Continuance, as for its first Institution. . . . And thus the sacred Order has been continued, for near 1700 Years.[65]

Further,

> The Constitution of the Church is founded in the Appointment of Christ; in that Commission which he gave the Apostles and their Successors: and consequently, does not derive its Authority from any Earthly Power. The Civil Magistrate never yet made a Bishop, Priest, or Deacon; nor ever can. . . .[66]

When Collier became embroiled in the famous Perkins case he defended his act of absolution by appealing to the priestly power derived from apostolic right. Otherwise, "where lies the Necessity of a Lay-permission"? His prevailing anti-Erastianism is voiced in his defence:

> If the Church is not *sui iuris* in matters purely Spiritual, and Independent in the Exercise of the Keys, Christianity lies at the Mercy of the *State,* and may be extinguished at pleasure. Call you these *Directions according to the Church of* England? God forbid! This divinity comes from *Selden,* or *Erastus,* or else from *Hobbes's Leviathan*; and makes Religion look like a Court-invention, a Politique Design.[67]

When a wide rift within the non-juring body of churchmen resulted from differences concerning observances of communion and prayer, Collier, here again a leading spirit in the dissenting group, struck a firm attitude that brought against him the charge

---

[65] *Upon the Office of a Chaplain,* pp. 207, 209.
[66] *Ibid.,* p. 205.
[67] *A Reply to the Absolution of a Penitent,* London, 1696, p. 9.

of popishness. Church ritual he held a necessity, its performance to be characterized by sincerity and sobriety: mere form and "religious address" are not sufficient to acknowledge God. The design of public worship is to confess visibly our dependence upon him, and the reason for "joining our bodies with our minds" in adoration is that the belief in one Deity may thus be confirmed by "external and sensible Acts,"

> For the generality are not always at leisure, nor possibly well prepar'd, to prove the Attributes of God by a Chain of Discourse, and Metaphysical Reasonings.[68]

The purpose of prayer is not to move God to greater mercy. He, in his infinite goodness, is without increase. Thus, it is not because God is "excited by our Importunity" that we receive blessings; the effect is psychological, for the act of prayer confirms faith and inspires hope and confidence. Collier's argument that worship is to be made to God alone he supports by scriptural doctrine, authority of the Ancients, and reason. To saints—"neither our Makers, nor Redeemers"—we owe no allegiance. Our adoration of saints would rather render them the less inclined to assist, "for venturing upon a Worship which has no Foundation in the Practice of either the Jewish or the antient Christian Church; which is disallowed by the Scriptures, and which some of themselves, when they were on Earth, condemn'd in the Heathens."[69] Collier pointedly objects to the "nauseous addresses" and "indiscriminate" worship of saints, angels, and God—in brief, to the devotions "customarily practis'd by the *Roman-Catholicks*." It is "plain by natural Reason, that there is but one God" and apparent from the Incarnation that Christ is the sole mediator between God and man. Then "what need we run after Daemons and departed Spirits for Patronage and Protection?"[70] Were it an act of humility to approach God through saintly mediation "we ought never to pray directly to any Person of the Trinity."[71] Particularly does Collier scorn Catholic "fulsome

---

[68] *Sermon IX*, p. 289.
[69] *Ibid.*, pp. 313, 314.
[70] *Sermon VIII*, p. 253.
[71] *Sermon IX*, p. 293.

Harangues," "Wonder-working Relicks," and easy intercession.[72]

Collier's interest in the form of worship included a recognition of the psychological value of music in the service. Since its purpose is to relieve weariness and compose the mind, and endear the offices of religion,

> It should therefore imitate the *Perfume* of the *Jewish Tabernacle,* and have as little of the Composition of common Use as is possible. There must be no Voluntary *Maggots,* no Military *Tatoos,* no Light and Galliardizing *Notes*; nothing that may make the Fancy trifling, or raise an improper Thought: This would be to Prophane the *Service,* and bring the *Play-House* into the Church. Religious Harmony must be Moving, but Noble withal; Grave, Solemn, and Seraphick; Fit for a Martyr to *play,* and an Angel to hear. It should be contrived so as to . . . take hold of the finest part of the Affections: To transport us with the *Beauty of Holiness*; to raise us above the Satisfactions of Life, and make us ambitious of the Glories of Heaven.[73]

He, like Sir Thomas Browne, distrusted "the symmetry of those heads which declaim against all Church-Music."[74]

Collier's activity in connexion with the writing and adoption of the new *Communion-Office* led to his publishing his *Reasons for Restoring Some Prayers and Directions . . . in the Communion-Service of the First English Reform'd Liturgy,* in which he defends the re-introduction of four usages: mixing water with sac-

[72] "Especially," he adds, "when the Favour of these powerful Mediators may be purchas'd upon such easy Terms; . . . when they are so surprisingly obliging, that they cannot refuse a Man that comes a great way to see them, though possibly he is more weary of his Journey than of his Sins; when a fair Present, though offer'd by a wicked Hand, raises their Compassion in such a visible manner, and makes them weep though they are in Marble. As if the blessed Saints, who were so far above the Temptations of Ambition and Popularity in this World, were alter'd to their Disadvantage since they went to Glory; and admir'd those Trifles now, which they despis'd before. But thus the fansy'd Interest and Indulgence of the Church *triumphant* slackens the Care and discipline of the *militant,* and Heaven is made instrumental to debauch the Earth." (*Sermon IX,* pp. 297, 298.)

[73] *Of Music,* p. 25. This passage is quoted by Arthur Bedford as an excellent expression of his own views, in *The Great Abuse of Music,* 1711, p. 246.

[74] *Religio Medici,* Part II, *Everyman* edition, p. 79.

ramental wine, prayer for the dead, prayer for the descent of the
Holy Ghost upon the· Sacramental Elements, and the oblatory
prayer, based upon the belief "that the Holy *Eucharist* is a proper
Sacrifice."[75] Careful to point out that his recommended "usages"
do not smack of popery, he supports the mixing of wine with
water as being a Jewish paschal custom, authenticated by general
practice in earliest times as well as by Catholic tradition. Primitive
and modern authority yield him copious citations. He notes that
prayer for the dead does not imply belief in purgatory; and though
the Church of England condemns the latter doctrine, "we can't
from thence inferr her Dislike of Prayer for the Dead."[76] On the
contrary, where the Church "has left her meaning doubtful, the
greatest Honour we can do her, is to interpret her to a Conformity
to Primitive Practice."[77]

The accusation of holding with Roman Catholic doctrine was
levelled at most of the non-juring body. Perhaps Bishop Burnet
and others found in the following passage excuse to attack Collier:

> The *Holy Catholic Church, and the Communion of Saints,*
> are Branches of the *Creed*: And the Notion of the Catholick
> Church, takes in the other World no less than this: Nay,
> those Deceas'd are certainly the biggest and the best Part of
> this *Society.* . . . And since the Church is but one, ought not
> the nobler Division share the common Privilege of the *Body,*
> and come within the Communion of Saints? But if we do
> nothing in their Behalf, if we decline Praying for them, if we
> don't remember them at the *Eucharistical* Sacrifice . . .
> the Correspondence fails on our Side. . . . And when we
> stand thus aloof from the noblest Part of the Catholick

[75] *Reasons for Restoring Some Prayers and Directions, as they stand in the Communion-Service of the First English Reform'd Liturgy.* London, 1717.

A full account of the ensuing controversy among the non-jurors, much of it characterized by the usual hair-splitting technique of the time, is given in Lathbury's *History of the Non-Jurors,* London, 1845, Chaps. IX, X, XI; other pieces of Collier's bound with his *Reasons for Restoring, etc.,* are *Defense of the Reasons; A Vindication of Reasons and Defense,* Parts I and II; *A Farther Defense, etc., Being an Answer to a Reply to the Vindication of the Reasons and Defense, etc.*

[76] *Reasons for Restoring, etc.,* p. 20.

[77] *Ibid.*

Church, may we not be said to maim the *Creed,* and strike off half an *Article*?[78]

In 1718 a piece entitled *Mr. Collier's Desertion Discuss'd* directly attacked him for having "deserted" the Church of England.[79] The author who, according to Lathbury, was himself a non-juror, "positively charges Collier with popery—with setting up as the head of a new schism, 'and so by unsuspected ways' leading 'his sequacious disciples, by degrees, at last into the communion of the Church of Rome. At least it seems to me, that he has his conscience so disposed, as perhaps his Library may be: at that end Papists, and at that end Protestants, and he comes in the middle, as near one as the other.' Such a passage," comments Lathbury, "was unwarranted by the circumstances."[80] Collier, had, it is true, in insisting upon the adoption of primitive usages, assailed the clergy from the Reformation on down. But he was not in sympathy with Rome. Defences from his faction ensued. Anglicans who desired the usages restored, yet who were not essentialists, began pamphleteering to prove the validity of Collier's stand, or to point distinctions between such doctrines as the Romish belief in purgatory and the Anglo-Catholic custom of Praying for the Dead. The literature of the controversy clearly reveals the non-jurors as a whole to have been of anti-popish sentiment. Most of the leading bishops and clergy of the time, Scottish as well as English, felt personally concerned to become active in the conflict. It has been said that the non-jurors deflected Anglicanism from its true course. But before they are branded as merely radical dissenters it should be remembered that they sincerely believed themselves to constitute the only true membership of the Church of England; and again, in noting charges against Collier, that Bishop Burnet and others—

[78] *Ibid.,* pp. 20, 21.

[79] The complete title is *Mr. Collier's Desertion Discuss'd: or the Offices of Worship in the Liturgy of the Church of England Defended: against the bold attacks of that gentleman, late of her communion, now of his own.* In a *Letter to a Friend.* First edition, 1718; second edition, 1720.

[80] The quotation from *Mr. Collier's Desertion Discuss'd,* p. 3, is taken from Lathbury, *History of the Non-Jurors,* p. 289. The pamphlet itself has proved unavailable.

hot supporters of William—had earlier for political reasons trumped up complaints against Collier.

Triumph of a kind was achieved in that in 1718, the year Collier's "desertion" was complained of, at Easter the New Communion Service (reputedly drawn up by him) was actually used, communion with those adhering to the Book of Common Prayer having been prohibited to the non-jurors.[81] With the new form, then, "the Holy Communion was celebrated by Collier's party . . . and by all the regular body, subsequent to the Union in 1733, until they became extinct."[82]

At variance with the dogmatism of this controversy and the censured "narrowness" of non-jurors is Collier's broad aim of unifying the Greek with the Western Church. Expression of his views pertaining to this issue is restricted to the correspondence between the Russian court and the non-juring bishops.[83] Elsewhere he frequently deplores the existence of factions and pleads uniformity in worship:

> if there were no *Divisions amongst us,* if Christians *were perfectly joyn'd together in the same Mind* . . . It would then be impracticable to *stalk* under a Holy Pretence; to set up the *Form of Godliness against the Power,* the *Name* against the Thing. . . . But alas! this Blessing is quite out of Prospect: What Diversity of Communions are we broken into? What's more ununiform, than christian Belief? More divided, than the *Church*? The Church, I say, which was intended for the Seat of Union, and the Cement of *Society*?[84]

He warns that zeal may destroy charity, and orthodoxy result in cruelty, and to serve the Church so is to mistake the design of Christianity; he urges tolerance for the inevitable doctrinal differences: "the best way is to live peaceably with People of different Opinions" even though "Belief is not always at Command."[85] But it is essential that the main articles of the Creed be professed:

[81] *Cf.* Lathbury, *History,* p. 291.

[82] Lathbury, *History,* p. 494.

[83] *Cf.* Lathbury's *History of the Non-Jurors,* Chap. VIII, for an account of the affair, and for the letters interchanged between the two groups promoting the union.

[84] *Of Peace,* pp. 383, 384.

[85] *Ibid.*

Thus where *Fundamentals* are the same, Difference in lesser Matters ought not to cut off Correspondence, to alienate Affection, or put a stop to kind Offices. For supposing Difference in Religion a just Ground for Disaffection, (which it is not,) yet where the Agreement, is much greater than the Disagreement, there, by our own Rule, the Predominancy should govern our Behaviour.[86]

To a deprecating comment of Congreve's upon the innumerable schisms Collier retorts:

Let them [sects] come from whence they will, we had better have them than some Peoples Opinions. 'Tis much safer to be of different Opinions than agree in believing nothing. Atheism is an ill Cure of Heresy and Schism: I admire Uniformity in Doctrine extreamly; but still must crave Leave to believe that a Mistaken conscience is more serviceable, than no Conscience at all.[87]

The atheist, Collier denounces as "a Heap of Organized Dust; a stalking Machine; a Speaking Head without a Soul in it. His thoughts are bound up by the Laws of Motion; his Actions are all prescribed"; according to his own creed

He is the Off-spring of *Chance*; the Slave of *Necessity*; danced by foreign Impulses no less than a *Puppet*: Ignoble at the End on't.[88]

Quite similarly the libertine, seeking an "easy Belief," "revolted to *Deism*," which "is bred out of Corruption of Manners, and like some *Insects,* has its Being from Putrefaction."[89] It gains proselytes through licence: "Appetite is let loose and Vice goes unrestrained by this Scheme: If Luxury and Debauching . . . were indulg'd by the *Gospel*; your Scepticks would be quickly won over. . . ."[90] But the deist will learn at Judgement the error of his belief that "our World was govern'd by Chance, and that God did not concern himself with Things below"; for then "it will appear that the Lord *is not slack, as some Men count Slackness*; that he

[86] *Of Peace,* pp. 384, 385.
[87] *Defense of a Short View, etc.,* p. 253.
[88] Preface, *Of the Office of a Chaplain,* p. 179.
[89] *Of Whoredom,* pp. 141, 142.
[90] *Of the Resurrection,* p. 412.

neither disdained nor neglected the Administration of human Affairs. . . ."[91] Meanwhile Collier, who in the main holds to the prevailing pragmatism of current theology, recommends the perusal of Pascal, La Bruyère, and Grotius.[92] All "Branches of Scepticism" he dismisses as ridiculously unsound; for "If the Success of our *Hobbists* were no better than their Reasoning, they would have few Disciples."[93]

This dislike of Hobbist materialism, which typifies the attitude of the body of churchmen, is given especially strong voice among the Platonists. While Collier attacks both atheism and materialism as springing from a common rejection of God and spirituality, he does not complain that science leads to atheism; nor does he hold the divine order to be opposed to Nature. On the contrary, he uses Nature in its widest interpretation to mean God—hence to explore its mysteries is not to be irreligious. Bacon too had believed God to be revealed through both the Word and the Universe. The common apprehension that investigating nature might shake the authority of religion he had scorned as savouring "utterly of carnal wisdom."[94] If, as it is frequently remarked, Bacon's method opened the way for scientists to reconcile science with religion, it must likewise have made it more possible for theologians to square

[91] *Sermon II*, p. 48. It is obvious that in several respects Collier is a theological descendant of the literalist school of Tertullian and Irenaeus; the gnostics, their abstractionist opponents, he condemns as heretics with "principles for immorality" and asks: "Are not *Atheists* and *Deists* altogether as bad as the Disciples of *Simon Magus*? Men who resolve Religion into *Fear* and *Fancy; deny the Lord that brought them*; and argue against those *Records* which stand upon the Evidence of Sense: . . . Such Persons, who publish their *Infidelity*, and make it their Business to poyson the Age, ought to be avoided in Conversation; and sham'd, if 'tis possible, into better Belief." (*Of Peace*, p. 386.)

[92] He advises "Monsieur *Paschal's Thoughts against Atheistical Indifference*: Monsieur *de la Bruyere Des Esprits forts* . . . A *Letter* to a *Deist*, written by the Learned Author of the *Snake in the Grass*: The *Article Christianity* in the Third Volume of *Morery's Dictionary*. These are all perus'd in a few Hours. And when this is done, I persuade my self, they won't think it loss of time to consult *Grotius of the Truth of the Christian Religion*." (*Of Whoredom*, p. 147.)

[93] *Of Thought*, p. 90.

[94] *The New Organon*, Spedding, Ellis, and Heath edition, Bk. I, Aphorism 89.

theology with science. It is no exaggeration to observe that Collier could well have said, in the words of Joseph Glanvill: "I have no design against Science: my indeavour is to promote it."[95]

[95] *The Vanity of Dogmatizing,* New York, 1931, facsimile edition of text of 1661, *Dedicatory Epistle,* A₃.

II. PSYCHOLOGY: FROM SPIRITS TO CERTAINTIES

Methinks, if it might be, I would gladly understand the Formation of a Soul, run it up to its *Punctum Saliens,* and see
it beat the first *conscious* Pulse. These *Thoughts!* whence do
they arise? What Stuff are they made of? And what Vigour
is it that gives them such an Instantaneous Production?
They are conceived in full Maturity, and step into Perfection
at first. They scorn the Gradations of Bodies, and the heavy
Successions of *Motion.*[1]

COLLIER, by his rejection of Platonic pre-existence and
epicurean atomism, and acceptance instead of Pauline
psychology, gained at once two important bases for his
concept of the soul—the divine birth of spirit and, through resurrection, its re-birth. Other questions he doubtless would have
satisfied by metaphysical postulates had his intellectual curiosity
been less wide and his mind of less scientific turn. Here, in an
attempt to characterize the temper of his thought, there irresistibly
arises his striking similarity to Joseph Glanvill: they have in common a zest for exploration, a delight in toying with bizarre notions,
a basic sympathy with Cartesianism, and yet the strength to reject
it when necessary. Both men were writing of matters supremely
interesting to their contemporaries; and Glanvill, as a Fellow of
the Royal Society, represented an attitude with which no literary
historian has ever bothered to credit Collier. But it is none the less
true that an almost identical approach is obvious in sections of *The
Vanity of Dogmatizing* and in that dialogue which affords the best
introduction to Collier's scheme of psychology, *A Thought.* In this
piece Lucretianus the atomist expounds the theory that thought
originates in the mechanism of the body; Hylarchus (the author's
mouthpiece) argues for immateriality of soul as distinct from
matter, and offers the Cartesian certainty, *cogito, ergo sum:*

[1] Hylarchus, in *A Thought,* p. 88.

Without *Thinking,* we can have no Sense of *Being*; and with it, we are we cannot tell what. So that the same Faculty seems to make us acquainted with, and Strangers to our selves.[2]

His opponent scoffs at such difficulty:

Thinking every Body knows is the Work of the *Brain*: That is the Forge in which all the Speculations of the Understanding, and the Appetites of the *Will,* are hammer'd out.[3]

And he launches upon a detailed explanation of the origin of ideas in nerves, animal spirits, and brain-fibres. Hylarchus then refutes this fantastic scheme and successfully defends his assertion that any mechanical solution of thought is impossible inasmuch as "both the *Fibres,* and *Spirits,* are *Material*" and matter cannot possess sensibility.

You may as well expect that two Bowls should grow sensible by *Rubbing* as that the Rencounter of any *Bodies,* should awaken them into *Perception* and *Reasoning.* The whole Force of *Mechanism,* consists in *Matter* and *Motion. Matter* is nothing but *Extention,* that is, Length, Breadth, and Depth. And *Motion* implies no more than a Change of Situation in the Parts of *Matter.* Now these two Ingredients, though never so well mix'd, will not rise into the Composition of a Spirit. *Thoughts,* and *Dimensions,* are the most incompatible, unresembling Things in Nature. To make the first out of the later, is a harder Metamorphosis than any is in *Ovid.* Who ever heard of an Ounce of Pain, and an Inch of Desire, or an Ell of Contemplation. . . . all your Transmutations can never hunt a Body out of *Extension.* You may divide, or consolidate; alter the Superficies, the Bulk, or Place; quicken the Motion, or interrupt the Quiet; but after all 'twill have Longitude, Latitude, and Profundity, in spight of Fate.[4]

Hylarchus concludes that "because *Extension* and *Cogitation* are unallied in the Ideas, and this later is not implied in the Notion of *Matter*," the faculty of thought cannot belong to what is material.

[2] *A Thought,* p. 73.
[3] *Ibid.*
[4] *Ibid.,* pp. 77, 78, 79.

Add to the three dimensions "what Dose of *Motion* you please, and then you have raised the whole *Posse* of Mechanism. And when you have disciplined it in all Postures, and Figures, 'twill be Matter and Motion still."[5] One may better suppose that "a Mouse may produce an Elephant, than that *Matter* and *Motion* should propogate out of their own Species," for "these Two Principles fall vastly short of the Notion of *Consciousness*; and are no more like *Perception,* than Colours resemble Sound."[6] Reasoning, then, proceeds from "an immaterial substance"; body and soul are quite distinct; since spirit has not extension it has no parts and is indivisible and immortal. Lucretianus complains that by such a scheme "all Communication between Soul and Body is cut off"; that "the Soul might have the same compass of *Sentiment* and *Perception,* and do every jot as well, if it were united to a Clod."[7] The difficulty is similarly put by Glanvill;[8] but whereas Glanvill, for all his speculation, tends to get not too far away from his admired Descartes, Collier, faced with the necessity either to declare a solution or to abandon the problem of the disjoined soul and body as inexplicable, chooses, as we have seen, to embrace the theory of occasionalism.[9] His spokesman concludes:

> I believe this mysterious Correspondence depends on the Laws of the Union; which by Sovereign Appointment are order'd to consist in a certain Reciprocation of *Thoughts* and *Motions,* and so *vice versa.*

Lucretianus asks, more explicitly,

> You mean, when I would move my finger, God directs the Organ for such a performance: And on the other hand, gives

[5] *A Thought,* p. 81.

[6] *Ibid.*

[7] *Ibid.,* p. 88.

[8] In a passage marvelling that "we are a Compound of beings distant in extreams" Glanvill exclaims: "But how the purer Spirit is united to this clod, is a knot too hard for fallen Humanity to unty. . . . How should a thought be united to a marble-statue, or a sun-beam to a lump of clay! The freezing of the words in the air in the northern climes, is as conceivable, as this strange union." *The Vanity of Dogmatizing,* p. 20. Mr. Basil Willey quotes this in his *The Seventeenth Century Background.*

[9] Collier never mentions Arnold Geulincx, and once only does he quote Malebranche.

me Ideas suitable to the Presence of sensible Objects, and
to the State of the *Union.*

Assent is given:

> Right. . . . 'Tis probable the Divine Oeconomy has setled
> such an interchangeable Train of *Thoughts,* and *Motions,*
> between Soul and Body, that as soon as the occasional Hints
> spring out, the other will as constantly follow, as if they were
> produced by the most immediate *Causality.*[10]

Resemblance of Collier's ideas to those of Malebranche does not
stop with this blanket solution; further similarity is seen in treatment of more particular problems of causality. For example, in the
Seventh of the *Metaphysical Dialogues* Malebranche declares that
experience teaches that pain results from a pin-prick, but not that
the prick acts on the mind; the latter, his sceptical opponent avers,
is possible because of the "conjunction" of body and mind. This
Malebranche refutes on the ground that the body is matter:

> Your body, then, cannot act *immediately* upon your mind.
> Thus, if your finger be pricked by a pin, though your brain
> be disturbed by its action, neither the one nor the other can
> act upon your soul or cause it to feel pain; for neither the one
> nor the other can act immediately upon the mind, since your
> brain and your finger are nothing but matter.

When the soul "suffers pain despite itself" the pain must come from
some external cause. And that cause is God, acting "in consequence
of the general laws of the conjunction of body and soul."[11] Collier
similarly explains the origin of pain:

> Since *Pain* is not the necessary result of *Matter* and *Motion*
> . . . we may from hence infer,
>   1st, That we may be reach'd by *Pain,* tho' we were noth-
> ing but pure Spirit: For since *Corporeity* can never be refined
> to *Thought,* nor *Atomes* made capable of *Consciousness,*
> 'twill follow that the *Soul,* tho' never so much disengag'd,
> and uncompounded, may be as liable to dolorous *Sensations,*
> as if she had the Body of a Giant about her. Thus we may be
> hungry without a *Stomach,* rack'd without Limbs, and

[10] *A Thought,* pp. 83-7.
[11] *Metaphysical Dialogues,* pp. 180, 181.

stabb'd without either the *Instruments* or the *Organs* of
Pain: In short, all those troublesome *Perceptions* which now
seize us through our *Senses,* may as intelligibly affect us
without them; since the whole Process and Force of the
Execution depends solely on the Pleasure of the *First
Cause.* For to speak plainly, *Matter* and *Motion* are but bare
Lookers on, the *Sentiments* both of *Pain,* and *Satisfaction,*
being immediately bestow'd by God himself.

2dly, If it be demanded whether a Thought can rack a
Man as much as bodily Pain, it may be answered in the
affirmative: For God who is perfectly Master of the *Creature,* can easily strike without the Intervention of *Matter.*
Omnipotence needs no Assistance either to punish or to
please. Besides, *Body* and *Spirit* are so very foreign, and
unresembling, that they can neither act nor suffer recip-
rocally, or entertain any Commerce with each other, by
virtue of their respective Qualities and Nature.[12]

The psychology of Collier is seen to be basically metaphysical.
But he and his contemporaries recognized, and in their attempt to
understand the workings of the human mind went far towards
utilizing, a principle thus expressed by Professor Max Dessoir:
while the "facts of consciousness do not themselves permit of
measurement," "if they are to be scientifically understood . . .
they must be referred to stimuli, and especially to the physiological
system. A parallelism between mental and bodily processes cannot
be proved metaphysically, but is an hypothesis indispensable to
psychology."[13] Study of mind and of body had always been more
or less allied, but the fact that this interdependence had gained in
notice by the seventeenth century can be ascribed to more elements
than the growing knowledge of Cartesianism in England. The shift
away from medieval scholasticism tended to focus emphasis upon
man himself rather than on far-flung astronomical schemes; there
was a corollary development of curiosity in the mechanism of the
body, for the Vesalian break with traditional Galenic physiology
and Harvey's observations had made their mark. Those who
accepted Harvey's conclusions naturally began to divest of meta-

---

[12] *A Moral Essay upon Pain,* pp. 22, 23.
[13] Max Dessoir, *Outlines of the History of Psychology,* New York, 1912, p. 99.

physical trappings their theories of the body and to reduce them instead to the more tangible level of mechanistic processes. But it is to Descartes that we here must turn as a key figure.[14]

In the face of Harvey's disclosures concerning blood-circulation, Descartes holds to a scheme of blood vapours that pass through arteries into brain-ventricles and extend to the seat of the soul, the pineal gland, there to cause perceptions or, on more violent collision, emotions. He adopts the current belief in animal spirits which effect bodily action; gaseous and distilled from the blood, these are "nothing but material bodies . . . of extreme minuteness" that "move very quickly like the particles of the flame which issues from a torch."[15] This popular misconception Collier ridicules by having his materialist defend it:

> The *Brain* has a great many small *Fibres,* or Strings in its Texture; which according to the different Strokes they receive from the *Animal Spirits,* awaken a correspondent Idea, and give us those Notices of Things which we call *Thoughts.* . . . Nerves, which are their Origin in the *Brain,* are branched out into a great many fine Subdivisions, and spread upon all the Surface of the Body, They are the Channels in which the Animal Spirits move: So that as soon as any foreign Object presses upon the Sense, those *Spirits* which are posted upon the Out-guards, immediately take the Alarm, and scower off to the *Brain,* which is the Head-Quarters, or *Office* of *Intelligence,* and there they make their Report of what has happen'd.[16]

[14] The chief contributions of Descartes to physiological psychology are contained in *The Passions of the Soul,* published in 1649, and in the *Traité de l'Homme,* 1662. Of the latter Franklin Fearing remarks that it is "probably the first attempt to present systematically a coherent description of bodily responses in terms of actual—or hypothetical—neuro-muscular structures." (*Reflex Action, A Study in the History of Physiological Psychology,* Baltimore, 1930, p. 19.)

[15] *The Passions of the Soul,* Article X, *Works,* Vol. I, p. 336. This concept is especially utilized in Elizabethan literature, in which the spirits are a highly attenuated and lively form of matter, acting as the go-between for man's spiritual part, rational soul, and body. *Cf.* pp. 317, 318, Edward Dowden's "Elizabethan Psychology," in *Essays Modern and Elizabethan,* London, 1910; also Ruth L. Anderson's *Elizabethan Psychology and Shakespeare's Plays. Humanistic Studies, Univ. of Iowa,* Vol. III, No. 4, 15 March, 1927.

[16] *A Thought,* pp. 73, 74.

Hylarchus, hearing that when the brain-fibres are struck they are "bent" and the object impressed upon the mind, satirically adds, "But I remember, some say the *Spirits* Tilt so violently, that they make Holes where they strike; which are no sooner open, but the *Ideas* run into them as fast as may be. And after they have lain there a little while, grow as drowsy as Dormice, unless they are rowsed by a new Summons." Since animal spirits are a "kind of little Pellets, wrought off the fine Parts of the Blood," and there-fore material, they could be "as Sleek and well Timber'd, as those *Atoms Epicurus* made his *Soul* of" and yet not create thought. Several difficulties stand in the way of such a theory—one of them the impossibility of singleness of representation:

> Supposing a Bird sits before me; these *Mercuries* imme-diately run up to the Center of *Sensation,* to give an Account of what is arrived. Now in doing this, either every single *Animal Spirit* must convey a whole *Representation,* which would multiply the Object, if not overload the Carrier; or else they must divide the Image among them, and so lug off every one his Share. . . . But then, when they have taken the Object to Pieces, how they will set it together again, is hard to imagine. For they cannot strike all upon one Point; and if they could, they would jumble the Proportions, and run the Object all on heaps; where the latter Impression would go near to deface the former. But if they impinge upon different Parts, and make every Part sensible with the Stroke; 'Tis true then they have it among them, but which way the whole should emerge, is still incomprehensible. For suppose the Image was painted in Order, without any Dislo-cation, vacant Intervals, or Interloping; yet the Parts of the *Fibres* being distinct, and impregnated by distinct Spirits, they can account no farther than their Share of Motion reaches. And therefore how they should club their particular Informations into a common Idea, is inconceivable.[17]

Another practical obstacle lies in the inevitable "counter-motions" which would result: "if any of the returning *Spirits* should happen to fall foul upon others which are *outward Bound,* (which is not unlikely) these Countermotions would overset them, or occasion a

---

[17] *A Thought,* pp. 75, 76.

later Arrival; either of which Accidents would maim the Image, and make it imperfect." Glanvill, pursuing a similar line of speculation, voices the same objection: "this motion would be quickly deadned even to an utter cessation, by *counter-motions*; and we should not remember any thing, but till the next impression. Much less can this *Principle* give an account, how such an abundance of *motions* should orderly succeed one another. . . . One motion would cross and destroy another; all would be clashing and discord. . . ."[18] Collier points out that if such difficulties lie in the way of sensation they would be the greater in the case of imagination, with "no external Impressions to begin the *Motion*."

Thus again Collier takes the stand of Malebranche in rejecting the theory that ideas originate in a mechanical source, and that animal spirits act as a causal link between body and soul; he ignores the Cartesian location of the pineal gland as the seat of the soul, and makes no more of an attempt to localize the soul than does Malebranche. The concept that the brain gives rise to motion is identical with renaissance theory; that it differs in phraseology is seen in Collier's use of the word *bent* to describe the action of *strokes* upon brain-fibres. Malebranche employs the term similarly: when the movement of spirits ceases "the Imagination remains polluted by the Impressions which they have made on the Brain, whose Fibres have been bent or broken by the violence of the Spirits which they have put in Motion."[19] Like usage occurs in Glanvill and other contemporaries.

As Collier reflects now and again certain elements of the older psychology of humours and spirits he at one time employs the terminology in all seriousness; at another, it seems that he but enriches his vocabulary with figurative language in the same way that modern diction savours of phrases picturesquely connotative of a once literal meaning. In his treatment of emotions we see his dependence upon this fiction which still colours our speech. In the Elizabethan view any operation of appetite is motion; responses that lightly disturb physical well-being are affections; responses that excite violently are passions. These concern thought-processes,

[18] *The Vanity of Dogmatizing*, pp. 38, 39.
[19] *A Treatise of Morality*, p. 123.

hence are maladies of the soul that corrupt judgement.[20] The humours are altered, and when the imagination has judged an impression, spirits pass from brain to heart to announce the object; by contraction or expansion of the heart the appetite either calls in or disperses the humours and spirits.[21] To this stimulus the entire body responds. Thus moderate joy brings health because a store of spirits is concocted and dispersed; vehement feeling may fatally overheat and swell the heart; and sorrow may shrink it.

Descartes defines "passions of the soul" as "the perceptions, feelings or emotions of the soul which we relate specially to it, and which are caused, maintained, and fortified by some movement of the spirits."[22] And to Malebranche passion means an agitation in the soul occasioned by a flow of animal spirits: "the Blood is impregnated . . . with Particles fit to raise such a fermentation as may produce abundance of Spirits agreeable to the nature of those Passions."[23] He defines passions as:

> Those Motions of the Soul which accompany that of the Spirits and the Blood, and produce in the Body, by the Mechanical Frame and Constitution of it, all the dispositions necessary to support and keep up the Cause from whence they arise. At the sight of any Object which moves the Soul . . . the Animal Spirits which come from the Brain to the other parts of the Body, divide themselves into two Branches or Courses.[24]

Collier grants that "*sensations* and *passions* seem to depend upon a particular Set of Motions";[25] that the "Powers of *Sensation* are

[20] *Cf.* Anderson, *Elizabethan Psychology*, p. 69.

[21] *Ibid.*, p. 80.

[22] *The Passions of the Soul*, p. 344. Of this definition Professor Brett says: "There are, therefore, psychophysical events, and the definition is so far from being revolutionary that it may be regarded as giving, in concise terms, what had been implied in every ancient or mediaeval view, namely that emotions belong neither to pure reason nor to mere matter. But the older doctrines were content to be negative and emphasize the antithesis between feeling and pure reason; the new doctrine was marked by new principles of classification and description." (*A History of Psychology*, II, 1921, p. 237.) *Cf.* subsequent discussion on stoicism for connexion between Descartes and stoic ideas.

[23] *A Treatise of Morality*, p. 123.

[24] *Ibid.*, p. 120.

[25] *A Thought*, p. 86.

contracted or enlarged . . . according to the Temper of the *Body*."[26] But he is mindful that these "circumstances are no more than occasional Causes of this Variety"[27]—another reflection of his denial of mutual agency between spirit and matter, and of his belief instead in the causality of supernatural will. The term "affections" he uses to mean "the Effects which may result from all the possible Combinations of *Matter,* and Motion."[28] What all the possible affections are he does not know, nor does he need to, he avers, to be sure that thought is non-material in origin; yet he, like many scientists of his age, still clung enough to animal spirits to attribute to them passional violence.

The gamut of emotional experience is critically examined by Collier for both psychological and physiological reactions. Despair he characterizes as "an uneasy passion" that "preys upon the *Vitals,* like *Prometheus's Vultur*; and eats out the Heart of all other Satisfactions";[29] it argues partially for a "defect of spirits," but he shrewdly labels it the result of fear, laziness, and impatience; contrarily, hope is "furnished with light and heat." Desire "is a conscious emptiness, an unsatisfied capacity" that he explains Platonically: desire arises from a painful lack and is so combined with an idea of the complementary state that volition becomes active. Since our wishes are consequent to the impotence and indigence of human nature they "awaken our Industry, and make us pursue our Advantage."[30] But man's failure to gain a wish "puts his Fancy into a Feavour; it drinks up his Blood, and fires his Spirits."[31] Fear, one of the strongest of passions, is rooted in the instinct of self-preservation; envy and ambition are despicable; surprise is a passion of neutral quality.

Collier's concept of anger shows close relationship to a traditional attitude.[32] This emotion he characterizes as the most forceful

26 *Ibid.,* p. 85.
27 *Ibid.*
28 *Ibid.,* p. 79.
29 *Against Despair,* p. 120.
30 *Of Eagerness of Desire,* p. 39.
31 *Ibid.,* p. 42.
32 Appetite to the Elizabethan psychologist was either intellective or sensitive (the one possessed by man alone, the other by man and beast) ; the latter was given to two inclinations—the concupiscible and irascible. Should the first gener-

one, and as arising from the instinct of self-preservation. Other passions develop more gradually, they "usually improve under Thought," and "their Objects must be made familiar to the Mind by frequent Representation before they grow to any considerable Obstinacy." But anger "is often perceiv'd to be in its full Strength, when first born. 'Tis a Tempest at the first Blast, and like Gunpowder discharges its Fury all together."[33] Physiologically, it "commands great Numbers of the animal Spirits to press in to its Assistance, which would never obey the Summons of cool and sedate Reason"; this violence of action results in "an unusual commotion of the Blood and Spirits." Failure to exercise reason keeps "our bodies almost always in an Uproar" for "whenever Occasions of Dislike return, it will not then be in the Power of the Mind to command the Motions of the Body, but the Blood will immediately boil up, and the whole Frame of Nature within us will be put into a Combustion."[34] Thus to Collier anger, or choler, is the old irascible appetite that the Elizabethans had considered the direct result of one humour. Charron observes that anger strongly, more visibly than other emotions, alters the human temper and frame. His description of such change is matched by one of Collier's:

> What wild Discomposure it causes in those who are under its Power, is easy to observe. What a furious and ill-natur'd Air does it paint the Face with? The Eyes are flaming out in Revenge; the Voice loud and boisterous, like a Storm; the Joints tremble by the tumultuous Motion of the Spirits; and when the Course of Nature is thus set on Fire, the tongue, that unruly Member, will be sure to put in for its Share of Extravagancy, and speak proud and foolish things.[35]

ate insufficient energy the irascible unites with it to give force to the soul. Accordingly affections resultant from such conjunction prove more dangerous than those springing from concupiscence alone. *Cf.* Anderson, pp. 95, 96, and Dowden.

[33] *Sermon VI*, p. 192.

[34] *Ibid.*; *cf.* pp. 170, 171, 200.

[35] Pierre Charron writes of the effects of anger: "Some of these Changes and Symptoms, are outward and apparent: Redness and Distortions of the Face, Fieryness of the Eyes, a wild and enraged Look, Deafness and Insensibility in the Ears, Foaming at the Mouth, Palpitation of the Heart; Quickness and Unevenness of Pulse, Swelling and Bursting Fullness of the Veins, Stam-

Anger, which is designed to support reason, supply courage, and lend intuitive power, usually overrides reason; this yielding to passion Collier deplores as an almost universal trait of human nature: he has too often observed emotional states "boil up the Blood to a Fever." But he believes that when "the Passions are not violent, we may check or quicken, change or extinguish the operation as we please."[36] Descartes had declared that no soul is so feeble as not to gain mastery over all passions if they are well trained.[37] Collier's admonition to "form our Desires in cool Blood"[38] remains quaint but, in the light of physiological comment, not paradoxical. He here is but putting in a phrase the warning that Descartes, at the end of his *Passions of the Soul*, offers against emotional excesses.[39]

At the same time that Collier asserts his belief in occasionalism he observes in more practical vein that contrary mental and physical states interact: the spirit strives to subdue the flesh, appetites war against reason, emotions destroy spiritual calm. Obviously an interplay of forces exists to a great degree. Collier's talk of this reality is as flavoured with traditional phrases of the older psychology as is the parlance of Burton. The humours, for example, not only cause illness; "unless we are careful, our Belief will have a complexional Tincture; bend toward the Passions, and follow the Bias of the Body." A man "of Melancholick Temper" will disturb his "imagination with unreasonable Fears concerning

mering in the Tongue, Gnashing and Setting of the Teeth, Loudness and Hoarseness in the Voice, The Speech thick and indistinct; . . . The whole Body is set on Fire, and in a perfect Fever." (*Of Wisdom*, London, 1697, Bk. I, p. 208.) The passage taken from Collier occurs in *Sermon VI*, pp. 199, 200.

[36] *A Thought*, p. 77.

[37] *Passions of the Soul*, Part I, pp. 355, 356.

[38] *Of Honesty*, p. 60.

[39] Descartes advises: ". . . when we feel our blood to be thus agitated, we should be warned of the fact, and recollect that all that presents itself before the imagination tends to delude the soul and causes the reasons which serve to urge it to accomplish the object of its passion to appear much stronger than they are, and those which serve to dissuade it to be much weaker. And when the passions urge us only toward things the execution of which necessitates some delay, we ought to abstain from pronouncing any judgment on the spot, and to divert ourselves by other thought until time and rest shall have entirely calmed the emotion which is in the blood." (Part I, p. 426.)

God Almighty" and "if he gives Way to the Spleen" may be "mis-led to the Doctrines of Superstition"; but "another of a bolder, and more sanguine Constitution" will presume upon "God's Good-ness, and carry the Notion of his Mercy too far. And if his Books, or his Company happen to be Ill, he'll be disposed to reform his *Creed* to his Humour, and reconcile it to Complexion. . . ."[40] Similarly illness may "so spoil the temper of the Blood and the Spirits" as to "impair Judgment and dull the Senses, which should give us Intelligence."[41] Ingenuity consists in the heat of the blood and the "plenty and fineness of the spirits"; courage likewise rises from heat, but dies when the spirits cool: an army captain hears a drum beat, his blood "charges in his Veins, his Spirits jump like Gunpowder, and seem impatient to attack the Enemy."[42] In gaming the spirits are virtually stirred up into a "storm," a "train" of them takes fire, they kindle and flash—and the passions are rampant.[43] Easy thoughts and an even temper "work kindly upon the Spirits, and throw Balsam into the Blood";[44] but guilt "flats" the senses. The spleen may affect the brain, though perhaps with no sensible impression elsewhere, and promote variable temper and a melan-choly that drives its victims into excesses so that "they become lost in a mist"—perhaps to be relieved "only by physick."[45]

In view of Collier's idea of the causality of pain he at least risks inconsistency in declaring that the will is not absolute in its control of the physical and that it is futile to resolve to feel no pain. That sensation he defines as "an unacceptable Notice arising from some

[40] *Of the Resurrection*, pp. 411, 412.

[41] Collier draws this idea from Pascal, concerning his reliance upon whom more is subsequently said.

[42] *Of Musick*, p. 21.

[43] *Cf. Upon Gaming.* This psychological reaction gamesters know, and use to their advantage: watching the current of passions, they observe when a man's head "grows misty" and "spleen overcasts his understanding," for "playing deep sets the spirits on float, strikes mud strongly into the Face, and discovers a Man's Weakness very remarkably."

[44] *Cf. Of Peace*, p. 346.

[45] *Cf. Of the Spleen.* Fear and anxiety, too, "darken the understanding, strike a damp upon the Heart, and clog the Spirits" and their victims turn lifeless and despondent. (*Of Solitude*, p. 356.) Such an inward malignity Collier has in mind when he writes that it "shoots into the Veins and poysons the Constitution." (*Of Peace*, p. 355.)

Disorder in the Body" and comprehended by the mind "when there's a stop upon the Spirits, when the *Parts* don't keep their *Ranks.* . . ."[46] Pain proves an impediment in that the mind is discomposed, the "Crasis of the Blood, or the Texture of the Brain is alter'd," the memory suffers, "the Head grows Muddy; the Imagination rambles, and the reasoning Faculty is impair'd."[47] On the other hand, the fact that a single thought can set the blood on fire, the spirits in action, Collier takes as evidence that generally "the Mind has a great Command over the Body; that it can rouze, or lay it asleep at Pleasure; that *Motion* is either begun or stopp'd, check'd, or reinforc'd, according as the Will directs" and as Reason dictates.[48] At any rate, the passive alliance of the soul with the body, and its liability to sensation that causes a sympathetic warding-off of physical decay, fit neatly into the scheme of divine causality. But, before thinking conclusively that here we find the interactionism of Descartes and Malebranche, it is well to be mindful that the same idea had existed elsewhere than in French thought. We need cite only one example familiar to Collier: a favourite of his among the Church Fathers, Tertullian, who wrote:

> But the soul certainly sympathizes with the body, and shares in its pain, whenever it is injured by bruises, and wounds, and sores: the body, too, suffers with the soul, and is united with it (whenever it is afflicted with anxiety, distress, or love) in the loss of vigour which its companion sustains, whose shame and fear it satisfies by its own blushes and paleness.[49]

[46] *A Moral Essay upon Pain,* p. 1.

[47] *Of the Resurrection,* p. 413.

[48] *Of Power,* p. 72. *Cf.* also *Sermons,* p. 383, and *Of Religious Temper,* p. 114. Apropos of this over-balance of flesh and blood, Collier in his dialogue *Of the Resurrection* paints the ideal state, attainable only "if Reason was more lively and enterprizing." He wishes that we "were quick enough to discover without being pricked forward by Passion" and that "the Thinking Part could make a Stand upon the *Mechanism,* and suffer nothing by the Heat of the Blood, and the Hurry of the Spirits." Then "we might raise, and check, and counter-change the Passions, at the beck of Thought"; with reason flourishing we could even enjoy strong delights without the usual attending violence.

[49] From Tertullian's *Treatise on the Soul,* in *The Classical Psychologists,* compiled by Benjamin Rand, Boston, 1912, p. 118. Collier's use of the idea may of course be largely ascribed to the French philosophers; it is to be found as well in the *City of God* of St. Augustine, whose writings Collier frequently cites.

Such sympathetic "blushes and paleness" suggest another traditional idea that with renaissance writers had been a stock motif
and in Collier's mind became a problem of the moot "causality."
His recommendation to study the face to determine emotions is
but a modification of the Platonic concept that the body mirrors
the soul, and that there is correspondence between external beauty
and virtue. "The Countenance seems designed not only for Ornament, but Information. The Passions there displayed . . . help to
let one man into the Sentiments and Affections of another."[50] Elsewhere he says, "Sometimes a Consciousness of Worth; a Nobleness
and Elevation of Mind; together with Fineness of Constitution,
gives Lustre and Dignity to the Aspect; and makes the Soul . . .
shine through the Body." Here "the Passions ebb and flow . . .
and are much better distinguished in their Progress, than the
change of the Air in a *Weather-Glass*."[51] Why, asks Collier, curiously, is this variety of change confined to one part of the body?
"What is the Reason a Man's *Arm* won't smile and frown, and
do all the intellectual Postures of the Countenance?"[52] The reason
is that God designed the face to be "uncloath'd" and has there
"fix'd the Seat and Visibility of the Passions." Still, "to metamor-
phose the *Blood* and *Spirits* thus *extempore,* is not a little strange.
It argues an amazing Fineness and Curiosity in the *Parts*; . . .
What can be more significant than the suddain Flushing and confusion of a Blush, than the Sparklings of Rage, and the Lightning
of a Smile? The Soul is as it were visible upon these Occasions."[53]
This flashing out of the soul like "a *Glory* upon the Countenance"
suggests an inner sun that shoots out rays with great vigour, a

[50] *Of the Aspect,* p. 113.
[51] *Ibid.,* p. 116.
[52] "The *Arm*," he continues, "seems to have a finer skin than the Face: 'Tis
less exposed to the weather; the Veins are larger, and more visible, and the
Pulse beats stronger. In short, If *Matter* and *Motion* would do the Business, the
Arm, excepting the Eye, seems to have the Advantage, and might put in for the
Index and Interpreter of the Mind. And yet we see 'tis strangely uniform and
unaffected upon every Accident and Turn of Thought; and Nothing but a Blow,
or a Pinch, can make it change Colour." (*Of the Aspect,* pp. 114, 115.)
[53] *Of the Aspect,* pp. 115, 116.

symbol of the divine essence within man.[54] The aspect is as obsequious to the mind as is the dial to the sun; sentiments are "drawn by the *Life* within." The language of the face is universal and comprehensive: " 'tis the Shorthand of the Mind." But Collier admits the rules of physiognomy to fail in attempting to determine thus upon virtue. Singularities of features may lend the innocent the semblance of knaves, and knaves, that of honesty. Too much of a realist not to admit that a man may "look a Lye, as well as speak one,"[55] he yet maintains, quoting Malebranche, that "when the Mind is thoroughly tinctured, the Face will hold the same Colour," and the key lies in the recognition that "Peoples Opinions of themselves, are commonly legible in their Countenances."[56]

If Collier's psychology on the one hand carries over certain traditional notions, on another it shows evidence of his acceptance of some ideas then foremost in scientific speculation. Physiologically, his interest must have led him into anatomical details; he exhibits, for example, surprising accuracy in tracing the blood stream over the body,[57] and he rightly conceives of the heart as a muscle and its valves as "sluices." "We may observe," he writes, "the *Valves* of this Muscle . . . secure the Blood from returning the wrong way. Like Sluices they open for Use, and shut against Inconvenience."[58] His inclusion of animal spirits is understandable

[54] This recalls Locke's figure, similarly used, of a "candle that is set up in us, [and] shines bright enough for all our purposes." (*Essay concerning Human Understanding*, Introduction.)

[55] *Of Lying*, p. 176. Bacon's attitude is suggested by this idea of human proneness to dissimulate; and Cicero writes of one's inability to measure honesty by facial expression.

[56] *Of Confidence*, p. 96.

[57] "What can be more admirable and commodious," asks Collier, "than the Circulation of the Blood? This vital Liquor is discharg'd from the Heart as from an Engine, and convey'd to the extreme Parts; Thus Warmth and Motion is spread thro' the Body, and the Functions of Life kept up. And when the Blood has gone the length of the Arteries, and begins to grow cool and disabled, 'tis receiv'd in the Capillary Veins, and brought back to the Heart and Lungs: From hence, after a recruit of Speed and Spirits, 'tis thrown out into the Arteries for the Purposes above-mention'd." (*Of Goodness*, p. 15.)

[58] *Of Goodness*, p. 15. Descartes, too, compares heart-cavities to sluices. (*Passions of the Soul*, p. 334.) His saying that the spirits are excited by the beat of the heart amounts to the same thing as Collier's "recruit of speed."

in view of their late rejection even among physiologists. Harvey's own position is somewhat uncertain on this point. He was unable to find "spirits" anywhere, and he several times breaks out in exasperation at the impossibility of their existence. Yet we run across such a passage as this—one which, of course, is not representative of his avowed position:

> Spiritous blood is none the less blood, as no-one denies that the blood, even that which flows in the veins, is filled with spirits. Even if the blood in the arteries is very gorged with spirits, it is still believable that these spirits are as inseparable from the blood as those in the veins. The blood and spirits comprise a single fluid (as whey and cream in milk, or heat in hot water) with which the arteries are filled, and for the distributing of which from the heart the arteries exist.[59]

Harvey's theory, which appeared in 1628, was not generally accepted for some time, and throughout the century animal spirits rather embarrassingly remained a factor somehow to be reckoned with. Other interest that Collier evinces is in the "stupendious Operations" of nutrition and digestion; and frequently he marks the constant change that goes on in the body,[60] and in the "furniture of the head." In *A Thought* Hylarchus, declaring the brain an "odd sort of Bog for *Fancy* to paddle in," says, "When I see people tread sense out of mud, as they do eels, then I may be inclined to believe that brains and reasoning are of kin."[61] Glanvill similarly discounts the physiological origin of thought: the brain "is of such clammy consistence, that it can no more retain it then a *Quagmire*."[62] Elsewhere he observes of animal spirits in the brain that "the making of one hole in the yeelding *mud*, defaces the print of

[59] Harvey's *Anatomical Study of the Movement of the Heart and Blood*, translated by Chauncey D. Leake, Baltimore, 1931, p. 12.

[60] Hobbes likewise says that "the constitution of a man's body is in constant mutation." Molesworth edition, 1839, Vol. III, pp. 40, 41.

[61] P. 73. Another time he speaks of "the fluid and pliable nature of the Brain." (*Sermon I*, p. 5.)

[62] *The Vanity of Dogmatizing*, p. 38.

another near it."[63] Remarks such as these suggest not only the current notion of the "muddy" consistency of the brain but, linked with speculation on the difficulty aroused by the counter-motions of spirits and their chance of collision, represent the writers' opinions upon the mechanics of memory.

As we work back to considering Collier's theory of knowledge it should be marked that while he virtually begins with the Cartesian certainty he does not literally say that "thinking equals being" but that "without Thinking, we can have no Sense of Being." Malebranche asserts that, because thought can be conceived of as existing independently of sense and volition, "Thought alone, is the essence of the soul, as extension alone is the essence of matter."[64] And thought originates in God. Thus, although Malebranche begins with this same principle of inner certainty, it is not for him as meaningful or as definitive of truth: one must add, not alone intuition itself, but as well an intuition of God; accordingly one can have no distinct idea of the existence of self, and our only reason for regarding as true any clear perception is based upon a vision of the reality of God. Once aware of this we realize the nature of cognition, and knowledge thus becomes pure perception or vision.[65] Collier comes to much the same conclusion as does Malebranche: we recognize the potentiality for knowledge, but that knowledge is actualized directly through God, not through any mediary cause. Intensely aware of the mystery of the soul and of human failure to penetrate that mystery, he yet can be definite in his ascription of spirit and mind to divine causality:

> The Mind is Heaven-Born, and comes immediately out of the Hands of God: So that to speak properly, we are nearer related to the Supreme Being, than to Father or Mother; *Nemo est tam pater,* says *Tertullian.* . . . And as the Soul is the immediate Product of the first Cause, so 'tis made in

---

[63] *Ibid.,* p. 35. This recalls a couplet from John Davies of Hereford:
  "Yet the moyst braine conceiuves more readily,
    But the drie braine retaines more steadily." (*Mirum in Modum*)
[64] *Recherche,* Vol. I, Bk. III, Part I, Chap. I, pp. 282, 283. Also quoted by Church, *A Study in the Philosophy of Malebranche,* London, 1931, p. 44.
[65] *Cf.* Church, *A Study in the Philosophy of Malebranche,* p. 259 ff.

his Likeness. Reason and Choice and Immortality, are images of the Divine Nature.[66]

Elsewhere, as we have already pointed out, Collier observes that the powers of the soul can be reduced to understanding and will; that understanding encompasses not material things alone but divine truths as well; that the will is free, stronger than reason, and impelled towards good.[67]

Chief among human faculties, declares Collier, stands reason,[68] which has as its function to govern thought and imagination and rule the appetitive part of man; and yet it is semi-dependent upon physical states. At this point Collier is associated with yet another French philosopher, and far more closely, in that he resorts to the "borrowing" so prevalent in the seventeenth century. The idea of the liability of reason to irritants Collier develops in his essay *Of the Weakness of Human Reason* which in structure and use of example he has drawn almost wholly from Pascal's chapter on the "Weakness of Man, and Uncertainty of his Natural Understanding."[69] One pair of citations will illustrate the closeness of Collier's rendering. Pascal writes:

> Set the greatest philosopher in the world upon a plank, even broader than the space he occupies in walking on plain ground, and, if there is a precipice below him, though reason convince him of his safety, his imagination will prevail; the very thought of it would make some perspire and turn pale. I will not relate all the effects of it. Who does not know that there are persons whom the sight of a cat or a rat, or the crushing of a bit of coal, will almost drive out of their senses.[70]

Collier slightly expands this:

> Another Instance of the Impotency of Reason, may be taken from the Prevalence of Fancy. For Example, Let a

[66] *Of Goodness,* p. 10.

[67] *Cf.* above in the discussion of metaphysics.

[68] *Cf.* Cicero in *De Finibus*: reason is the most exalted of faculties, and the soul of man is consummate in his rational power. (S. Parker's translation, London, 1702, p. 309.)

[69] *Thoughts,* Part I.

[70] *Ibid.,* p. 100.

Bridge, somewhat Broader than the space a Man usually takes up in walking, be laid over a Precipice, or deep River; desire some eminent Philosopher to take a Turn or Two upon it for Meditation sakes; I warrant you for all the Strength of his Notions, he begs your Pardon. For though he can demonstrate himself as safe as if he was upon a *Bowling Green*; yet he is so Ridden by his Imagination, that he dares not venture. And some are so struck, that the very Thought of such an Undertaking, will make them turn Pale, and fall a Sweating. . . . 'Tis well known, that the Sight of a Cat, or the scratching of a *Plate,* will discompose some People almost into an Agony; and throw their Reason quite off the Hinges.[71]

Other than the effects of illness, old age, and emotional states, climate may impair reason and disturb the imagination. "A Cloud is enough to overcast thought and good humour," which "rise and fall with the *Mercury* in the *Weather-Glass*"; some men can "scarcely talk *Sense,* unless the Sun shines out. Understanding requires a kind Climate, as well as Plants." Further, says Collier, "One may almost tell in what *Latitude,* Season, and Circumstances, a Book was writ. Generally speaking, *Northern* and *Southern* Wit differ almost as much as Fruits; by Consequence, Summer and Winter must have a proportionable Influence."[72] This recalls Milton's plaint of the English lack of sun that "ripens wits as well as fruits."[73]

Reflection of a contemporary attitude is to be found in Collier's idea of imagination: this he considers not a "higher" faculty but rather one that proceeds out of the connexions of the soul with the body and hence becomes associated with such sensuous operations as instinct; imagination is juxtaposed to reason in both function and end-results. The cool tone of the coming eighteenth-century prose is heard in his advice against eager pursuit of the fancy:

[71] *Of the Weakness of Human Reason,* pp. 236, 237.
[72] *Of the Spleen,* p. 35.
[73] *The History of Britain*; this lifelong opinion that the chill English climate was unfavourable to his muse he reflects again in his poem *Mansus* and elsewhere in his prose. *Cf. Reason of Church Government,* Preface to Bk. II. Malebranche likewise treats the matter of climate in his *Recherche.* For treatment by Elizabethan psychologists, *cf.* Anderson, *op. cit.,* Chap. III.

"Make much of your Imagination; for you'll scarcely ever Pattern it. 'Tis not possible to build up to the Model of the Brain: Nature does not Furnish so fast as we can Think."[74] And from the same essay *Of Eagerness of Desire,* "The Object is over-flourished by the Fondness of Imagination, which usually paints beyond the Life, and sticks in the outward Varnish, without having either Leisure or Capacity to Discover the Coarseness underneath."[75] To "genuine" pleasure that, founded in reality, "will stand the Test of Reason" he contrasts a "fantastick pleasure" that is a "kind of flushing of the Imagination, and kept up by a confus'd superficial way of Thinking."[76] The former only is "agreeable to the Powers of the Mind rightly constituted."[77] The same idea is found in John Smith: imagination is a faculty which obscures and dims a higher kind of perception:

> We cannot here see . . . *in speculo lucido;* here we can
> *see but in a glass,* and that *darkly* too. Our own imaginative
> powers, which are perpetually attending the highest acts of
> our souls, will be breathing a gross dew upon the pure glass
> of our understandings, and so sully and besmear it, that we
> cannot see the image of the Divinity sincerely in it.[78]

Descartes had likewise considered imagination a sensuous operation and limited it to arising only in the case of corporeal things. And Malebranche, who devotes all of the second book of his *Recherche* to a discussion of this faculty, censures the human tendency to be ruled by "sensation or imagination" rather than by reason or by pure thought.[79] This attitude is characteristic of other

[74] *Of Eagerness of Desire,* p. 41.
[75] *Ibid.*
[76] *Sermon X,* p. 339.
[77] *Ibid.*
[78] *Select Discourses,* p. 25. This passage is also quoted by Willey, *The Seventeenth Century Background,* p. 141.
[79] Malebranche comments that the mind (*esprit*) is "called sensibility or imagination whenever the body is the natural or occasional cause of one's thoughts"; mind is called "intellect whenever it itself is active or rather when God is active in us." The attitude here represented is in its essence not far removed from the conception of such earlier psychologists as La Primaudaye, John Davies of Hereford, Coeffeteau, Burton, and Phineas Fletcher, all of whom considered imagination, or fantasy, and common sense and memory as internal senses. Although there was among these writers much confusion as to

Cambridge Platonists, especially of Cudworth. Considered as one of the high points in the development of the function of imagination in art, this phase in its history offers possibilities not usually suspected of the metaphysical negativism of these intellectuals; but it is precisely here that we see the relatedness of Coleridge and sections of his *Biographia Literaria* to the Platonists.[80]

Belief in an exalted intuitive power, as held by Malebranche for example, does not in Collier's scheme account for the *inception* of knowledge; at this point he diverges from mystical interpretation and turns towards the new empiricism. Sense perception is of first importance. Although to him the operations of all the senses are "in some respect incomprehensible" he holds those of hearing and sight superior to the others. "*Taste* and *Touch* are . . . more narrow spirited" for they "engross an Object to themselves, and won't let the Company share with them."[81] But whatever their defects, or however distasteful if indulged to excess, the senses are indispensable in the learning process. In extreme youth

> we pronounce upon the Quality of Things, according to the
> Pleasure or Dislike they are receiv'd with by the Body. In

the function and points of location of these powers, they were apparently one in thinking imagination the faculty of continuing to handle the images collected through the rudimentary perception of "common sense." *Cf.* Anderson, *Elizabethan Psychology*, pp. 13-17.

[80] *Cf.* Willey's *The Seventeenth Century Background*, pp. 158, 159, for comment on this point.

[81] *Of Musick*, p. 20. Collier is very much interested in speculating about the sense of hearing. "The Manner of the Conveyance of Sounds," he writes, "is unintelligible. For what can be more strange, than that the rubbing of a little *Hair* and *Cat-gut* together should make such a mighty Alteration in a Man that sits at a Distance? But this Wonder of *Perception* is not peculiar to the *Ear*. . . ." Hearing "commands a Satisfaction at a greater Distance, strikes a finer Stroke, and makes a single Object divide it self without lessening. For Instance: A Man may see the Light of a Candle, and hear a Voice or Instrument, as well if there be Ten in the Room, as if he was there alone. The Stream of Sounds, though cut into several Rivulets, comes as full to the Ear as if it had but one Channel to feed." In the same essay *Of Musick* he amusingly considers whether "there may not be some *Counter-Sounds* which may give the Mind as high a Disgust, as the other can a Pleasure. . . . I believe 'tis possible to invent an *Instrument* that shall have a quite contrary *Effect* to those *Martial Ones* now in Use. An *Instrument* that shall sink the *Spirits*, and shake the *Nerves*, and curdle the *Blood*, and inspire *Despair*, and *Cowardice*, and *Consternation*, at a surprizing Rate" (pp. 23, 24).

the State of Childhood, smooth or rugged Perceptions, are the only Test of Good and Evil. . . . Matters are wholly referr'd to our Senses, for several Years at first; since we find them in Possession for deciding the Question, concerning Choice, or Aversion; . . . This pre-engages our Judgment, creates a Partiality, and makes the Business of Reason more difficult than it would be otherwise.[82]

Gradually, as understanding and reason develop, another type of perception enters into the process of gaining knowledge; here the term means not *sensory* perception, but *recognition,* or realization, of ideas. Like Cudworth, who in refuting the Hobbesian "mind is nothing but local motion" declared that perception itself must be accounted for, Collier asks:

For how can the Distinction of Substances be known, but by the different Properties and Operations which proceed from them; and which way can these be discovered, but by the distinct Notions, and *Sentiments,* we have of them?[83]

He is then asked, "You take the Differences of Ideas, for Demonstrations of Distinction in Things; will that hold?" To this he rejoins:

If clear and distinct *Perception,* is not the infallible *Mark* of Truth, 'tis impossible to know any Thing. For all Reasoning is at last resolved into Self-evident Principles: Now these Magisterial Propositions don't dispute for Belief, but demand it: They flash Conviction so powerfully that there is no resisting them, unless you will suppose our *Faculties* are false: And then it will be Madness to argue about any Thing.[84]

It is fairly obvious that it is to this "clear and distinct *Perception*" that Collier refers in speaking of revelation as a means of gaining knowledge. Thus he takes into account two steps in the process of learning: sensory perception, at first the only means of receiving ideas; and a later perception to be reached through reasoning, reflection, and intuition or revelation. Nowhere perhaps is Collier more personally representative of his century than in his declaration

[82] *Of the Resurrection,* p. 398.
[83] *A Thought,* p. 80.
[84] *Ibid.,* p. 81.

of faith in an inner certainty; it reveals rather conclusively his sure solution of the problem of external authority versus intuitive guidance; his "distinct Notions" and "Self-Evident Principles" that "flash Conviction" connote arrival—however different the process —at the same conclusion as do the "clear and distinct ideas" of Descartes, the "light of reason" of the Platonists, the "clear intuitive knowledge" of Locke. It is significant that from yet another viewpoint comes the similar conclusion of a contemporary scientist, Jan Swammerdam: "I believe we shall find it not unjust to dignify with the name of reason that faculty of our minds, by the assistance of which, we form clear and distinct notions of things. . . ."[85]

What concern Collier evinces for education is for the psychological development of the child, not the social aspect of the problem. He deplores the static mental condition during the physical growth of adolescence and the formation then of wrong impressions because "the Fibres are weak, and the Texture of the Brain unusually yielding."

> And over and above this Disadvantage, we have neither Judgment to discover, nor Strength to resist an unacceptable Object: And thus thro' our own Weakness, and the Indiscretions of those we happen to converse with, we are apt to be prepossess'd with odd Prejudices, and seiz'd with unaccountable Fears: Now these *Mormo's,* and Impositions sometimes engage the Fancy so far, and strike so deep into the Constitution, that the Reason for our whole Life finds it impossible to deal with them.[86]

It would be desirable, thinks Collier, to grow with a conscious, objective knowledge: "if we carry'd the Man and the Child about us at the same Time; if we had one Soul, little more than a Blank, without any Characters of Knowledge in it, and another, grown to its full Maturity in Judgment and Experience . . . the Folly . . . of the Infant Part" would be both instructive and interesting to

[85] Quoted by Fearing, *Reflex Action,* p. 52.

[86] *Of the Resurrection,* pp. 398, 399. The term *mormo,* meaning *terror* or *bugbear,* was used very rarely. John Smith, in his *Select Discourses* (1660), speaks of "frightful apparitions of ghosts and mormos." (*Of Superstition,* p. 37.)

the other.[87] He observes the variety of humours in children and advocates treatment according to the fineness of temper. Since *"Manners* are generally the Result of Education," through discipline, good example, and careful management any "Bias should be set right at first" and the mind "prepossess'd" to virtue. "This is the way to smooth the Passage to a happy Life; to reconcile Appetite to Reason, and make the Affections more manageable afterwards." Childhood is "the best time for Improvement":

> Now the Memory is strong, and the Body capable of Application, there's no need of Long Intervals of Refreshment . . . or waiting the Leisure of a weather-beaten Constitution. . . . As yet the Mind is not over-charg'd with *Cares,* the Power of *Interest* is not grown up, and the Baits of *Pleasure* hang somewhat out of sight. Now, if ever, the *Paper* is blank, the Scales even, and the Affections most indifferent.[88]

Collier warns against over-educating, or setting "Nature upon the Tenters." Health must be taken into account; without it, "the Measures for Education are broken, the Instruments of Thought are lost, and the Progress of Knowledge impracticable."[89] Montaigne had written, "Books are pleasant companions, but if by associating with them we end by losing gaiety and health, our best possessions, let us leave them."[90] Observing the tendency of parents to force offspring beyond their capacities and into a picked profession almost from the cradle, Collier urges that aptitudes of the

[87] Cicero wrote, too, that for some years we have no understanding of ourselves, that not until maturity do we learn of what our souls are made. In the first part of life we are "spiritless," "tender," and incapable of judging. He says that the mind is given *sensories,* whereby it is accommodated with perceptions, to work itself up to the use of its powers. (*De Finibus,* pp. 314, 328, 329.)

[88] *Of Infancy and Youth,* pp. 78, 79.

[89] *Ibid.,* p. 79.

[90] *The Essays,* Trechmann's translation, 1927, Vol. I, p. 243. Collier was impressed by the case of Pascal's over-driving himself and becoming ill through study—"As if 'twere honourable to fall a Sacrifice to *Sense,* and die for Love of the Muses!"

child be studied and his natural bent discovered before the decision is made—advice that still issues from modern quarters.[91]

With his plain implications of belief in a "blank soul," Collier obviously rejects the theory of innate ideas and instead accepts the mind as the *tabula rasa* so familiar in current writing. Descartes had held, but Malebranche rejected, the notion of innate ideas;[92] Glanvill remarks that "our initial age is like the melted wax to the prepared Seal, capable of any impression from the documents of our Teachers."[93] And Locke's characterization of the mind as "white paper, void of all characters, without any ideas" has become classical. He likewise believed ideas to rise from experience— directly out of sensation and also from reflection—or from intuition, or the "perception of self-evident truths":

> Such kind of truths the mind perceives at the first sight of the ideas together, by bare intuition . . . and this kind of knowledge is the clearest and most certain, that human frailty is capable of. This part of knowledge is irresistible, and like bright sunshine forces itself immediately to be perceived, as soon as ever the mind turns its view that way; and leaves no room for hesitation, doubt, or examination, but the mind is presently filled with the clear light of it. It is on this intuition that depends all the certainty and evidence of all our knowledge.[94]

Thus for Locke the *tabula rasa* by virtue of inherent intuitive power becomes the medium for establishing between reason and

[91] William Petty's *Advice* (1648), a letter on education, had insisted on the need to consider the natural dispositions of children and to follow "natural propensions." Much earlier, Roger Ascham, in his *Scholemaster* (written between 1563 and 1568), had recommended that the scholar's "natural aptness" be taken into account. The opposite view is seen in Bacon's *Of Parents and Children*: "Let parents choose betimes the vocations and courses they mean their children should take; for then they are most flexible; and let them not too much apply themselves to the disposition of their children, as thinking they will take best to that which they have most mind to." (*Essays,* Spedding, Ellis, and Heath edition, New York, 1869, Vol. XII, pp. 100, 101.)

[92] *Recherche,* Vol. I, Bk. III, Part II; *Works of Descartes,* Vol. I, *Principles of Philosophy,* pp. 222, 223; also *Passions; Notes directed against a Certain Programme, etc.*

[93] *The Vanity of Dogmatizing,* p. 128.

[94] *Essay concerning Human Understanding,* pp. 228, 230.

its object the connexion which Malebranche believed impossible (because the soul alone is incapable of connecting an idea and its object) but which Collier recognizes in his acceptance of the compelling claims of those "self-evident principles" that derive through contact of the mind with experience. By his resolution of the reasoning process into the terms of sense-experience intuitively perceived, Collier in this respect allies himself to the British school of empirical philosophy of which Locke was the founder.

III. MORALITY AND THE SOCIAL SCENE

A SOCIAL instinct," wrote Aristotle, "is implanted in all men by nature"; man "is the only animal whom she has endowed with the gift of speech."[1] Cicero found in nature "the first beginnings of society"[2] and Hooker declared: "Civil society doth more content the nature of man than any private kind of solitary living, because in society this good of mutual participation is so much larger than otherwise."[3] Like Bacon, Collier concurs in Aristotle's dictum, "He who is pleas'd with Solitude must be either a wild Beast, or a God."[4] Had we been made "not to intercommon with any Mortal . . . this articulate Pronunciation were in vain: for to what purpose should a Man have a Tongue to talk only to himself?"[5] The design of society is to make men the better for each other's company; consequently happiness must derive largely from social intercourse.[6]

Collier draws on metaphysical argument to prove the equality of men; since all descend from God, none less directly than another, "the best Part of the Nobility is common to the whole Kind."[7] They have natural affinity in thought, emotions, sensations; their bodies have been divinely moulded by the same Cause, their souls endowed with the same powers of reason and immortality.

[1] *The Works of Aristotle,* Ross edition, Oxford, 1921, Vol. X, p. 1253ᵃ.

[2] *De Officiis,* p. 25. He adds: "Nature with the aid of reason likewise binds man to man, unites them by the bond of language and of social life, inspires them with a strong love of offspring, and impels them to multiply the occasions of meeting and consorting with their fellows" (p. 6). *Cf.* also Seneca's *Letters to Lucilius, Epistle Six.*

[3] *Ecclesiastical Polity,* seventh edition, Church, Bk. I, p. 250. *Cf.* also p. 239.

[4] From Aristotle's *Politics, op. cit.* Quoted in Collier's essay *Of Friendship,* p. 47, and in Bacon's essay of that title.

[5] *Of Solitude,* p. 273.

[6] Collier looks back to agree with Seneca, Cicero, and Tacitus in the view that "the furniture of the mind must be brought out" for the companionship of man in his "poverty-stricken" nature.

[7] *Of Honesty,* p. 65.

But as Collier scrutinizes man and his world he becomes less demo-cratic—or less metaphysical—and practically concludes that social classes result from a cleavage very natural, and essential. Consis-tently a tory in attitude and action, he is contemptuous of majori-ties and majority standards; their rule is, he declares, inapplicable to both divine and moral law. "Universal Applause, is seldom little less than two Thirds of a Scandal" and "A Man may almost swear he is in the Wrong, when he is generally Cryed up."[8] As for the vulgar—here aristocratic bias dictates—

> Either Incapacity or Prejudice, Negligence or Imposture, disorders the Judgment of the Multitude. Their Under-standings are often too Weak, or their Passions too Strong to Distinguish Truth, or pronounce upon the Right of a Case.[9]

They are "more smitten with Appearances, than Things"[10] and exhibit no interest in the "Amusements of Learning, the Researches into Nature, and the Entertainments of Reason."[11] Indulgence in sensual appetites is the alternative, with consequent immorality and licentiousness. Collier graphically portrays the vicious circle: the common man over-rates and apes nobility and yet cries for distinc-tions to be destroyed; social superiors, widening the breach, expe-diently handle their underlings and encourage their fawning lest they grow rebellious from ill treatment.

Collier has little good to offer for nobility *per se*. Hereditary rank smugly held through antiquity of family he scoffs at. In his *Essay Upon Pride* one gullible speaker asks, "Don't you think it is a great Addition to ones Birth, to stand at the Bottom of a long Parchment Pedigree, and be some Yards removed from the first Escutcheon?" The cynic replies: "If you go but one Inch farther than the Gentleman at the Top you spoke of, it is ten to one but you take old Goodman, *etc.* by the Leathern Breeches." Position has too often been gained through "servile Compliance with whatever is uppermost."[12] At the same time that Collier admits the utili-

[8] *Of Popularity*, p. 71.
[9] *Ibid.*
[10] *Of Confidence*, p. 97.
[11] *Of Theft*, pp. 324, 325.
[12] *Upon Pride*, p. 56.

tarian gain of high position he firmly preaches the doctrine of *noblesse oblige* and deprecates the popular notion that a gentleman can lightly indulge his fancy: "Persons of Condition have no unlimited Range, no Exemption from Duty, no peculiar license for Folly and Distraction: So far from this, that Dissolution of Manners is more criminal in such Persons than in *Peasants*."[13] Their loose living is the faultier because it is infectious in example :

> if none but the *Vulgar* were licentious, the Sin would look clownish and despicable, and the Barrenness of the Soil would almost starve it. But when the *Weeds* take root in a rich Mould, they shoot up amain; when Appetite and *Mode* meet, the Infection spreads, and the Disease becomes Epidemical.[14]

Further, the man of figure shares in the privileges of government: and he who "enjoys Honour and Estate by a Society, has greater Engagements to Regard it, than he who receives only a common Protection. One has perhaps a 1000 *l. per Annum* for keeping the Laws; and the other, nothing but his Labour for his Pains."[15]

Collier observes an almost universal tendency in times of leisure towards licentiousness; and he deduces from the divine decree of manual labour for the majority of men the aim of averting some of the ills to which flesh is heir. While he recognizes poverty to be for the individual an evil he declares inequality of wealth a social good:

> Now if all People were equally rich, and could go on without Working; who would you get to till the Ground, or dig Mines? . . . An Equality of Estates would bring on an Equality of Conditions; confound Degrees, and melt down the Distinctions of *gentil* and *simple*.
>
> And when Things were thus brought to a Level, People would be too proud to serve any Body but themselves; and thus no mutual Assistance could be expected.[16]

[13] *Of Riches and Poverty*, p. 111.
[14] *Of Whoredom*, p. 135.
[15] *Of Duelling*, p. 129.
[16] *Sermon III*, p. 88.

These observations are tempered by Collier's suggestion that the poor, having spent themselves in drudgery, should be cared for after their usefulness ends. Beyond the utilitarian advantage patent in the very existence of the lower class he implies a cultural value in rule by pedigree in preference to purse-strings—unless a vitiated aristocracy should permit wealth to pass into sturdier, perhaps more shrewd, *bourgeois* control.

Collier voices a constitutional dislike of communal schemes. The well-advertised plans of Lycurgus, Plato, and More he declares impracticable because the abolition of private possessions is incompatible with human nature:

> There will always be a Disproportion as to Strength, Industry, and Consumption. Some will labour less, and some spend more than comes to their Share. . . . The Active, the Skilful, and the Strong, will expect a Preference; the Unserviceable, will be grudg'd their Maintenance, and the Old and Infirm look'd upon as a publick Grievance.[17]

Again, Collier, like Hobbes recognizing self-love as a determining force in human nature,[18] advocates the situation most likely to develop social virtues. There is, for example, no demand for benevolence or generosity when one man has no greater need than another. But in a non-communal state altruism can flourish at the same time that self-interest satisfies itself in possessions *willingly* shared. Besides, growing out of the selfish instincts, there is inherent in human nature a love of property—"a strange Relish in calling something one's *own*."[19] This trait as well as the quarrelsome, passionate nature of man is overlooked by the "levelling projects" of Plato and St. Thomas More which Collier brands as "no better than pretty Amusements, and a Sort of philosophical *Romance*."

[17] *Of Theft*, p. 270.

[18] Hobbes declared that every voluntary act has for its end some selfish good, and Collier, that "where there's most to be gotten or lost, 'tis natural to attend closely. . . . We are apt to love those things best, which belong to ourselves." (*Of Theft*, p. 272.)

[19] *Of Theft*, p. 272.

This jumbling of Fortunes, and throwing all into *Plato's Hotch-potch*, would make way for a *civil* chaos, and produce nothing but Strife and Confusion. The more Pretensions are intermix'd, the more they are entangled; and the farther we retire from *Property*, the nearer we border upon Disputes. To give a faint Image of this *Utopian* Contrivance; What Complaints and Quarrels are frequently seen amongst Partners in Trade . . . ? When all's done, separate Right, and single Enjoyment is the best Expedient for Peace and Quietness. Division of Estates makes Union of Minds, and People are most pleas'd when their Interest lies within themselves.[20]

Rather does Collier agree with the political theory of Aristotle[21] and the view of Cicero that a statesman's first duty is "to provide for the security of private property and prevent it from being alienated by public authority." The latter characterizes socialism as "the most pernicious system that can be conceived."[22] Once the wealth of a group has been pooled, reasons Collier, it must somehow be reapportioned, and then, practically, the socialistic structure has crumbled.

Collier's violent toryism consisted in neither mere lip-service nor bare theory. His firm belief in the principle of divine right, evinced in controversial writings as well as in stubborn loyalty to James, was voiced at the expense of his own comfort and public position.[23]

[20] *Of Theft*, pp. 270, 271. Collier's lack of comment upon the *New Atlantis* may indicate his disapproval of its fanciful pictures; on the whole he shows his approval of Bacon by either quoting or borrowing from him.

[21] Citing numerous disadvantages attendant upon community of possession, he maintains that "Property should be in a certain sense common, but, as a general rule, private; for, when everyone has a distinct interest, men will not complain of one another, and they will show more progress, because every one will be attending to his own business." (*Works*, Vol. X, pp. 1262^b, 1263^a.) Collier likewise sympathizes with the attitude that the only community that is ethically significant springs from friendship, not mere political organization.

[22] *De Officiis*, p. 117. Grotius, whom Collier now and then cites, quotes in his *De jure belli ac pacis* (ii, 3, 4) the words of Seneca: "Ad reges potestas omnium pertinet, ad singulos *proprietas*." (*De benef.*, vii, 4.)

[23] Collier was Lecturer and Preacher of the Rolls at Gray's Inn; but, "the Revolution coming on, the public exercises of his function became impracticable," he wrote. (From *Biographia Britannica*, Vol. IV, pp. 1406, 1407.) Through his ability and the favourable attention attracted by his first volume of sermons, 1686-7, he was well set on the path towards high ecclesiastical honours. It was

James I had declared in a speech to Parliament: "The State of Monarchie is the supremest thing upon earth: For Kings are not onely Gods Lieutenants upon earth, and sit upon Gods throne, but even by God himselfe they are called Gods . . . and so their power after a certaine relation compared to the Divine power."[24] Collier too believed the divine origin of the king to be implicit in the express words of God, and as well to be concluded from a reasoned observation of nature:

> if God had not so plainly declared the Persons of Princes Sacred and Inviolable . . . we might in great measure have inferred his Commands from the Reason of things: And that he expected we should continue firm to our Engagement, tho' under the greatest Discouragements: For without Steadiness in this Point, Societies must break up; and the *Foundation of the Earth* put out of *course*.[25]

Subjects have no right to depose rulers nor to incite rebellion,

> For if deposing of Kings, and dispensing with Oaths, and resolving Conscience into *Publick Good,* that is, *Convenience,* are not Tenents of a flaming Malignity, the Distinctions of Right and Wrong are Unintelligible.[26]

That subjects have no justification for creating a new ruler is Collier's thesis in *Animadversions upon the Modern Explanation of . . . a King de facto* (1689), a scathing attack upon the legitimacy of William's claim to the English throne. Collier's stubborn

in defence of James, with *The Desertion Discussed in a letter to a Country Gentleman* (1688), that Collier began his career as a controversialist.

[24] James I, "A Speach to the Lords and Commons of the Parliament at Whitehall," 1609, in *The Political Works of James I* (ed. McIlwain), p. 307. In this passage James declares: "Kings are also compared the Fathers of families: for a King is trewly *Parens patriae*, the politique father of his people. And lastly, Kings are compared to the head of this Microcosme of the body of man."

[25] *A Persuasive to Consideration tendered to the Royalists, particularly those of the Church of England,* London, 1695, p. 6.

Collier declares in a sermon that kings deserve more homage than angels: "Now, because we are certain God has given the Prince Authority over us, but we have no Assurance that we are Subjects to the Angels; therefore though the Prince falls short of the Perfection of those glorious Spirits, yet he deserves a greater Respect from us, because we are under his Jurisdiction." (*Sermon VIII,* p. 263.)

[26] *A Persuasive to Consideration,* pp. 15, 16.

loyalty is seen in his refusal to term James's flight an abdication since "his Majesty before his withdrawing, had sufficient grounds to make him apprehensive of danger . . .";[27] this and other declarations aroused bitter controversy and rankled in the swelling bosoms of Dr. Burnet and his defenders of William. Collier's hotheaded support of the theory of divine right culminated in his refusal to take the new oath of allegiance to William and Mary; he turned into a non-juring leader and, through the ridiculous outcry over his dramatic absolution at the gallows of Friend and Perkins, was outlawed for life. The hopelessness of the political situation in his day he describes in his *Persuasive to Consideration*:

> We see in what a *Tempest* the Nation is tossed. What a Torrent over-bears all Regards, both Human and Divine. Neither Nature nor Obligation, Crown nor Mitre, Law nor Gospel, can stand before it. No Moral Difficulty can stop its Passage. It breaks through all the Opposition of Blood, Heights of Station, and Defences of Right. So that now, if ever, we may make the Prophet's Complaint, *Truth is fallen in the streets, and Equity cannot enter.* . . . And when this Civil *Chaos* will settle, He only knows who brings Light out of Darkness, and Order from Confusion.[28]

More specifically he deplores the state in which kingship has fallen; "the Power of Princes . . . is little more than imaginary: The Crown gives no proper Strength to those that wear it. . . . As the Case stands, their Empire consists chiefly in the Submission of other Men's Wills; which is in a manner but reigning by Courtesy,"[29] actually in a position but "borrowed from little People."[30]

Consistent with Collier's monarchism is his distrust of rebellious multitudes and of flatterers of princes, hangers-on who endanger the reputation of majesty. "What," he asks, "can be more destructive to crown'd Heads than a Libertine Favourite? A Creature that shall blow up their Passions, and poyson their Pleasures? A Man that shall make a Jest of Conscience, and whisper Licen-

---

[27] *The Desertion Discuss'd*, p. III.
[28] *Persuasive*, p. 17.
[29] *Of Power*, p. 57.
[30] *Of Religious Temper*, p. 121.

tiousness in their Ear?" But such villains "find their Account
too often to be discourag'd" and, "Like some Sort of Meat, they
shine in Putrefaction, make a Figure out of foul service, and grow
rich upon Infamy."[31] In addition to this warning Collier is equally
frank to set the limits of the king's power and policies: he has
no right to use spies, to receive deserters and thus utilize an
enemy's subjects; rather should he send out his own ambassadors,
merchants, and travellers for information;[32] he must observe all
religious and churchly duties, for "a Christian peasant is more
noble than a heathen prince."[33] Any tendency towards tyranny
must be suppressed.

As for magisterial and legal problems, Collier evinces more
interest in theories of law than in instruments of enforcement. He
observes that any civil right can be limited or taken away by
Parliament—"not that 'tis impossible for them to act Unjustly,
but only that what they Determine hath the Force of a Law;
because every Man is supposed to have given his consent to it."[34]
Similarly popular consent vests power in the magistrate to maintain
peace and the common good of the state; while his concern is not
with the transgressing of divine law, he must do nothing contrary
to the commands of God. Laws were designed to restrain human
insincerity and passion, to render injustice "an uncreditable, as
well as an unprofitable Practice."[35] Collier's account of the origin of
law can thus be seen to resemble that of Hobbes: both are based on
the theory that human nature is fundamentally selfish and predominantly passionate, both qualities in turn necessitating a strong
external control, to be lodged most satisfactorily in a monarch.[36]
(Here Collier is at one with both James I and Hobbes in recognizing that in the best form of government complete freedom
of subjects would be anomalous.) Civilization, declares Collier,
depends upon law enforcement: "Discipline is as necessary in Gov-

[31] Of Flattery, p. 256.
[32] This idea suggests the New Atlantis.
[33] Cf. James I on the difference between a good king and tyrant, Of a Kings
Dutie in his Office.
[34] Upon the Office of a Chaplain, p. 205.
[35] Sermon I, p. 2.
[36] Hobbes, Works, Vol. III, Chap. XVII, p. 153 ff.

ernment as Lancing and Burning in Surgery. If the Sword of Justice was always in the Scabbard, the World would be strangely out of order."[37] He recommends obedience to national laws so long as they are consistent with precepts of Revelation.[38] The inadequacy of civil strictures, owing to lack of legislative foresight, proves itself in the crimes unprovided for and passed over in practice. Collier is strongly anti-Erastian; spiritual and civil rule, because of absolute separateness of church and state, can each be supreme within its own limits; it is no more in the power of the state to deprive church leaders of spiritual authority than it is in the province of the church to remove the magistracy or disincorporate the state. Selden's dictum flatly typifies the opposing view, that of Hobbes and others advocating a state-dictated religion: "There's no such thing as spiritual jurisdiction; all is civil, the church's is the same with the lord mayor's."[39]

Collier condemns as one of the evils of his day the malpractices of lawyers—outrageous fees, twisting of statutes and wills from their purposes, the betraying of trusts in court. Like Bacon,[40] he generalizes upon the elements that hinder the administration of justice: misinformation of the judge, his bias, and his inability to execute his sentence; but "where the Judge is above the Influence of Favour or Disaffection, and has Force enough to maintain the Award given, there it's impossible for Justice to fail."[41] "Judges ought to remember," wrote Bacon, "that their office is *jus dicere,* and not *jus dare*";[42] similarly Collier reminds the "*Bench,* the *Bar,* and the rest" that "they are not the *Makers,* but the *Ministers* of *Law*; they are the Servants of the Government" and "When the Reason of Things is good, 'tis not material though the Latin proves otherwise."[43] Selden likewise censures current corruptness of legal machinery: "The king's oath is not security enough for our property, for he swears to govern according to law;

[37] *Of Goodness,* p. 3.
[38] *Cf.* Hooker's treatment of civil law as one expression of divine law. (*Ecclesiastical Polity,* Bk. I.)
[39] John Selden, *Table Talk,* 1892, LXVIII.
[40] *Cf. Of Judicature,* in *Essays.*
[41] *Sermon II,* p. 33.
[42] *Of Judicature,* Vol. XII, p. 265.
[43] *Of Duelling,* p. 120.

now the judges they interpret the law; and what judges can be made to do we know."[44]

Certain cardinal virtues are in Collier's mind essential to a good state. For his ideas on the social importance of honesty and justice he looks to Cicero's *De Officiis* and Plato's *Republic*; Cicero had held to the stoic doctrine that "everything that was *Honest,* was for a Man's Interest, and that nothing unjust could possibly be serviceable":

> For if Plunder was the main Point, and everybody might rob another to enrich Himself, the common Confederacy of Mankind, . . . must break up of course. . . . So in the Body Politick, if we should all lie at catch upon each other, and carry off what we could get, *Society* must of necessity fly in pieces. . . . And what is Nature in this Sense but the Maxim of Reason, the Law of God and Man? Justice is the Cement of the World, all *Societies* stand upon this Basis, and therefore Fraud and Violence are every where punish'd."[45]

This passage Collier quotes as representative of his own attitude; and it is a sincere one as he contemplates the matter theoretically— and with enthusiastic idealism. But he would scarcely be a man of his century without showing a tinge of expediency. He admits that with "Distrust, and Vigilance, and Skill" as "defensive Arms, I believe we may maintain our ground," and adds:

> that you may not think me too strait-lac'd; I'll allow in some Cases a Man may indemnify Himself, and return untoward Usage: for instance, if I can pass Brass Money where I received it, I know no harm in the Dexterity.[46]

Another advantage to organized society is peace, which furthers the common good, strengthens the state, and in general adds to the significance of all phases of life. Public measures, Collier points out, are vitiated when subjected to political feuds. War causes dissolution of manners, prevents law-enforcement, and results in famine, tragedy, barbarity, and disgrace; history is marred by animosities that have become both notorious and im-

[44] *Table Talk,* p. 95. Selden, as his editor remarks, had good reason to know, having been committed to prison and to the Tower.

[45] From *De Officiis,* Bk. III, it stands in Collier's *Of Honesty,* pp. 46, 47.

[46] *Of Honesty,* pp. 34, 35.

mortal. In peace law may take its course, for authority is recognized and wartime issues do not cramp the administration of justice. Again, peace is desirable because it furthers commerce, whereas war proves a paralyzing deterrent.[47] Flourishing trade not only augments the wealth necessary for running the body politic but encourages industry and sociability and is potentially a way of importing knowledge and religion along with commodities. In short, the "cement of the commonwealth" consists largely in good will and general benevolence and their accruing benefits. Collier advocates severe punishment for him who holds doctrines destructive to the commonwealth or who in policy or act would rob his king. In effect he echoes Cicero's dictum: "It is infamous, outrageous, execrable to exploit the state."[48]

In Collier's observations upon trade are reflected certain conditions peculiarly characteristic of the turn of the century. He writes of the gain of benevolence through business and in the next breath shows the mark of his utilitarian age:

> 'Tis Trade which imports the Growth of distant Countries, furnishes Life, and cements *Society*. Without this Assistance, the Pleasure of an Estate, the Grandour of Courts, and the Equipage of Authority, would shrink almost to nothing. In a word, we are polish'd, and subsisted upon *Commerce*; and every thing that's Useful, is so far Honourable.[49]

But too frequently the mystery of trade is the mystery of iniquity. While tradesmen are necessary to the convenience of life and there can be found, Collier admits, much good faith and generosity among them, they are too mercenary: from the handling of small coins they tend to develop a corresponding smallness of spirit, and they resort to unscrupulous methods of buying and selling. Collier flays such dishonest practices as the use of false weights and measures; the sale of one amount and delivery of another; the over-vouching for values and glossing them over by deceptive

[47] Collier writes, though, that war is just when necessary; this recalls counsel of James I to be "slow in peace-making" because an "honourable and iust warre is more tollerable, then a dishonourable and dis-advantageous peace." (*Works*, p. 29.) The same idea occurs in *De Officiis*, and in the history of Tacitus.

[48] *De Officiis*, p. 119.

[49] *Of Theft*, p. 278.

lights, applying of varnish and gums, and clouding shops with perfumes and incense. The buyer becomes the victim of "Imposition and Legerdemain; and the *Seller* wants nothing but a little Jargon to make him a Juggler."[50] More vicious is the adulteration of commodities by unwholesome ingredients:

> Thus a Man buyes a Sickness instead of Provision. *His Table is made a Snare to him.* His Satisfaction is balk'd, and his Blood poison'd: And in short, he loses Health and Life sometimes as well as Money, by the same Bargain. . . . They that can put *Death into the Pot,* and prey upon the Vitals, what Mischief are they not prepar'd for? What if their *Trade* is not as mortal as a Bullet? What if they work like an *Italian* Dose, and take some Time to send a Man into the other World? . . . Are People's Constitutions to be practis'd on, are they to suffer in their Health, to enrich Injustice? Must they be treated like a *Mountebank's* Man, and take off unfriendly Draughts, ·for the Benefit of the *Tavern* or the Brew-house? Nay in one respect they are used worse: For here's no-Preservative . . . the Poyson is given without the Antidote.[51]

In short, Collier would ask with Mandeville:

> But who can all their Frauds repeat?
> The very Stuff, which in the Street
> They sold for Dirt t'enrich the Ground,
> Was often by the Buyers found
> Sophisticated with a quarter
> Of good-for-nothing Stones and Mortar;[52]

in such cases, exclaims Collier, is "all Regulation impracticable . . .? Is it not in the Business of some Persons to redress the Grievance?"[53] He goes on to condemn the rascally treatment of apprentices, mere dupes in their masters' hands; indeed, "except an Apprentice is fully instructed how to Adulterate, and Varnish, and give you the Go-by upon occasion, his Master may be charged

[50] *Of Theft,* p. 284.
[51] *Ibid.,* pp. 285, 286.
[52] *The Fable of the Bees,* ed. Kaye, Oxford, 1924, Vol. I, p. 23.
[53] *Of Theft,* p. 286.

with Neglect; and sued for not Teaching him his Art, and his Trade."[54]

Jonathan Swift also voices this note of protest:

> I believe there is hardly a nation in Christendom, where all kind of fraud is practised in so unmeasurable a degree as with us. The lawyer, the tradesman, the mechanic, have found so many arts to deceive in their several callings, that they far outgrow the common prudence of mankind, which is in no sort able to fence against them. Neither could the legislature in anything more consult the public good, than by providing some effectual remedy against this evil, which, in several cases, deserves greater punishment than many crimes that are capital among us. The vintner, who, by mixing poison with his wines, destroys more lives than any one disease in the bill of mortality; the lawyer, who persuades you to a purchase which he knows is mortgaged for more than the worth, to the ruin of you and your family . . . do surely deserve the gallows much better than the wretch who is carried thither for stealing a horse.[55]

"The vendibleness of the commodity," writes Collier, "cannot justify ill practices." An example he censures is the publicizing by booksellers of "vicious authors"; this is so "horrible" in result "that had these Men kept *Shop* in the *Sickness* Year, they had better have retail'd the Plague, sent it into the Country by all the Carriers, and given it Vent and Passage to the best of their Skill."[56]

As a general principle of trade Collier advocates an established price not to vary with the customer's purse; for a man's need does not alter the quality of the article nor lessen the gain. The buyer is dishonest if he offers the seller less because the latter is in pressing circumstances.[57] The worth of a thing is to be determined by the general rate of sale, unless a price is fixed by the government; and scarcity, which usually increases the value of com-

---

[54] *Upon Pride,* p. 71.

[55] *Works,* ed. by Sir Walter Scott, London, 1883, Vol. VIII, p. 101.

[56] *Of Authors,* p. 56.

[57] This recalls Selden's remark that "Every tradesman professes to cheat me, that asks for his commodity twice as much as 'tis worth." *Table Talk,* CXXXVI, p. 182.

modities, should not be artificially increased.[58] On the whole, Collier recommends a modest profit; alertness, circumspection, honesty, justice; and if one still is robbed, philosophical acceptance of misfortune. He sarcastically points out that "we are a *Trading* People . . . and must have no interfering between Business and Religion." Yet if "the *Pulpits* and the *Exchange* will not agree, we must *Live,* and there is an End on't."[59] Justice both at home and abroad is an ideal to be striven for, one to which the achievement of a monopoly, for example, is contrary because it works on the poor severe hardships; it violates the principle of commerce:

> *Trade* is design'd . . . to carry Convenience to every Quarter, and furnish our Wants, upon a reasonable Exchange. Now these Ends are best secur'd by keeping Business in a great many Hands. To draw this Stream into a private Channel, is to be an ill Commonwealth's-man: 'Tis to baulk the publick Interest; 'Tis to disserve the *Society,* to which as Members we are bound to be true.[60]

Collier recommends the practice of usury as one means of preventing concentration of wealth. His dialogue *Of Usury* reflects, with greatly expanded treatment and sources, several ideas found in Bacon's essay of the same title. Both agree that total suppression of money-lending is fit "only for an Utopian Government."[61] Both discount the argument that it "is against nature for money to beget money." Collier writes:

> Silver and Gold is by no means so barren a Commodity as you suppose. Money is a strange fruitful Thing, provided the Soil, and the Season hits; carry it but to *Turkey* or the *East-Indies,* and it commonly exceeds the Product of Grain.[62]

He declares it as reasonable to expect rent from a borrower of money as from a tenant of land which is but another form of

---

[58] Collier has in mind the barbarity of Dutch traders who made a practice of destroying in the East Indies the export materials they had to leave behind. (*Of Theft,* p. 303.)

[59] *Of Popularity,* p. 68.

[60] *Of Theft,* pp. 308, 309.

[61] Bacon writes: "Therefore to speak of the abolishing of usury is idle. All states have ever had it, in one kind or rate, or other. So as that opinion must be sent to Utopia." (*Of Usury,* p. 220.)

[62] *Of Usury,* p. 181.

wealth, and therefore as legitimate to profit from guineas as from pastures. Here he matches Selden's practicality: "I see no reason why I may not as well take use for my money as rent for my house. 'Tis a vain thing to say, money begets not money; for that no doubt it does."[63] Further, says Collier, the lender should share in the borrower's gain, or hold some guarantee against possible loss of principal and recompense for permitting his gold temporarily out of his own service. Among disadvantages of usury Bacon comments that "were it not for this lazy trade . . . money would not lie still, but would in great part be employed upon merchandizing; which is the *vena porta* of wealth in a state."[64] Similar phrasing shows Collier's indebtedness in proffering the objection: "were it not for this grasping at Interest, Money would not lie dead so long in the Miser's Coffers; 'twould circulate farther in Trade, and flow more freely in the Veins of the Commonwealth." He mentions the idea only to refute it:

> For those who won't venture their Cash upon an Advantage, would never lend *gratis*. At this rate, Money would sleep and rust in the Bag. . . . For, who will run Hazards without Profit, and help other People to get Estates for nothing? Who will set his Fortune a sailing, and lend it over the *Line,* without a Farthing Consideration? If the Owner's Money will earn nothing in a Voyage, he'll make it keep the House, and not ramble about the World to no purpose. Consider, on the other side, how *Trade* subsists upon Credit, and sets up with *Crutches*: So that take away the Allowance of *Interest,* and you stop the Course of Traffick, shut up part of the *Exchange,* and lay an Embargo on the *Merchantmen* in the *River.*[65]

Like Bacon, he finds a basis for usury in human selfishness; Bacon had said that the giving of interest is "a *concessum propter duritiem cordis*: for since there must be borrowing and lending, and men are so hard of heart as they will not lend freely, usury must be permitted."[66] And Collier, on the assumption that lending liquidates

[63] *Table Talk,* CXLV, p. 188.
[64] *Of Usury,* p. 219.
[65] *Of Usury,* p. 186.
[66] *Of Usury,* p. 218.

money and thereby facilitates trade, is willing for the individual to profit that public property may at the same time increase in value.[67] With more specious argument he defends usury on the ground that it satisfies a natural law of gratitude and is consistent with the rule of doing as we would be done by; accordingly the rate of interest must be kept reasonably low and special allowance made for the poor. To the objection that usury entails sabbath-breaking he, like Bacon, answers that interest accumulates on all days of the week inasmuch as tenants pay rent for holy days, and on them the land does not cease to be productive. Collier concludes that wherever money-lending has been frowned upon the disapproval was peculiar to the time and not rooted in evils inseparable from the practice itself. It is man's prerogative to formulate laws to meet his present need and to ignore the strictures of tradition: "Why should the *Mosaick* Restraint oblige, when the Circumstances are so much changed, and the Practice be the same, where the Reasons are different?"[68]—the reasons chiefly being individual gain and economic advancement of society. Hence it becomes "a Civil Question, concerns a Branch of *Meum* and *Tuum,* and by Consequence belongs wholly to the Cognisance and Regulation of the State."[69]

Swift and Mandeville have not denounced social evils more scathingly than has Collier. Throughout his essays and dialogues there is woven, often directly, sometimes incidentally, a vigorous arraignment of manners, morals, and amusements. Keenly aware

[67] He thus concurs with Mandeville's notion that private vices and public prosperity are necessarily concomitant:

> . . . Fools only strive
> To make a Great an Honest Hive . . .
> Without great Vices, is a vain
> *Eutopia* seated in the Brain.
> Fraud, Luxury and Pride must live,
> While we the Benefits receive . . .
>
> *(The Grumbling Hive)*

[68] *Of Usury,* p. 205.

[69] *Ibid.,* p. 212. This dialogue affords an example of Collier's learning and his painstakingly thorough method of assembling proof upon a matter that permits several-sided discussion; he chronologically presents historical variance of opinion ranging from the ancient Hebrews, commands of Scripture, canons of Church Fathers, statutes and customs of English and other governments down to such modern authorities as Beveridge, Selden, Hammond, and Grotius.

of the hypocrisy and selfishness that not only coloured the surface but rose deep-dyed from the bottom of the social structure, he rails at the libertinism and mercenary principles reflected about him. Distinctions between good and evil were almost lacking; the notoriously wicked prospered, and the virtuous suffered dire calamities; cut-throat competition ruined merchants, crime flourished, and daily there was heard complaint of theft and murder. The degeneracy of the times was such, declares Collier, that

> We are now fallen back to *Pagan* Liberty. There's not only Impunity, but Reputation in being Vitious. 'Tis with some People counted an Argument of Brains, and a Test of Quality. To be afraid of being damn'd is a vulgar Fancy, and Conscience passes for Cowardice.[70]

In spirited dialogues—such as *Of Gaming, Of Drunkenness, Of Whoredom,* and *Of Duelling*—he severely lashes specific evils as having neither personal nor social justification. Gambling is "commonly scandalous in the Motive, foul in the Management, and frightful in the Consequence":[71] indicative of greed in those at play, it results in brawls, murder, even madness and suicide. Collier describes a scene when the dice "are snatch'd too quick," and "the *Loading* and *Legerdemain* is discover'd":

> Upon this they run to Arms, and after some Artillery discharg'd in Swearing, come to a close Encounter. And thus one of them is run through the Lungs, and left agonizing upon the Place: Or, as it happen'd not long since the Gamester is knock'd down with a Pint-Pot, and his Skull broken! He is forc'd to be Trepan'd, and then relapsing into Play and Drinking, dyes of a Frenzy.[72]

Feverish gambling among women dissipates their husbands' funds and wild betting even strips their studies of books; men are thus challenged "to go farther in Danger, and appear more brave." The ill company met in dicing circles is a corrupting moral influence; and practically the custom is vicious because of its effects upon family, business, and personal character. Gambling, declares Col-

[70] *Of Goodness*, pp. 23, 24.
[71] *Of Gaming*, p. 13.
[72] *Ibid.*, pp. 21, 22.

lier, is—unlike drunkenness or debauchery—an incurable evil. His black pictures of the methods of fleecing *bubbles* and the sorry end of the gambler, he avers, are only too realistic.[73]

Equally pernicious in result is duelling. This Collier condemns as a practice *malum in se*. The eagerness of opponents, and the willingness of attendants to assist in complete ignorance of the issue, argue for their contempt of mankind: they often act "without any Provocation; except the Vanity of complying with a barbarous Custom. As if it was as indifferent a Thing to cut a Man's Throat, or let it alone, as to wear a broad or narrow brim'd Hat; And that these little Concerns of *Blood* ought to be perfectly governed by the Fashion."[74] Duellists are thus murderers by principle and butchers in philosophy. Further, the custom is not only dishonourable but "not improved unto common law." In the dialogue *Of Duelling* the libertine scoffs at legal procedure:

> Do you think a Parcel of starched Lawyers, with a *Jury* of *Haberdashers,* and *Chandlers,* are proper Judges in the Case? Are such *Pedants,* and *Mechanicks* as these, fit to give Rules to *Men of Honour*?[75]

The antiquity of the custom avails nothing; Collier strikes at the very reason held dear—satisfaction of a code of honour:

> when you have given the best Proof of your Sufficiency, and *killed your Man,* you are seized into the Hands of *Justice;* treated like Assassins; and condemned to Die with Circumstances of Ignomiy. You are not *Indicted* for acquitting your selves like Gentlemen; but for disturbing the Publick Peace, and murthering the King's Subjects.[76]

Courts hold the plea in ridicule and grant no damages, for in the eyes of justice methods of highwaymen and duellists are alike. The whole affair, tempestuous, absurd, irrational, is "as contrary to the Tendency and Temper of Christianity, as *Hob's Creed* is to the *Apostles;* as Light is to Darkness, as God is to the Devil."[77] The

---

[73] For a very similar picture *cf.* Robert Burton's *The Anatomy of Melancholy,* Vol. I, pp. 336, 337, of the Shilleto edition.

[74] *Of Duelling,* p. 120.

[75] *Ibid.,* pp. 116, 117.

[76] *Ibid.,* p. 119.

[77] *Ibid.,* p. 143.

English, advises Collier, should look to the French, who are not blinded by false notions of honour, but suppress duelling and refer grievances to the government.

Collier censures still other matters of mode that root themselves in personal conduct but spread infectiously to corrupt society. Libertinism leads to debauchery and immorality; it lowers, or burlesques, among other values, those of the institution of marriage, which Collier considers radically needed for social regularity. The marriage contract should be mutually held to, its sanctity defended, its violation by either sex punished. Even suggesting the safeguarding of family honour by legal protection, he holds up an ideal of domestic peace undisturbed by quarrels and pettiness, and of a security that would hearten one against poverty and age. Practically, domestic hostilities result in neglect of business, dissipation of fortune, and in general a disordered, libertine way of living. Whoredom constitutes one of the worst of social ills, one that in turn creates the problem of illegitimate children. Privately handled, their maintenance is even then no trifle, observes Collier, for it amounts to feeding an adulterous brood that, sucker-like, starve and impoverish a worthy family. The innocent victims are only burdens upon society. Collier condemns as one of the worst of sins sodomy: "this Wickedness is Felony, without Benefit of Clergy, by our Statutes. . . . Indeed, such Monsters ought to be the Detestation of Mankind, pursued by Justice, and exterminated the Earth."[78] Balls and romances fall into the class of glaring vices. The latter are "dangerous Entertainment for Youth" and "Stuff People's Heads with Visionary Prospects": they lack realism, furnish no useful knowledge, corrupt the judgement, and dwell so much upon the intrigues of love that their impressionable readers are deluded into imitation.

The one position taken by Collier which is widely known—and which has made him famous or infamous, according to the bias of the critic—concerns the late seventeenth-century stage. It is enough to note here only that in his catalogue of social evils plays and playwrights stand in the very first place. He is convinced that

[78] *Of Whoredom*, p. 154.

"nothing has gone farther in Debauching the Age than the Stage Poets and Play-house."[79]

Collier's condemnatory judgements often are based on moral grounds; but sometimes they rise from class consciousness. If gentlemen, he declares, "must run counter to the Vulgar in every Thing, I wonder they don't leave off Swearing, Drinking, &c. These, by their Assistance, are grown *Plebeian* Vices: Insomuch that Porters and Footmen, are as perfect in them as themselves."[80] Certainly what is beneath a man is beneath a gentleman. Luxurious living is offensive when observed among "the vulgar." Even common man, notes Collier, furnishes his house as richly as his superior's. Those of low station should not dress well, for it "looks like an illegal Aspiring into a Forbidden Station."[81] Persons of culture and true refinement will exhibit good taste: "They pitch upon nothing that is tawdrey and mechanick, staring, or ill matched. One may know a Gentlewoman almost, as well by seeing her chuse a Mantua, or a Ribbon; as by going to Garter, or Clarencieux."[82] No public person has any reason to value himself on the possession of "Gold Chains, Velvet Caps, or Sables"; such com-

[79] Preface, *A Short View of the Immortality and Profaneness of the English Stage,* 1698 (Preface dated 5 March, 1697).
Discussion of this invective and of Collier's subsequent pieces during the stage controversy that ensued of course constitutes a long chapter in itself which, in as complete and as broad an account as it should be, has not been written. For this attack upon Restoration wits critics have generally either condemned Collier for a muddy-minded fanatic, as Montagu Summers has in his ranting introduction to Congreve, or for an "egregious jackass," as has Strachey; or, like Macaulay, have eulogized him as a moralist lifting English literature from the muck and mire before the sentimental comedy set in. With one exception they have failed to scrutinize closely the actual fabric of *A Short View,* and to see that Collier really supports his comment upon thorough knowledge of seventeenth-century classical criticism—that of Corneille, Rapin, Boileau, Molière. Collier's connexion with contemporary French literature on several scores, two perhaps important ones still undetermined, has through study become too obvious for anyone to credit the charge that the "criticism" of *A Short View* came second-hand by way of Rymer. *Cf.* Joseph Wood Krutch's *Comedy and Conscience after the Restoration* (New York, 1924), and Dr. Johannes Ballein's *Jeremy Collier's Angriff auf die englische Bühne, ein Beitrag zur Geschichte des englischen Dramas* (Marburg, 1910).
[80] *Of Duelling,* p. 132.
[81] *Concerning Cloaths,* p. 112.
[82] *Ibid.,* p. 107.

pliance with the weakness of the masses is "an innocent Stratagem
to Deceive them into their Duty; and to Awe them into a just Sense
of Obedience."[83] Richness of habit is both unnecessary and insufficient to keep up the distinctions of degrees, and a great man will
contemn this sort of finery. A prudent magistrate possessed of
power need not doubt his own influence, for "A Gentleman's Mien
and Behaviour is sufficient to discover him, without any great
Dependance upon *Shops* and *Taylors*!"[84] A rich habit is at best
only a sign of wealth, and argues no more for the wearer's worth
than it does for the contrary; it amounts to a ridiculous vanity that
often robs a family of necessities, and gives credit only to the tailor.
Care of one's person must not be carried to obtrusive extremes;
"here, as in most things, moderation is best." The misuse of
ornamentation is deplorable:

> To see Gold and Scarlet condemn'd to Liveries, the Coach-
> Box furnish'd like the *Council Chamber*, and the Horses
> wear as good *Velvet* as the *Company*, . . . This Prostitu-
> tion of Finery, is enough to make it nauseous; and to ruin
> it's Reputation to all Intents and Purposes.[85]

Collier goes on to point to the folly of squandering huge sums of
money on magnificent buildings, furniture, and equipages. On the
whole he advises moderation and common sense, and avoidance of
truckling to appetites and social foibles. Particularly does affecta-

---

[83] *Ibid.*, p. 99.

[84] *Ibid.*, p. 101.

[85] *Ibid.*, p. 193. Cicero advises moderation in dress and in ornament, and recommends spending funds for useful improvements, not ornamental colonnades and
theatres. (*De Officiis*, pp. 63, 110.)
Mandeville satirizes luxury that

> Employ'd a Million of the Poor,
> And odious Pride a Million more: . . .
> Their darling Folly, Fickleness,
> In Diet, Furniture and Dress,
> That strange ridic'lous Vice, was made
> The very Wheel that turn'd the Trade.
> Their Laws and Clothes were equally
> Objects of Mutability;
> For, what was well done for a time,
> In half a Year became a Crime; . . .

(*The Grumbling Hive*, Vol. I, p. 25, in *The Fable of the Bees*, ed. Kaye.)

tion in manner arouse his contempt. Graceful conversation and "address in the Modes" are pretty enough accomplishments, he grants, but they are only a veneer gained through education and not to be overvalued. These "little Formalities are often magnified beyond all Sense and Reason; And some People are so Fantastically fond of them, as if . . . it were in Reality a more valuable and gentile Quality to dress well, and come handsomely into a Room, than to take a Town, or to be fit to discharge the Office of a Privy Counseller. . . . I am not," he concludes, "of their Mind in this Matter, but think it much better for a Man's Parts to lie in his Head, than in his Heels."[86]

In his survey of social conditions Collier concludes that no worse form of injustice exists than the treatment of curates and chaplains. This group he first strongly championed in his essay *Upon the Office of a Chaplain,* which was written to arouse self-respect among the profession and, in readers, the deference befitting clergymen. These poor priests, he observes, had been treated contemptuously by Milton in *Eikonoklastes:* "The Scripture owns no such *Order,* no such function in the church. . . . Bishops or Presbyters we know, and Deacons we know, but what are Chaplains?" Collier retorts, "He might have answered in his own Words, That they were *Household Priests;* and given an Instance from the Old Testament."[87] Because chaplains have been commissioned by God[88] they are not servants, and hence should be accorded more freedom and less contempt than they receive. Traditionally priesthood has in all ages been held in high esteem:

[86] *Upon Pride,* p. 58.

[87] From the preface to *Upon the Office of a Chaplain.* Here Collier quotes from *Eikonoklastes,* shortening it inaccurately. Milton answers his own question: "In state perhaps they may be listed among the upper serving-men of some great household, and be admitted to some such place as may style them the sewers, or the yeoman-ushers of devotion, where the master is too resty or too rich to say his own prayers, or bless his own table." (*Eikonoklastes,* Patterson's edition, p. 845.)

[88] The clergyman receives his authority "from God himself, whose Deputy he is in Things pertaining to Religion; He is not entertain'd upon any secular Account; or to manage any other Business but what relates to another World; and is Consecrated to this Function by the Divine Warrant and Appointment; and consequently he is God's Minister not Man's." (*Upon the Office of a Chaplain,* p. 194.)

The holy *Order* is appropriated to the Divine Worship, and a *Priest* has the peculiar Honour to *belong* to *nothing* less than God Almighty. . . . Christian *Priests* are the Principal Ministers of God's Kingdom. They represent his Person, publish his Laws, pass his Pardons, and preside in his Worship. To expose a *Priest,* much more to burlesque his Function, is an Affront to the Deity.[89]

There is, moreover, an immediately practical reason for respecting the clergy:

The Functions and Authorities of Religion have a great Influence on *Society.* The Interest of this Life lies very much in the Belief of another. So that if our Hopes were bounded with *Sight* and *Sense,* if *Eternity* was out of the Case, general Advantage, and publick Reason, and secular Policy, would oblige us to be just to the *Priesthood*: For *Priests,* and Religion always stand and fall together.[90]

Collier advocates higher salaries to improve the learning and status of the profession, for poverty exposes them to contempt and "scurvy temptation." Further, out of holy revenues, one-half should go to the curate, or, if the living be small, two-thirds to him who supplies it. It is uncanonical and sacrilegious for clergymen to enrich themselves through labours of others in their own order. Chaplains attached to private homes and estates Collier warns against servility and flattery lest they cheapen their trust; too often they harbour erroneous ideas about wealth and greatness at the expense of regard for their station. Advancement should depend upon more than favouritism or mechanical succession; Collier suggests the holding of preferments by tenure of knights' service and as well the granting of pensions for age-disability. He presents in *Upon the Office of a Chaplain* a veritable guidebook for curates who would remain unmercenary, who "prefer a homely, unornamented Liberty, to a splendid Servitude."[91] He never tires of emphasizing the sordidness in those consecrated to the church who betray honour for "handfuls of barley." This essay has a special

[89] *A Short View,* p. 83.
[90] *Ibid.,* p. 84.
[91] From George Herbert's *Country Parson* Collier cites a passage advising proper conduct on the part of the clergy. (*Upon the Office of a Chaplain,* p. 230.)

importance in view of the fact that Collier had himself held such
a position, and an historical significance in that it casts light upon
the conditions among a large class of stipendiary clergymen who at
that time were as a group poorly used by their superiors. Some of
his ideas are found in the writings of Swift who, likewise aware of
a social need for higher regard for prelates, writes in his *Project
for the Advancement of Religion*:

> It so happens that the men of pleasure, who never go to
> church, nor use themselves to read books of devotion, form
> their ideas of the clergy from a few poor strollers they often
> observe in the streets, or sneaking out of some person of
> quality's house, where they are hired by the lady at ten shil-
> lings a month; while those of better figure and parts, do
> seldom appear to correct these notions. And let some reason-
> ers think what they please, it is certain that men must be ·
> brought to esteem and love the clergy, before they can be
> persuaded to be in love with religion.[92]

On yet another score Swift and Collier are of the same mind:
both mercilessly satirize the follies of women, their extravagance,
affectation, ignorance (except for the incomparable Stella). Yet
both rise to their defence. St. Chrysostom had called woman a
"desirable calamity"; and Collier would not soften the epithet. But
we find him complaining that women have not had fair "Trial to
discover their Worth."

> They are by Custom, made Incapable of those Employments,
> by which Honour is usually gain'd. They are shut out from
> the Pulpit and Barr; from Embassies, and State Negotia-
> tions; so that notwithstanding (as I believe it often happens)
> their Inclinations are generous; and their Abilities Great, to

---

[92] *A Project for the Advancement of Religion and the Reformation of Manners*, in Sir Walter Scott's edition of *The Works of Jonathan Swift*, p. 92. In 1697
Swift read the *Essays* then published by Collier.

In the third chapter of Collier's *Short View*, "The Clergy Abused by the
Stage," he offers a defence of the profession at the· same time that he attacks
those playwrights he considers scurrilously to have represented the clergy. He
endeavours to show on three grounds the right of the latter group to fair treatment: because "of their Relation to the Deity, because of the Importance of
their Office," and because of their having "prescription for their Privilege."

serve the Publick; yet they have not an Opportunity of shewing it.[93]

Three years later Defoe wrote *The Education of Women,* in which he stigmatized denial to women of the advantages of learning as "one of the most barbarous customs in the world";[94] and still later Steele opportunely informed his readers that he was of the same mind.

Collier is seldom content merely to condemn social ills. We have noted his protest against the common adulteration of foodstuffs and his advocacy of control of their sale. Again, he would provide for the poor by housing them in comfortable retreats; he has studied and admires the Athenian systems, and those of the French and Dutch, the latter having hospitals for aged soldiers and seamen. He recommends provision for labourers and tradesmen, and, especially when he considers the total absence of beggars in countries like Holland, he hopes for an intelligent means of handling poverty and need. "It might not be amiss," he suggests, "if Parishes in great Towns were carefully inspected, Vice and Necessity better discover'd, and the Impotent distinguish'd from the Lazy."[95] He points to the difficulty involved in telling actual want from counterfeiting, but advises generally a liberal attitude. Still, charity should not be given indiscriminately; treatment of the poor should depend upon the cause of their indigence—whether debauchery, extravagance, conscience, or casualty. By all means is it wrong for one to be haughty in dispensing his alms.[96]

93 *Upon Pride,* p. 82.
94 Defoe continues: "If knowledge and understanding had been useless additions to the sex, *God* Almighty would never have given them capacities; for he made nothing needless. . . . The capacities of women are supposed to be greater, and their senses quicker than those of the men; and what they might be capable of being bred to, is plain from some instances of female wit, which this age is not without." In *Later Stuart Tracts,* edition of George Aitkin, p. 282. Collier's essay *Upon Pride* first appeared in *Miscellanies in Five Essays,* 1694; Defoe's tract in 1697.
95 *Of Riches and Poverty,* p. 109.
96 Cicero had written: "Let us therefore give of our substance to the deserving poor, but with thrift and moderation. For many have run through their patrimony by indiscreet giving. . . . Besides, robbery often follows profuse liberality." (*De Officiis,* p. 106.) He adds that "A form of generosity to the State is the ransom of prisoners and the relief of the poor" (p. 111).

Thus Collier deals with social interests that range from toryism, utilitarian matters of trade and wealth, needed reforms, to luxurious living, the prevalent libertinism and immoderateness even to diet and livery for horses. No perpetrator of vice is spared, whether he errs through immorality, irrational conduct, or violation of simple rules of guidance. Yet along with Collier's rather inclusive condemnation there runs a vein of tolerance, and his unequivocal plain-dealing is as often cloaked in nice satire as it is served up in hammer-and-tongs style. Suggesting through current parlance the flavour of contemporary life, he brings into his dialogues conventional types, the rake, the coxcomb, the drunken sot, the "bubble," the die-hard antagonist—but withal the same human stuff that Swift utilizes in propounding his *Serious And Useful Scheme, to make an Hospital for Incurables.*

IV. *MODUS VIVENDI*

L IFE was not calm in London during the second half of the
    seventeenth century; nor, really, in the first two decades of
    the eighteenth. Within this span of Collier's years he had
thrust upon him deprivation, imprisonment, outlawry; he exercised
himself to thwart political machinations; he became the key-figure
in three controversies and yet found periods to enjoy the quiet of
scholarly seclusion and to labour at his varied literary projects
other than pamphleteering. Such turbulent experiences nurtured a
constitutionally dynamic spirit and helped, no doubt, to clarify a
philosophy of living that to him would have meaning and durability.

It is wholly natural that this philosophy should be an admixture
of stoic and Christian doctrine with hedonistic elements: wholly
natural in view of Collier's own vigour and sanity; of the prevailing renascence in the seventeenth century of stoicism and its
almost imperceptible fusion with traditional Christianity. Again,
Collier's familiarity with Church Fathers and with Greek and
Roman thought was that of a scholar; his knowledge came at first-
hand, not through the convenient maxim-book. And further, unlike
the divines of his day who were turning more and more to English
nationalism and away from continental culture, Collier, as we have
seen, evinces decided affinity for French literature.[1] This tendency

---

[1] There is obvious discipleship in literary style and in his use of the maxim
and epigram; he ultimately reflects much of the Port Royalist polish of expression
as manifested in Pascal and La Rochefoucauld, although Collier was natively
possessed of a style that in vigour, terseness, and liveliness of image is seldom
found among comparable contemporaries. Bossuet he resembles in manner of
character delineation. (That he and Bossuet were distinctly on common political
ground is seen in the latter's studied defence of James's writings.) Collier's
attack on the stage, usually criticized as wholly irrational and attributed to an
ingrained demand for morality, was motivated to a vast degree by rationalism
and common sense. This attitude in criticism is closely allied with Cartesianism
in philosophy and science; Collier's embracing of French critical tenets has been
noted. But his philosophical leanings towards Descartes and Malebranche are
no greater than his dependence upon Pascal and his delight in the Jansenists.

completes the cycle rather than deviates from it: in Descartes is to be found a strong revival of the later stoicism; its dualism he found acceptable, and he clearly shows the influence of Cicero and Seneca. Cicero succeeded in making of his writings a well of material invaluable because through his exposition of early stoic doctrines he kept certain old fragments nowhere else preserved. Collier draws from the *De Finibus, De Officiis,* the *Laws, Paradoxa Stoicorum, Tusculan Disputations,* and the essays on friendship and old age.[2] His own translation of the *Meditations* of Marcus Aurelius[3] conveniently shows how closely he was acquainted with that Roman stoic; he knew as well Juvenal, Lucan, Seneca, Horace, and Epictetus.

In the neo-stoic doctrine of self-sufficiency is rooted much of the advice in Collier's essays. True felicity, says the Anglican divine, rests with God and the Eternal, not the mundane here and now. Yet somehow the earthly span must be lived with credit and control. Accordingly

> A wise Man should be satisfied with himself, and live upon the Fund of his own Sufficiency. He should keep his Inclinations within the Compass of his Power, and wish himself always just what he is. There is a Freedom, and Greatness, and Pleasure, in such a Management as this.[4]

After the manner of Cicero, Collier upholds as the first requisite to purposeful living the stoic virtue of fortitude, to be guided by reason and moderation.

> Fortitude implies a Firmness, and Strength of Mind, which enables us to do and suffer as we ought. It puts us into a condition to maintain our Reason, to stand by our best Interest, and act up to Decency and Conscience. It keeps a

---

[2] Collier wrote for S. Parker's translation of the *De Finibus* (1702) a recommendatory preface which he makes a critique of both the work itself and the art of translating.

[3] *The Emperor Marcus Aurelius Antoninus, his conversation with himself, from the Greek, together with the preliminary Discourse of the learned Gataker, etc. to which is added, the Mythological Picture of Cebes the Theban, etc. Translated into English from the respective originals.* 1701. Other editions 1708, 1726, 1887, 1889, 1891, 1903.

[4] *Of Fortitude,* p. 205. Cicero had called fortitude "that great and sublime spirit which scorns the chances of life." (*De Officiis,* Bk. I, p. 30.)

Man steady to a wise Resolution and gives Life and Perfection to all great Designs.[4]

To arrive at the right "pitch" of fortitude one must cultivate "indifferency" and "keep appetites low." Even here extremes are to be avoided; while "we should be careful to maintain the Sovereignty of the Mind," the soul is not to be tyrannized over, "that being the way to make it both troublesom and unserviceable."[5] For him who reads, the middle way is pointed in stoic doctrine; but the "learned Coward makes a wooden Appearance":

> For a Man to converse with the Hero's of former Ages, and to be bred to the Notions of Fortitude. To have the Memory furnish'd with the Reason and Rhetorick of the greatest Philosophers, and like *Achilles,* to feed as it were upon the Marrow of Lions: To fail under all this . . . Discipline and Demonstration, must look very untoward . . . To have Armour of Proof and not dare to use it: To get no Heat by the warmth of *Plato's* Dialogues: To desert from *Epictetus,* and *Tully;* and make *Seneca* and *Antoninus* cry Quarter! To manage in this manner is double Infamy.[6]

Collier does not make Seneca and Antoninus cry quarter: his prose is clothed in the armour of proof of both.[7]

It is with the same quiet insistence met in the *Meditations* that Collier argues for acquiescence in the *status quo.* Discontent is not only useless, it implies either a lack of reason or weak reflection upon providence. Most of our troubles are never realized, but in any event calamity catches us soon enough without our running to meet it. Vain fears will not alter nature. God expects us to supply our wants through prudence and industry; therefore, advises Collier, seize opportunities that present themselves, trust in providence, and submit to the unalterable. It is to be remembered that lasting

---

[5] Sermon, *Difference between the Present and Future State of our Bodies,* London, 1686, p. 28.

[6] *Of Fortitude,* p. 218.

[7] In the preface to his translation of the *Meditations* he compares in quite a detailed way the thought, logic, and methods of Seneca and Marcus Aurelius. He particularly praises the comprehensiveness, just reasoning, and convincing morality of the latter who, he says, has "drawn up an admirable scheme of natural religion" (p. xv).

life out is only a matter of endurance. In a comparatively short while death comes. This view is common to epicurean and stoic; Epictetus and Seneca declare that if pain can be borne, it will be light; if not bearable it cannot be long.[8] Epicurus, reiterating that "Great pain cannot be Long; nor Long pain Great," believes that "nothing doth so alleviate, mitigate, and blunt the edge of any pain, as Constancy, and Custom of suffering."[9] Hence the Wise Man, "used to diseases and pains, doth very often rejoyce and smile even in the highest fury of his sickness." Similarly Collier insists that "to bear Pain decently is a good sign of inward Strength, and a handsome proof of a great Mind."[10] Courage must support virtue:

> He that can't stand the Shock of Pain, and part with his Limbs, or his Life upon Occasion, can never be firm in his Duty. . . . I grant 'tis no easie Task to come up to this Pitch of Fortitude: However, the force of Custom and Principle, Vigour of Thought, and Nobleness of Resolution, will go a great way in the Matter.[11]

Yet some feeling is permitted. Cicero and Seneca "will give us leave to groan a little in the Case"; but, says Collier, "we must not cry *Craven*; the Noise must be bold, and surly; it must be only to throw more spirits into the Muscles, and help us to repel the Attack with greater Vigour."[12] While in orthodox stoicism the dogma that "pain is no evil" stands as a primary postulate, true epicureanism found pain, as the antithesis of pleasure, the only evil in nature. Collier flouts the extreme of both attitudes: why "maintain an impracticable Post" that gives "Sense and Experience the Lye"? The stoics, in declaring nothing but immorality an evil, and thus "chopping a little Logick," would "make the *Patient* insensible of his malady." "A mighty Discovery!" he exclaims, to find "no Vice and Wickedness in Pain: . . . Who knows not that there's noth-

---

[8] Cf. Seneca's *Letters to Lucilius*, Vol. I, Letter 24, p. 83.

[9] Epicurus, *Morals, Collected Partly out of his own Greek Text, in Diogenes Laertius, and Partly out of the Rhapsodies of Marcus Antoninus, Plutarch, Cicero, & Seneca*. London, 1670, p. 131.

[10] *Of Pain*, p. 10.

[11] *Ibid.*, p. 12.

[12] *Ibid.*, p. 20.

ing of moral Turpitude in the Headach, and that the *Cholick* is neither Felony nor Treason?"[13] Cicero had said that "no one can be brave who declares pain the greatest evil, or temperate who maintains pleasure to be the highest good."[14] With the first half of this dictum Collier agrees; for him the evil lies not in the recognition of pain but in the cowardly bearing of it since the divine purpose back of imposed suffering is to test our integrity or to punish our misdemeanours.

As Edwyn Bevan has pointed out of the ideal Wise Man of the stoics, "he was not to *concern* himself with his brethren . . . he was only to serve them";[15] to have benevolence, but not love; to engage in action, shrink from no hardships; but his success must remain a matter of indifference. According to Epictetus he may sigh, but only if the sigh is superficial. His tranquillity must remain intact. Here, pity, in that it is a feeling aroused by the suffering of another, becomes a vice. Collier recommends an attitude approaching this stoical indifference:

> A wise well-wisher will consider there is a necessity of Discipline; both to secure the Orderly, and reclaim the Evil. . . . As things stand, 'tis not conceivable how Providence can Govern without Punishing. Upon this Contemplation, a good Man will no more be disturbed at the Methods of Correction, than by seeing his Friend take unpalatable Physick, which he knows to be proper for his Health.[16]

Antithetical as this may sound to certain Christian preachings it is but a notion deduced from a concept of divine methods: man, patterning after the perfect example of God's punishment through discipline, will cultivate self-control. The self-denial that we find here is not that rigorous product of the early school but rather that germane to and compatible with the eclecticism of Cicero, the sturdiness of Seneca, the patient endurance of Marcus Aurelius. Their common rejection in its extremity of the ideal of the man who could only feign benevolence relates to Collier's philosophy

[13] *Ibid.*, p. 7.
[14] *De Officiis*, p. 3.
[15] *Stoics and Sceptics*, Oxford, 1913; *cf.* pp. 66, 67.
[16] *Of General Kindness*, p. 174.

in that its model figure is Christ, a man of passion. Aurelius had named three relationships for "every man to acquit himself in," his body, his deity, his neighbours. In the main the stoic ignored this third obligation or, like Cicero, paid his allegiance to the state. Collier, mindful of his duty to God, to his neighbour, and to himself, as strongly individualistic as his Roman forbears, expounds a morality humane but not humanitarian.

The admonitions to "know thyself" and "look to the deity within," so gently emphasized throughout the *Meditations,* grow out of the belief that man, independent of circumstances, can find his true good in the sovereignty of his own will and reason. Here, at this point of power in an "inner citadel" stoic and Christian values differ. And here, however much he may argue for self-reliance, Collier points to the necessity for complete faith in God, and looks through ultimate knowledge of him to realize happiness. Thus he stands in the tradition of Hooker and Pascal, the one voicing a reasoned, the other a mystical faith. Pascal writes:

> The Stoics say: Turn in upon yourselves, and there you will find your repose. This however is not true. Others say: Go forth from yourselves, and seek for happiness in diversion. Neither is true. . . . Alas! happiness is neither within us, nor without us. It is in the union of ourselves with God.[17]

Hooker had observed that human desire always embraces the infinite and that man's chief good is communion with God.[18] Only through divine grace can he become invincible; even the "heathen" were aware that supernatural aid was a necessity. Human frailty Collier sees as part of the plan of God that our ideals will rise above vulnerable bodies, our aims encompass spiritual attainment; to the same end our powers will ultimately find a complement in

---

[17] *Thoughts,* p. 87.

[18] "No good is infinite but only God; therefore he is our felicity and bliss. Moreover, desire tendeth unto union with that it desireth. If then in Him we be blessed, it is by force of participation and conjunction with Him. . . . Then are we happy therefore when fully we enjoy God, as an object wherein the powers of our souls are satisfied even with everlasting delight; so that although we be men, yet by being unto God united we live as it were the life of God." Hooker, *Ecclesiastical Polity,* Bk. I, p. 255.

the divine soul. Thus for him, as for many a professed stoic, the virtue of self-sufficiency falls short.

Somewhat, it would seem at superficial glance, at odds with the acquiescent strain in Collier's philosophy is his hedonism. A positive and hardy temper is at once obvious in his declaration that pleasure is the ultimate end of living:

> The only Reason why *Being,* is better than *Not Being,* is because of the agreeable *Perceptions* we have in the first, which are impossible in the latter. Without Pleasure either in *Hand,* or in Remainder, Life is no Blessing, nor Existence worth the owning. Were I sure never to be pleased, my next Business should be to *unwish* my self, and pray for annihilation. For if I have nothing which delights me in my *Being,* the very Sense of it must be acceptable; and then I had better be without it. He that can prove himself *Something,* by no other Argument than *Pain,* will be glad to be rid of the Conclusion. For to suppose that Misery is preferable to Not Being, is, I believe, the wildest Thought that ever entred the Imagination.[19]

Epicurus, emphasizing the doctrine that "Pleasure in the General is the end of a happy life, or the Chiefest Good," distinguishes between "*Two* Kinds of Pleasures," those spiritual and those physical; the first consists in "*the Indolency of Body, and Tranquillity of the Mind.*"[20] Collier makes the same distinction: the "general Division of Pleasure, is into that of the Mind, and the other of the Body." The first is "the more valuable": the causes of spiritual satisfaction are more "reputable" than those of physical pleasures; satisfactions of the mind are more at command than those of the body; intellectual delights are "nobler" than others. He employs the same psychological argument as that of Epicurus:

[19] *Of Pleasure,* pp. 177, 178.
[20] Epicurus describes the "two kinds of pleasure; *One,* that may be considered as dependent upon, or radicated in *Quiet*; and so is nothing else but a constant Placability, Calmness, and Vacuity or Immunity from all perturbation and dolour; and *Another,* that may be considered as resident in *Motion*; and so consisteth only in a certain sweet affectation, or pleasant titillation of the sense, as may be exemplified in joy, hilarity, eating and drinking when we are hungry and thirsty, the pleasures of all which doth arise only from a pleasant motion in the Organs." (*Morals,* p. 24 ff.)

desire supposes a lack, or want, which is painful. Accordingly we act to remove the pain and thus gratify our desires. He observes that corporeal pleasures are rooted in imperfection;[21] but "rational delights" spring from generosity, knowledge, virtue, and their reward is great:

> When the Mind is well awaken'd, and grown up to the Pleasures of Reason, they are strangely affecting. The Luxury of *Thought,* seems no less than that of the *Palate.* The Discovery of a great *Invention,* may be as moving as Epicurism. The Entertainments of Plato were as high-season ... as those of Apicius.[22]

There can be no middle ground between pleasure and pain. One or the other gains ascendency. That, for instance, which "some Philosophers call *Indolence,* is properly a state of *Pleasure.* For though the Satisfaction may be somewhat Drowsie; yet, like the first Approaches of Sleep, it strikes smooth and gently upon the *Sense.*"[23] It is pleasure that reconciles us to pain. "Who would submit to the Nauseousness of *Medicine,* or the Torture of the *Surgeon*; were it not for the Satisfaction of receiving our Limbs, and our Health?"[24] This ultimate purpose may motivate the most ascetic regimen:

> *Pleasure* is pursued where it seems most renounced, and aimed at even in Self-denial. All voluntary Poverty, all the Disciplines of Penance, and the Mortifications of Religion, are undertaken upon this View. A good Man is contented with hard Usage at present, that he may take his Pleasure in the other World.[25]

It is natural for every one to aim at perfection. And since "Contemplation is the Delight of the *Deity,* we may be assured the Flower and Exaltation of Bliss, lies in the operation of the Mind."[26] None

---

[21] *Cf.* Collier: "Desire is a conscious Emptiness, an unsatisfied Capacity." He adds, "It implies want in the very Notion, and supposes the Absence of the Thing desired." (*Eagerness of Desire,* p. 39.)

[22] *Of Pleasure,* p. 183.

[23] *Ibid.,* p. 178.

[24] *Ibid.,* p. 179.

[25] *Ibid.*

[26] *Ibid.,* p. 182.

is allowed this privilege, however, but "such as keep within the Order of Nature." Here again Collier voices a tenet of Epicurus. He recognizes the danger of valuing too highly pleasure lightly interpreted. "He that buys his satisfaction at the Expense of Duty and Discretion, is sure to over-purchase."[27] Further, "when Virtue is sacrificed to Appetite, Repentance must follow; . . . All unwarrantable Delights have an ill *Farewel,* and destroy those that are greater."[28] God, we are reminded, has not been pleased to make "a sensual man's capacity" measure up to his desires. Religion forbids few actions "but such as are naturally prejudicial to Health, to Reason, or Society."[29] And the "Heathen Philosophers, excepting some few of the Cyrenaicks, and Epicureans, were all agreed in the folly of forbidden Pleasure."[30]

It is obvious that in his insistence upon pleasure as the end of life and the identification of happiness with pleasure Collier's philosophy becomes identified with the hedonism of Epicurus.[31] When from certain basic doctrines of epicureanism and stoicism there are sloughed off garbled expansions little fundamental discrepancy remains. Accordingly, to find in Collier honest sympathy with both is not to uncover an inconsistency of thought. He selects from the two systems what he finds good and harmonizes these elements without quibbling over labels. That his attitudes are those of an introspective man, his ideas those of one who knows his own mind and has learned self-control, is clear ; and that these standards are scarcely to be adopted by that vast "generality" who need specific guidance Collier recognizes. An ethical scheme built up in ignorance of the very object it seeks to aid remains generally useless

[27] *Ibid.,* p. 179.
[28] *Ibid.*
[29] *Ibid.,* p. 180.
[30] *Ibid.*
[31] It is quite evident from marginal references and comments on Epicurus that Collier knew his writings, but in what form it is impossible to say. He may have read a Greek version; again, possibly he was familiar with some such collection of Epicurean thought as the *Morals,* published in 1670, the contents of which were drawn from a wide variety of Greek and Roman sources. The suggestion that Collier's knowledge came by way of Cicero is negated, for one reason, by the latter's almost consistent disapproval of Epicurean doctrine. Collier's derogatory reference to "Epicurism" implies that he distinguished to some extent between its true meaning and the popular notion, or pseudo-Epicureanism.

or becomes even injurious. At this point of offering practical advice for right conduct Collier did not blunder. As a spectator of society and its foibles he is first an interested student of human nature.

Curiosity over man and his motives and attempted analysis have from the time of the gnomic poets of the sixth century B.C. given rise to a kind of pseudo-psychological literature. In this history of self-scrutiny the *Rhetoric* of Aristotle marks a high spot, as do such documents of the soul as Augustine's *Confessions*; later Montaigne and Charron, Pascal and Gracian and La Rochefoucauld wrote in this tradition.[32] Another, exerting perhaps more influence, was La Bruyère with his *Les caracteres de Theophraste*.[33] All these Collier knew well. Considering man a being of impulses, emotions, needs that impel him to master himself, they make up a long line ushered in by Aristotle and his *entelechy,* joined by Plato, Descartes, Leibnitz, Nietzsche, Bergson, and finally by James with his pragmatism. The Democritean concept of man as a mechanism guided by matter found an able exponent in Hobbes. We have seen that Hobbes and Collier hold in common their hedonistic doctrine of self-interest as the basis of conduct and therefore that of social structure. Both point to the instinct of self-preservation as the most powerful principle motivating passional life; both discover in man a prevailing tendency towards folly, pride, excess. Collier, divided on the point of man's benevolence, prefers to prove an inherent universal goodness "an acknowledged and practicable Disposition." Generally a lack of benevolence, he holds, is due to a lack of reason, to prejudice, to poor environment. Self-love is not a fault except when developed to excess.[34] Man, foolishly concerned over his

[32] Professor Dessoir calls La Rochefoucauld's volume of *Sentences and Maxims* "a serious attempt at practical psychology, a reduction of carefully observed facts to concrete principles." *History of Psychology,* Introduction, xxl.

[33] First edition, 1688. In 1592 in England there had appeared Isaac Casaubon's Latin translation of the extant *Characters* of Theophrastus. Collier uses La Bruyère's version.

[34] *"Nature,* like Narcissus," remarks Collier in his essay *Of Friendship,* "is strangely taken with its own Reflection." Again, in *A Short View,* he says, "People love to see their *Passions* painted no less than their *Persons*: And like

future, is yet conservative, lacking in plasticity, vain, remarkably vacillating—on the whole, determined by forces outside his control. While many of these ideas immediately suggest Hobbes, it were short-sighted indeed to pounce upon them as Hobbesian because they are contemporary, or to infer that to begin with Hobbes's concept would be to end with Hobbes's materialistic scheme. Collier was probably only indicating his common sense and practical observation. Certainly he had encountered the same notions in Cicero.[35] Aside from his attacks in the stage-controversy, Collier's voiced disapproval centres about Hobbes more than any other contemporary. Much of his dialogue on *Pride* consists in a refutation of Hobbesian theory. In their general positions the two men had no real affinity of thought. A choice epithet of Collier's is "Mr Hob's Ghost! . . . a Satyr upon your whole Kind!" Yet he can quote Hobbes to his own purpose, ignoring for the moment his rôle as a tool of the Adversary.

While on the whole Collier advises the cultivation of Christian virtues of kindness, humility, charity, tolerance, with firm insistence upon social sympathy and aim, in more specific rules for conduct we glimpse an utilitarian attitude. "To decline any trouble which leads to advantage or accept a satisfaction with misery annexed is folly."[36] Further, "to endeavour not to *Please,* is Ill-nature; altogether to neglect it, Folly; and to overstrain for it, Vanity and Design."[37] The Golden Rule is a good but not absolute standard: its validity depends upon rational interpretation. Hence one should follow it advisedly. As he looks at the glitter and empty pretence of his world Collier cynically concludes that " 'tis good to move warily, and not Trust without Reserve; to believe People Honest, and manage as if they were otherwise."[38] In short,

---

Narcissus, are apt to dote on their own Image. This Bent of self Admiration recommends the Business of [stage] *Amours,* and engages the Inclination" (p. 184).

    [35] Cicero in his *De Finibus* evolves his whole discourse on what constitutes the *summum bonum* from a recognition of the natural principles of self-love and self-preservation. The same viewpoint is found in his *De Officiis.*

    [36] *Of Religious Temper,* p. 98.

    [37] *Of Popularity,* p. 71.

    [38] *Of Lying,* pp. 175, 176.

> We must endeavor to preserve a Superiority of Reason, a
> Command of Appetite, an Independance of Thought. The
> Possession of an Object does not make it eligible, if any ill
> consequence hangs upon it. Before we determine our Choice
> we should look forward to the Issue, and compute upon the
> Profit and Loss.[39]

Add the constant injunction to moderation, and we find it essentially the counsel of Cicero.[40] To the stoic through the centuries
passion has always been a derangement of reason. To Collier this
was no less true. He could approach the problem of ethics declaring
with the Roman moralist that every question of duty has two sides,
one relating to the "sovereign good," the other to practical and
detailed rules for governing conduct.

We see the mark of his age on Collier as he defines the broad end
of pleasure in life. While he argues that happiness does not consist
in "Abundance, or in being the Owner of large Possessions"[41] it
is with Hobbesian utilitarianism that he declares happiness to depend upon power: when power goes, happiness goes, for the want
of power is the immediate cause of all misery.[42] Weakness, not will,
causes suffering; human beings lack strength to seize what they
like or dismiss what they abhor. In their impotence lies their undo-
ing. Hence

> Power is a noble and majestick Attribute, and gives Life and
> Perfection to all great Designs; wise Contrivances and
> virtuous Dispositions, without correspondent Force to back
> them, signify nothing. Wisdom and Goodness unfortify'd by
> Power, are but vain Speculations and charitable Dreams. A
> kind Wish relieves no Man, for it's one Thing to think, and
> another to effect; without Power we can neither oblige our

[39] *Of Religious Temper*, p. 98.

[40] "Whatever you undertake," wrote Cicero, "there are three rules to be
observed. In the first place, it is necessary to subject appetite to reason, for that
is the surest means of fulfilling your duty; again, you must estimate the importance of the object you wish to accomplish that the effort you bestow upon it may
be neither greater nor less than the case demands. Finally, observe moderation in
all that concerns the aspect and dignity of a gentleman; and moderation is best
attained by observing . . . decorum. . . . But the most important of these three
rules is to subject appetite to reason." *De Officiis.*

[41] *Sermon X*, p. 329.

[42] *Of Power*, p. 64.

selves nor others, neither prevent an unforseen Evil, nor pursue an Advantage. The most virtuous Mind, if it has no Strength but that of Zeal and Inclination, can never keep the World in Order.[43]

Collier again echoes Hobbes[44] in saying that "knowledge is power in a great measure" because "it puts us in a Capacity to make Nature serviceable, and to command the Creation";[45] we recall too that Hobbes (in the manner of Gassendi) regarded pleasure as a positive end, as something which because it is the object of a desire is good.

In the same practical spirit Collier advocates a dynamic, meaningful existence: life, a time for trial and effort, should be lived dangerously and bravely. To realize this ideal, health and strength are important, but too great solicitude for the body is to be scorned:

> To make it our main Concern therefore to keep our Bodies in Repair; To Avoid Business, and doze over Life, for fear of wearing them out too fast, is an inglorious Management. Some People are wonderful cautious in this affair: Any thing extraordinary in Thought or Action, is a dangerous Experiment! Accidents may break in; the Blood and the Humours may be disturb'd this Way. They dare scarcely move out of their Pace, or venture to speak Sense, for fear of spending their Spirits, or making their Pulse beat too fast.[46]

This to Collier "is to be a Cypher in the World":

> I grant Straining above Strength, Rashness, and unnecessary Hazards, are indefensible Sallies: Prudence and Precaution are good Things: But then our Care should not carry us to Insignificancy: Let us be prudent to do something: To shrink from Business, to slumber in the Shade, and lie always under Shelter, is to mistake the Point, and overrate our present Security.[47]

[43] *Sermon II*, p. 42.
[44] *Cf.* Hobbes, *Leviathan*, Vol. III, p. 61, *English Works*, ed. Molesworth.
[45] *Of the Resurrection*, p. 410.
[46] *Ibid.*, p. 439.
[47] *Ibid.*

In brief, we must indulge ourselves in no ease, but use our bodies "generously, and to good Purpose."[48] Withdrawal from the world and reality is not justifiable on grounds of preserving one's integrity; temporary seclusion must be, not an end in itself, but a means of girding one's loins against living an active life among men.

Collier's definition of ethical standards derives partially from his theory of knowledge. When he writes of the "clear and distinct *Perception*" and "Self-evident Principles" that "flash conviction" he is but postulating the validity of inner certainties, hence implying an absolute standard for the individual. Selfish interest as a moral criterion he condemns because a judgement of conscience moved by desires could justify any fault; there then could exist no fixed values and the moral scheme would be as variable as human fancies. True, often a man seems to fare the worse for his integrity, the better for his iniquity.[49] But "Virtue and Vice are utterly uninterpretable by Success. The Fate of the Righteous and the Wicked is shuffled in common and promiscuous Events, as if the Distinctions of Good and Evil were nothing but empty Names, and Terms of Philosophy."[50] On the contrary, virtue and vice are not mere "empty names"; their "lines . . . are struck out by Nature in very legible Distinctions; they tend to a different Point, and in the greater Instances the Space between them is easily perceiv'd. Nothing can be more unlike than the original Forms of these Qualities." Some evils proceed from "the Niceness of our Imagination," others

[48] *Of the Resurrection*, p. 440. The old orthodox Stoic of the school of Zeno had maintained that the Wise Man would be indifferent to pleasure and pain, as well as to health and wealth. But in the later eclectic stoicism preached in Rome by Panaetius of Rhodes this rigid teaching became softened to include these attributes as essential to happiness. Since Cicero's *De Officiis* is based upon a lost treatise of Panaetius, we find in this guide-book the expression of doctrines not too severe and too rigorous to be of practical benefit. Cicero holds that "in the food we eat and the care we bestow on the body we should aim at health and strength, and not a sensual pleasure." (*De Officiis*, p. 51.) And to Collier, health is desirable not chiefly "for the sake of Pleasure, and the Benefit of the Senses" but because "we are then in the best Condition to serve God, and be useful to Society." (*Of the Resurrection*, p. 439.) This attitude is based on the same social interest expressed by Marcus Aurelius.

[49] In Chapter IX of his *Meditations*, Marcus Aurelius expresses the same idea.
[50] *Sermon II*, p. 50.

from a "real Foundation in Nature." In explaining man's inability
to perceive truth Collier borrows this figure from Pascal:

> There is but one precise point proper to shew a Picture in:
> the rest Misrepresent by Nearness, or Distance; by being too
> High, or too Low. *Perspective* will tell us this Nice place in
> Painting; but in *Thinking* and *Morality* 'tis not so easily
> fixed.[51]

Pascal had written, "There is but one indivisible point from which
we should look at a picture; all others are too near, too distant, too
high or too low. Perspective fixes this point precisely in the art of
painting; but who shall fix it in regard to truth and morals?"[52] In
1712 Shaftesbury, in Italy, used the same figure: "The rules of
perspective lie hid (under the *je ne sais quoi*) like the rules of
morals, right and wrong, equity and inequity, etc."[53] Collier warns
that the search for truth is too often defeated through laziness or
prejudice (or through the senses, which as we have earlier seen, he
believed to "want Force to distinguish" right and wrong until reason develops) ; too often a value is established, ideas given set, by
petty truckling to leaders of fashion. Thus is erected opinion or
common sentiment, which stands in opposition to reality, or truth.
All this Collier draws from Pascal who wrote:

> We see scarcely anything, just or unjust, which does not
> change its quality with the climate. Three degrees of latitude
> upset all the principles of jurisprudence; a meridian, or a

[51] *Of the Weakness of Human Reason*, p. 234.

[52] Pascal, *Thoughts*, Chap. VI, "Weakness of Man," p. 95.

[53] *Plastics, An Epistolary Excursion in the Original Progress and Power of
Designatory Art*. In *Second Characters*, ed. by Benjamin Rand, Cambridge,
1914, p. 177.

Collier, by his recognition of the comparative state of morality and perspective,
would thus save himself from being condemned as barbaric in the eyes of Shaftesbury, who brands Hobbes and Locke as exemplars of aesthetic numbness: they
declare that "beauty is nothing," "virtue is nothing," and so "perspective nothing,"
and "music nothing." But "these," says Shaftesbury, "are the greatest realities of
things," and accordingly "these philosophers together with the anti-virtuosi may
be called by one common name, viz. barbar[ians] . . ." (p. 178).

few years of possession, determines what is truth. Fundamental laws vary. Right has its epochs.[54]

Collier's rendering is but slightly expanded:

> And which is more surprizing, the Standard of *Just* and *Unjust,* is often alter'd with the Climate; Two or three Degrees of *Latitude,* is enough to Ruin a Lawyer; to make the *Twelve Tables* Useless; and Repeal the *Statute Book.* A meridian upon the Globe, or a few Years of Possession, decides a Cause; for it seems *Right* as well as *History,* has its Chronological Epoch's.[55]

He concludes elsewhere that one would think "Right and Wrong lay rather in the Fancies of Men, than in the Reason of Things; and was bounded more by Seas and Rivers, than by any unalterable Limits of Nature; that Virtue and Vice were minted by the Civil Magistrate."[56] He feels that the "heathen philosophers," in debating the criteria of truth, have but presented a plethora of "summum Bonums," a tedious spectacle of "the diferences one Sect had with another; their Inconsistencies with themselves, and the ridiculous and ill-supported Tenets some of the most famous of them have held."[57] However much Collier may have learned of moral evil and of good from the sages he reiterates that we must depend upon an inner certitude of right and wrong. Conscience is not to be overruled by custom—for custom and tradition prove inadequate. Collier must have realized full well in his non-juring experiences just how "cramping a thing" it is to be tied to a "set of notions."

Through classical and renaissance literature the theory of friendship remained definitely a philosophic concept that lent itself to some fine writing but never really became a moot question. Collier's treatment of this stock theme is worth noting—not because of any fresh convictions of his on the matter, but precisely because his handling of sources typifies the borrowing so prevalent in seventeenth-century prose. His essay *Of Friendship* he has neatly woven from the versions of Bacon and Cicero. Like Cicero, Collier,

[54] *Thoughts,* p. 98.
[55] *Of the Weakness of Human Reason,* p. 236.
[56] *Upon Pride,* pp. 21, 22.
[57] *Sermon II,* p. 37.

employing the dialogue, introduces the situation of grief over the
death of a friend and concludes that such emotion argues for self-
love; for "to be sorry a Friend is not with us, when he is better
from us, is a Sign we rate our Convenience highest, and Mourn
more for the *Living* than for the *Dead*."[58] From this point he
explains the relationship of friendship as one springing out of the
imperfections of human nature, which lacks "Fund enough to
furnish out a Solitary Life." Man "has not every thing growing
upon his own *Soil,* and therefore is willing to Barter with his
Neighbour. This Exchange of Offices, when 'tis managed with
Frankness and Fidelity, excites native Generosity, and improves
into Confidence and Affection." When men see their thoughts and
inclinations reflected, their good opinion of themselves is confirmed
and they are grateful: "A Conformity of Opinion and Desire, looks
like a Multiplication of ones Self. A Man sees his own *Being,* as
it were, doubled and extended in his Friend; and then 'tis no
wonder if he loves him," an *alter idem.*[59]

Cicero declares friendship to spring "from an inclination of the
soul joined with a feeling of love rather than from calculation of
how much profit the friendship is likely to afford."[60] Everyone is
dear to himself on his own account, and "unless this feeling were
transferred to friendship" the *alter idem* would never be found.[61]
Bacon, interpreting this phrase with his usual utilitarian atti-

[58] Cicero, in the person of Laelius, laments the death of Scipio, but, believing
that ill has befallen to himself instead of his friend, remarks that "great anguish
for one's own inconveniences is the mark of the man who loves not his friend but
himself." *Laelius on Friendship,* trans. by W. A. Falconer, London, 1923. Loeb
Classical Library, p. 119.

[59] *Of Friendship,* p. 52. It is in this passage that Collier remarks, "*Nature,*
like *Narcissus,* is strangely taken with its own Reflection." *Cf.* Glanvill: "*Love*
as it were *uniting* the Object to the *Soul,* gives it a kind of *Identity* with us; so
that the beloved *Idea* is but *our selves* in another *Name*: and when *self* is at the
bar, the sentence is not like to be impartial: For every man is naturally a *Narcissus,* and each *passion* in us, no other but *self-love* sweetned by milder *Epithets.*
We can love nothing, but what is agreeable to us; and our desire of what is so,
hath its just inducement from within us: . . . We love our *friends,* because they
are our *Image,* and we love our *God,* because we are *his.*" *Vanity of Dogmatizing,* pp. 119, 120.

[60] *Laelius on Friendship,* p. 139.

[61] *Ibid.*

tude,[62] names his famous "fruits" of friendship: a man cannot
commend himself with modesty, supplicate as he might find it
helpful to do, nor speak for himself as effectively as can his proxy;
further benefits are peace in emotional life, and support of one's
judgement; the friend serves as a vent in relating misfortunes, and,
since the grief is halved by the telling, the friendship is doubled.
Thus conversation and counsel are psychologically and selfishly
invaluable. With scant change Collier takes over into his essay
these advantages and makes use of the same examples.[63] "Those,"
he writes, "who have no Friend to discharge their Cares, and their
Grievances upon, are . . . a sort of *Cannibals* to themselves; and
prey upon their own *Vitals*."[64] But friendship "relieves our Cares,
raises our Hopes, and abates our Fears. It doubles our Joys, and
divides our griefs. A Friend who relates his *Success,* talks himself
into a new Pleasure," for "friendship, like some universal Medicine, works contrary Ways; but always to the Benefit of Nature."[65]
Bacon had employed the same striking figure: "Certainly, if a man
would give it a hard phrase, those that want friends to open themselves unto are cannibals of their own hearts."[66] "In a word," he
adds, "a man were better relate himself to a statua or picture, than
to suffer his thoughts to pass in smother."[67] This Collier varies
with, "In a word, the Advantage of Conversation is such, that for

[62] "Here the best way to represent to life the manifold use of friendship, is to
cast and see how many things there are which a man cannot do himself; and then
it will appear that it was a sparing speech of the antients, to say, *that a friend is
another himself*; for that a friend is far more than himself." Bacon, *Of Friendship*, p. 173.
[63] Bacon, for example, writes: "It is not to be forgotten what Comineus
observeth of his first master, Duke Charles the Hardy; namely, that he would
communicate his secrets with none; and least of all, those secrets which troubled
him most. Whereupon he goeth on and saith that towards his latter time *that
closeness did impair and a little perish his understanding*" (p. 169).
Collier utilizes the illustration: " 'Tis somewhat Remarkable what *Commines*
observes of *Charles* Duke of *Burgundy*: This Prince was so very reserv'd, that
he would impart his *Secrets* to No-body; especially those which troubled him
most. Whereupon the Historian tells us, that this Closeness did *Impair and a
little Perish his Understanding*" (p. 59).
[64] *Of Friendship*, p. 60.
[65] *Ibid.*
[66] Bacon, p. 170.
[67] *Ibid.*, p. 171.

want of Company a Man had better talk to a *Post* than let his Thoughts lie Smoking and Smothering in his Head."[68]

Other ideas Collier draws from Cicero: virtue is the measure of friendship, and will bring about affection between correspondingly virtuous men; without this relationship life is almost impossible even to great persons. Collier's position is Cicero's rather than Bacon's in condemning the sacrifice of virtue to expediency and in refusing to regard friendship primarily in a mercenary light. Dishonesty, base motives, insincerity are ruled out. But there are certain requisites for friendship: frankness, a granting of privacy, freedom from passion and self-conceit; a sense of honour, courage, constancy, agreeableness of temper; "Cowardice will betray friendship; and Covetousness will starve it. Folly will be nauseous; Passion is apt to ruffle; and Pride will fly out into Contumely and Neglect."[69] There must be willingness to receive a kindness, as well as to do one, for "he who always refuses, taxes the Profferer with Indiscretion."[70] An "inoffensive pleasantness" conveys advice with "better Success than naked Reprehension" because "this guilding of the Pill, reconciles the Palate to the Prescription, without weakening the Force of the Ingredients."[71] A friend must not be subjected to distrust or observation; we should anticipate his desires and "scarce give him time to think he wanted an assistance." "Friendship, to make it true, must have Beauty as well as Strength: Charms to endear, as well as Power to Supply."[72] To break off such a connexion, "one of those few things which are the better for the Wearing," is "unreasonable Levity": caprice, chagrin, curiosity, "an ambiguous Expression," none of these is sufficient cause. Nothing but "plain Malevolence can justify Disunion."[73] In that case the way "is to draw off by Degrees, and not to come to an open Rupture. Let the Acquaintance be Decently buried; and the Flame rather Go out, than be *Smother'd*. For as *Cato* observes, though in the phrase of a Taylor, *Friendship* ought not to be

[68] Collier, p. 61.
[69] *Ibid.*, p. 53.
[70] *Ibid.*, p. 54.
[71] *Ibid.*
[72] *Ibid.*
[73] *Ibid.*, p. 65.

Unrip'd, but Unstitch'd."[74] Again, there is little of substance in Collier's essay that is original. In this dialogue we see the most glaring case of "borrowing" in Collier, except for the material taken from Pascal on *The Weakness of Human Reason*.[75] Nothing of Montaigne, incidentally, is reflected except where both writers depend upon Cicero. The general view given in Plato's *Lysis* and

[74] *Of Friendship*, p. 65; *Laelius on Friendship*, p. 185. Laelius quotes Cato in saying that the ties of friendship "should be unravelled rather than rent apart"— *dissuendae magis quam discindendae.*
There remains for mention one passage that in one form or another appears frequently in literature—and that has been erroneously ascribed, by implication, to Sir William Temple. Collier cites Alphonsus the Wise as saying "That all the Acquisitions and Pursuits of Men, excepting Four, were but Bawbles; *i.e.* old Wood to burn, old Wine to drink, old Books to read, and old Friends to converse with." E. N. S. Thompson (in *The Seventeenth-Century English Essay*, Univ. of Iowa Humanistic Studies, Vol. III, 1926, p. 113) selects for praise of fine writing a passage in Temple's prose that contains this particular quotation woven into the context. One of the *Apophthegms* of Bacon varies it slightly: "Alonso of Aragon was wont to say in commendation of age, that age appears to be best in four things,—old wood to burn, old wine to drink, old friends to trust, and old authors to read." The sentiment is found earlier in collections of Spanish apophthegms. Goldsmith uses it in Mr. Hardcastle's "I love everything that's old— old friends, old times, old manners, old books, old wine." (*She Stoops to Conquer*, I:29, 30.) A version preceding Collier's occurs in Shakerley Marmion's *The Antiquary* (1640-1641).
[75] As a rule, Collier suggests in the context the source. He is prolific in marginal annotations and references. And when he is guilty of omission, he is but doing what one of the most notorious borrowers of them all did—except that Bacon calmly culled from others' wit quotation after quotation with no hint of origin and thereby gained a reputation for clever aphorisms.
With respect to Collier's development as an essayist, it is significant that *Of Envy*, which has earmarks of resemblance to Bacon's *Of Envy*, and *Of Friendship* appear in his first volume of essays, as does *Of the Weakness of Human Reason*. There is no doubt that the stylistic influence of Bacon expanded into one of thought as well; but in the main Collier was no disciple of Bacon. In writing these first essays he was just as well aware then as later that "'tis no very easie Business not to miscarry" and the "Matter . . . not without Disadvantage." He observes in the preface to his third volume of *Moral Essays*: "The Ground is beaten, as well as slippery, and the Subjects either barren, or seiz'd. Theophrastus and Tully, Montaigne and Bacon, Bruyère and Bellegard, not to mention others, have exercis'd their Fancy this way. . . . I grant, 'tis possible to raise New Notions out of an Old Theme: There's no constant Necessity of Borrowing, or Coincidence. Different Inventions, and later Discoveries in Philosophy and Religion, are some Relief this way. But then these Succours won't always do. I must confess, I found some Difficulty to gain fresh Quarters, and get into a Track by my self."

the slighter summary in Plutarch's *Moralia* must have been known to Collier. But he turned, and wisely, to that piece of classic Roman prose in which the views of the ancients upon friendship found their culminating expression, and upon which moderns have, knowingly or not, since drawn for ideas to voice their own attitudes.

Another literary theme holding steady allure for writers has been the ages of man, from mewling infant to mere oblivion. Especially did the possibility of drawing analogies appeal to the renaissance love of figure and conceit; and later, essayists found the topic rich for moralizing. Collier's essay *Of Infancy and Youth* relies upon Bacon's *Of Youth and Age*.[76] But his dialogue *Of Old Age* deserves to be known among good essays : its mellow tone, the tolerant observation of human foibles, the genial style—these combine to produce a piece of his best prose. In contrast to his close following of Cicero on friendship, Collier here draws only very generally from the *De Senectute* and through that upon Plato's *Republic*.[77] Balancing the liabilities of old age against its advantages, he reminds us that while physical decay is inevitable, mental and moral imperfections can be avoided, and disagreeable factors obviated :

> A brave Mind is always impregnable. True Courage is the Result of Reasoning. A just Sense of Honour, and Infamy, of Duty and Religion, will carry us farther than all the Force of *Mechanism*. . . . Innocence of Life, and Consciousness of Worth, and great Expectations, will do the Business alone. These Ingredients make a richer *Cordial* than youth can prepare.[78]

Old age has its privileges : knowledge and wisdom, benefits from well-husbanded talents, and freedom from violent passion—that *domino agresti ac furioso*. There is consolation in the fact that declension of vigour is slow, almost imperceptible. "To go to bed at Thirty," observes Collier, "and rise with all the Marks of

[76] The result is actually an interesting admixture of Collier, Bacon, Cicero, and La Rochefoucauld.

[77] Collier utilizes the introductory section of the *Republic,* passages that concern a discussion between Socrates and Cephalus on old age.

[78] *Of Old Age,* pp. 160, 161.

Eighty, would try one's Patience pretty severely."[79] We are permitted to "walk down the Hill so gently, that the Change of Situation is scarcely perceiv'd, till we are near the Bottom." Preparation for pleasant old age lies in moderation in youth:

> This is the way to make both the Mind and the Body more easy. I say the Body, for Intemperance antedates Infirmities, and doubles them. It averages its own Excesses, and plunges us sooner and deeper in the Mire, than otherwise we should fall. He that would have his Health hold out, must not live too fast. A Man should husband his Constitution, and not throw it away till he has done living, if he can help it. Not to provide thus far is to betray our Senses, and prove false to the Interest of Ease and Pleasure.[80]

The mind as well will reap the rewards of a carefully managed life. The more "disengag'd from the Entertainments of Sense" one is, the less one will be troubled by impracticable wishes, since "strength and desire will fall off together." In short, "Habits of Virtue, and handsome Performances, are the best Preparatives. Let's lay in a Stock of good Actions before-hand. These will secure our Credit *without,* and our Peace *within.*"[81] So to the last, reason and moderation must serve as ethical guides. Throughout the dialogue there runs a tone of acquiescence, a desire to bear trouble "with decency" —both essentially of the spirit of Cicero and Marcus Aurelius.

> He that charges an Enemy, does not shew himself more brave, than he that grapples handsomely with a Disease. To do this without abject Complaints; without Rage, and Expostulation, is a glorious Combat. To be Proof against Pain, is the clearest Mark of Greatness: It sets a Man above the Dread of Accidents. 'Tis a state of Liberty and Credit. He that's thus fenced, needs not fear nor flatter any thing. He that distinguishes himself upon these Occasions, and keeps up the

[79] *Of Old Age,* p. 170.
[80] *Ibid.,* p. 171.
[81] *Ibid. Cf.* Marcus Aurelius: "The best provision for a happy life is to dissect everything, view it on all sides, and divide it into matter and form; to practice honesty in good earnest, and speak truth from the very Soul of you: and when you have done this, live easy and cheerful, and crowd one good action so close to another, that there may not be the least empty or insignificant space between them." (*Meditations,* p. 268.)'

Superiority of his Mind, is a Conqueror, though he dyes for 't; and rides in Triumph into the other World. And when we are . . . proving the most formidable Evils to be tolerable; are we Insignificant all this while?[82]

No, answers Collier: "Thus to teach Resignation and Greatness, and appear in the Heights of Passive Glory, is, I hope, to live to some Purpose." Hope in a future life is sustaining, for "the more we sink into Infirmities of Age, the nearer we are to immortal Youth."[83]

All People are young in the other World. That state is an Eternal Spring, ever fresh and flourishing. Now to pass from Midnight into Noon on the sudden: To be decrepid one Minute, and all Spirit and Activity the next, must be an entertaining Change. Call you this Dying? The Abuse of Language! To fly thus swiftly from one Extream to another; to have Life flow in like a Torrent, at the lowest Ebb, and fill all the Channels at once; this must be a Service to the Case in hand. For this Reason old People will go off with Advantage.[84]

To "be afraid of growing old," says Collier, "is to be afraid of growing Wise, and being Immortal."[85] The things of this world ultimately fail; "And as long as Thoughts are too big for Things, we shall always be craving."[86] Would God create an appetite without an object? The "Being of Happiness is more than a Dream," not to be realized here. So well is it worth our inquiry that "Curiosity should almost carry us into the other World."[87] To be unwilling to embark upon unknown seas in search of so noble a state "is to be over-fond of our Native Country, and to hang about Life a little too meanly."[88]

The manner of meeting death is the last admonition to right conduct that Collier can offer; beyond lies the realm of theological

[82] Of Old Age, p. 173.
[83] Ibid., p. 174.
[84] Ibid.
[85] Ibid., p. 175.
[86] Ibid.
[87] Ibid., p. 176.
[88] Ibid. Collier observes that on the whole "People are not so apt to be too big to live, as too little to die." (Of the Value of Life, p. 27.)

speculation. Death is our final scene to be enacted, and it behoves us to make it our best performance. All life, says the stoic, is but preparation for this moment which serves as a release from pain. Seneca wrote to his friend Lucilius:

> The man who fears death . . . is as much a fool as the man who fears old age, for as age follows youth, so death follows age. He who's shy of dying has been shy of living, for life's given subject to the discount of death; to death we go. Only a mad-man, then, fears death: anticipation is for certainties, fear for uncertainties. Death's an impartial and invincible Must. Who can grumble at being on the same terms as everybody else? . . . the only man who welcomes his coming cheerfully is one who has long prepared himself for it.[89]

And Marcus Aurelius asked: "Where is the hardship if Providence, that planted you here, orders your removal?"

> You cannot say that you are sent off by a tyrannical and unrighteous sentence; no, you quit the stage as fairly as a player does, that has his discharge from the master of the revels. . . . He that appoints the entertainment is the best judge of the length of it; and as he ordered the opening of the first scene, so now he gives the sign for shutting up the last . . . therefore retire in good humour, for he by whom you are dismissed means you no harm.[90]

He who has lived well will know how to die well. Collier achieves this same calm acceptance, and, thus gaining in objectivity, gains both a point of departure and an end.

It is, perhaps, unfortunate that the seventeenth century was an age so rich in intellectual genius that it could squander its talents, and fix their possessors in obscure niches, to remain unrecognized witnesses of their time. Several reasons are apparent why Collier has been relegated to one of the dustier corners of the gallery. Not the least is that such an attack as his *Short View* naturally exasperates those critics whose literary gods are aesthetic figurines and who noisily ignore "morality in art." Impressionism and romantic

[89] Seneca, *Letters*, Vol. I, pp. 102, 103.
[90] *Meditations*, p. 270.

pique have no place in judging a man like Collier. Late seventeenth-century England watched a scientific critical temper supersede the creative, and reason and common sense take the reins. The confusion and change of his day Collier was able to regard with objective clarity, with freshness, usually with tolerance. Credited—if it be creditable—with having hastened the onset of sentimental comedy, and thus closely allied with Steele in a common aim of propriety for the stage, Collier is akin to him in a more significant way: he adopts in his essays a mellowed seriousness of tone which we can fairly think of as helping to prepare the way for the genial *Spectator*; he could be said to write with like purpose, "to enliven morality with wit, and to temper wit with morality." The coldness and bloodlessness of the classic age ahead he escapes. While historically he is important both as a forerunner and as a representative of his time, he has intrinsic merit very rewarding to one who can stop to read well-written essays of substance. To peer suspiciously at Collier because he can preach to others the vanity of human wishes and at the same time express a personal eudemonic philosophy; because he withered late artificial comedy beyond repair, even though he as audibly hated the narrowness of Puritan recrudescence; because he fought for Christianity above Anglicanism and yet permitted ritual to loom so large as to bring on the charge of popishness; because he could embrace the mysticism of Malebranche and still utilize the new empirical philosophy; to deplore, in short, the reflection in one seventeenth-century mind of such variation in interest and attitude, is tacitly to confess indifference to a significant age rich in speculation and eager in curiosity, and to lament the successful activity of a man vitally close to his age. A scholar in whom the renascence of true classicism blends with an instinctive acceptance of the modern, Collier was primarily neither a literary critic nor a theologian: he was first a critic of living, his aim both an end and a means of life.